MANAGEMENT
THEORY, RESEARCH, AND PRACTICE

SECOND EDITION

EDITED BY AFZAL RAHIM
WESTERN KENTUCKY UNIVERSITY

Bassim Hamadeh, CEO and Publisher
Michael Simpson, Vice President of Acquisitions and Sales
Jamie Giganti, Senior Managing Editor
Jess Busch, Senior Graphic Designer
Angela Schultz, Senior Field Acquisitions Editor
Natalie Lakosil, Licensing Manager
Allie Kiekhofer, Interior Designer

First published in the United States of America in 2016 by Cognella, Inc.

Cover image copyright © Depositphotos/justinkendra

Printed in the United States of America

ISBN: 978-1-63189-541-8 (pbk) / 978-1-63189-542-5 (br)

www.cognella.com   800-200-3908

Contents

Departure from Tradition

By Afzal Rahim
Center for Advanced Studies in Management

The first edition of Management: Theory, Research, and Practice was created specifically to address the following critical issues in the content and purpose of academic business texts.

- Existing texts are much the same. They cover the same topics, are written in the same academic style, and often include very similar reference lists.
- The authors of the existing texts are trained to write in traditional academic language and not to address what a student audience needs. Accordingly they are often dry, dull, and unreadable. In general, these are books written by professors for other professors, not for students or general readership.
- Textbook authors are experts in certain areas, but not all of the topical areas. For instance, Harold Kerzner's excellent and widely read project management text still incorporates a 1964 conflict management methodology which makes it appear wholly ignorant of more recent advances. Thus, academic authors are not always able to present cutting-edge materials in many chapters, and some chapters or sections may be considerably dated.
- For these reasons, many existing textbooks simply turn students off. Moreover, the overabundance of citations and references distract from learning.
- Further, most texts lack practical guidance to the instructor on teaching the subject at hand. This is a serious deficiency, given that most instructors and professors are specialists in a single area and may not know how to teach outside their specialties.
- Finally, most texts are written from a theoretical and abstract perspective without a practical, real-life approach to the subject matter. This fault is made even more problematic because so many students are actually kinesthetic, or hands-on, learners.

This second edition remains focused to address these critical issues in the content and purpose of academic business texts. First, I approached the authors and invited them to contribute based on their expertise and qualifications in their respective fields. I shared with them this book's goal of being in an undergraduate vernacular that would appeal to 19-year young, non-management majors, instead of one written in typical academic jargon. My purpose was to introduce undergraduate students to business and management leadership thought and practice in a way that would interest them, rather than turn them off. This goal was unique in itself and meant jettisoning much of the typical dry, technical-academic jargon in which professors and scholars are accustomed to conveying ideas.

Second, management is a hands-on, practical discipline, needing input from practitioners as well as scholars. This text attempts to remedy this problem in that a number of the authors are successful practitioners in their fields as well as being published scholars.

Third, this text seeks to remedy the problem of overly dry, abstract, technical texts by including practical exercises and cases from experienced instructors in these fields at the conclusion of each chapter.

Fourth, to maintain consistency, I was heavily involved in the editing process of each chapter. Chapters were revised 1−4 times before they were accepted for publication. This process has lent a high degree of consistency throughout, so that the work does not stand as simply a compendium of individual compositions.

Thank you for selecting this text in your efforts to create better leaders. I look forward to your comments and criticisms to improve subsequent editions.

PART I
Individual Differences

1. Individuals in the Organization

Michael R. Carrell
Northern Kentucky University

Robert D. Hatfield
Western Kentucky University

Aditya Simha
University of Wisconsin–Whitewater

Would Apple be Apple without the influence of Steve Jobs? Would another individual at the helm of affairs have led Apple to be a success? While individuals are similar to each other in some ways they are also different from one another in other ways. These differences are what makes each person distinct and gives them "individuality." These differences can help groups by infusing them with diverse viewpoints, and therefore, multiple perspectives and ways to solve problems. But on the other hand, these very same differences can also cause group conflicts because the individuals may fail to share a common view. To manage people is to manage individuals. Every manager, team member, and coworker needs an understanding of how individuals are different and also how they are alike.

This chapter examines four ways in which individuals differ and how these differences matter to the manager, coworker, and organization. We discuss these differences based upon:

- Personality
- Perception
- Attitudes and Values
- Competencies and Abilities

Differences based upon personality and perceptions provide some of the clearest contrasts between employees, and therefore we present whole sections on these two topics. We then collate the remaining two sections into one subsequent section, based upon values, attitudes, demographics, competencies, and abilities.

Nature of Personality

Definition

Personality is the set of traits and attributes that is relatively stable over time and can influence one's attitudes and behaviors. These traits and attributes can be used to compare and contrast individuals. Each set or constellation of traits creates individuality. These differences can also make working with, and managing, individuals sometimes fulfilling and sometimes frustrating. Managers can benefit from possessing a basic understanding of personality traits. These traits are not the same as a person's abilities, motivation, or moods. Personality traits are behavior patterns which are relatively stable over time. When introverts are slow to speak in meetings that does not imply they are unintelligent, mean, or in a bad mood. Introversion is simply a behavior pattern which manifests itself in their being hesitant to speak in meetings. If coworkers and managers have a better understanding of the individual differences among their associates they can better attribute motivation and interact with others more effectively.

Components of Personality

Personality has been a very popular research area. Therefore, there are several different models describing components of personality.

The Big-Five Model of Personality. The "Big Five" model of personality has been described as being the best model of personality. It is both reliable as well as valid. It has demonstrated reliable and steady relationships with important workplace outcomes. This model is also called the "OCEAN" personality model because its traits are Openness, Conscientiousness, Extraversion,

Agreeableness, and Neuroticism (McCrae & Costa, 1987; Rushton & Irwing, 2008). Each trait actually has two anchors or opposite points. For instance, the anchors of Openness are "open to new experience" and "closed to new experience" at the other end. For Conscientiousness the opposite anchor is "undirected." Each trait is seen as a continuum or scale between the two anchors. Each individual generally has a pattern of behaving in a way that's closer to one end of a scale or the other, although of course, some individuals may be right in the middle. On Openness, a person nearer the "closed" end could be described as "low on openness" to new experiences. An individual could also be exactly in the middle of a scale, for instance a "5" on a scale of 1–10 on Openness. We would then conclude that this trait of Openness does not describe that individual's general behavior, and that person is equally likely to either try or not try something new. Personality traits are often assessed by an individual filling out a questionnaire (self-report), and in some cases, individuals filling out questionnaires about others (peer-report). A popular and quick questionnaire which measures one's personality along the Big-Five is presented in the appendix of this chapter.

Openness to experience vs. Closed to experience. Questions relating to openness on questionnaires use adjectives such as imaginative, creative, broad interests, curious, analytical, and daring. Adjectives such as traditional, conforming, narrow interests, unanalytical, conservative, and down-to-earth are used to describe someone at the "closed" end of the scale. The shortened version of the big 5 scale does not use as many adjectives as the longer version does.

Conscientiousness vs. Undirectedness. Conscientious is associated with the behavior most desired at the workplace. Conscientiousness is described as careful, reliable, hardworking, energetic, well organized, and punctual. Undirected behavior is described as careless, lazy, disorganized, aimless, unperceptive, and thoughtless. The shortened version of the big 5 scale does not use as many adjectives as the longer version does.

Extraversion vs. Introversion. Extraversion is considered the personality trait on which people are most easily categorized. Extraverted behavior is described as sociable, fun-loving, friendly, spontaneous, talkative, and people-oriented. Introverted behavior is reserved, inhibited, cold, passive, timid, and task-oriented. The shortened version of the big 5 scale does not use as many adjectives as the longer version does.

Agreeableness vs. Antagonism. Agreeable behavior is described as good-natured, courteous, helpful, cheerful, humble, and forgiving. Antagonistic behavior is described as irritable, rude, suspicious, critical, cynical, and stubborn.

The shortened version of the big 5 scale does not use as many adjectives as the longer version does.

Neuroticism vs. Emotionally Stable. Neurotic behavior is described as worrying, nervous, high-strung, emotional, vulnerable, and a subjective. Emotionally stable behavior is described as calm, at ease, relaxed, unemotional, hardy, and objective. The shortened version of the big 5 scale does not use as many adjectives as the longer version does.

If you are a manager in a department you will likely have employees who demonstrate all of these different behavior pattern anchors. One employee's constellation of personality types might be Open, Conscientious, Extraverted, Agreeable and Neurotic. A second employee might be similar but be Introverted and Emotionally Stable. A third employee might have a completely different constellation of traits and fairly consistently behaves in a Closed, Undirected, Introverted, Antagonistic, and Neurotic manner. Essentially, all these employees will be identifiable as distinct individuals.

Leaders and managers are interested in learning about personality because they manage people and personality helps predict the reactions and other behaviors of individuals they manage. An introverted subordinate will often react less verbally than an extroverted subordinate. When a manager interacts with a subordinate the manager wants to maximize his/her communication success and impact, and therefore would be wise to adopt different communication styles with different individuals. For instance, there would be no point in speaking harshly or gruffly with a neurotic employee, as that would only hinder communication. Similarly, managers need to take into account employee personality types before assigning them duties. For example, there would be no point in expecting an introverted and shy employee to be the company's spokesperson in front of a large and unknown crowd. Therefore, the wise manager takes the individual's personality, and the behavior that is predicted, into account while making decisions.

Other Personality Types

Jung's Personality Types. There are other personality models that also seek to describe not one, but many, aspects of behavior that is relatively stable over time. The Myers-Briggs model, based on the work of Carl Jung, has multiple personality types within its model. Myers-Briggs has been called the "Coca-Cola" of personality tests since it is a for-profit test generally marketed to employers. The model classifies individuals into extroverts or introverts (I or E), sensing or intuitive (S or N), thinkers or feelers (T or F), and perceivers or judges (P or J)—so people could get various combinations. For instance, someone may be an INTJ and the other an ESFP, or other such type. Various combinations are possible, and each combination is associated with differences in behaviors and attitudes. It then combines these into patterns perhaps more descriptive of cognitive styles than personalities. This test, while a fun one to take, and we urge you to seek out free MBTI tests online, is not as effective nor considered as valid as the big five personality test.

Locus of Control. Locus of control is associated with the degree to which a person thinks that their own behaviors influence what happens to them in life. This, like other traits, varies between two poles or anchors. At one pole are those that believe that their own behaviors determine what happens to them in life. Persons with this trait are called "Internals" since they believe they themselves generally control their life. On the other hand, "Externals" believe that fate, luck, and other external factors generally determine what happens to them. Think of someone you know who's always blaming others for their misfortunes—chances are that individual is an external.

Many managers think locus of control is important at the workplace. Internals are more likely to believe that their efforts will lead to performance, they perform better on learning and problem-solving tasks when performance leads to rewards, they engage in less risky behavior, their job satisfaction and performance is more strongly related, they display a greater work motivation, they are more independent and more reliant on their own judgment, and they receive higher salaries and raises (Lefcourt, 2014; Spector, 1982). Having said that, it is also important for individuals and managers to realize that sometimes, external situations can influence performance, and so they should not be too willing to discredit 'externals' at their workplaces, and should instead, focus on being able to communicate with and motivate both Externals and Internals.

Self-Esteem. This is the degree to which people have positive or negative views about themselves. Self-esteem has become controversial. Do you have high self-esteem because you experienced success in the past on something that raised your self-esteem or were you successful because you already had high self-esteem? Perhaps it cannot be determined what comes first—a bit of a chicken-and-egg situation, this. However, we believe that those with high self-esteem are more satisfied and motivated at work, attracted to high-status jobs, and have higher levels of job performance. Skillful managers may wish to consider providing opportunities for success, and reinforce that success, with an eye toward maintaining or increasing self-esteem. On the same line of thought, if managers perceive that some of their employees are displaying signs of low self-esteem, then it may behoove them to think of ways to increase the self-esteem and therefore increase performance

Type A and Type B Personalities. Using "Type A" to describe high-strung individuals and "Type B" to describe more laid back individuals is part of workplace culture. It is relatively easy to observe how competitive, aggressive, impatient, and fast-working a coworker or subordinate might be. Neither A nor B personality types have a general advantage at the workplace. Type As may perform better on tasks with important time pressures or that allow solitary work. Type Bs may perform better on tasks requiring complex judgment or require working as a team (Baron, 1989). Some have said that Type As get more work done early in their careers but die younger that Type Bs. There may be something to that, at least in part, due to the influence of stress on those individuals.

Cardiologists noticed that patients falling into the Type A set of behaviors were twice as likely as others to suffer from coronary heart disease (CHD). When the individual components of the Type A are examined, the factor of "hostility" was found to be the most correlated with CHD. Therefore, there are "hostile" and "non-hostile" Type As. Recent studies on the relationship between CHD and personality have identified a Type D personality, "D" for distressed (Versteeg, Spek, Pedersen, & Denollet, 2011). Type D is a personality type with two important aspects: *negative affect* (irritable, worrier) and *social inhibition* (lack of self-assurance).

Whether managers are concerned about CHD or not, the conflicts which arise between Type A and Type B employees can be substantial. Managing two employees on a project where one is fast working and impatient and the other is working at a slower pace and is not concerned about getting an early start on the work can be difficult for all concerned. Students working on teams may have noticed the conflict between "rabbits," those focused upon the start and jump quickly and try to get ahead of the assignment, and "tortoises" those more focused upon the deadline and pace themselves at a slower pace to reach the goal. Each is suspicious of the other and rarely harnesses the strengths both approaches could offer if coordinated properly.

Outcomes of Personality Differences

Do personality traits predict important workplace outcomes other than these interpersonal communication and reaction behaviors? The answer is yes, but only in limited ways. Other factors are more important.

Selection research shows that cognitive ability and *work sample* tests are two of the best pre-employment selection tests. This means they are best for determining who will be the highest performers once hired. Personality tests, on the other hand, are relatively poor at predicting who will be a high performer if hired. Yet, some employers use a personality test as a pre-employment test.

Why do employers persist at using indicators known to be less valid than others? Sometimes it might be because employers do not know about research on tests and other predictors. Other employers might have convinced themselves that tests that are actually poor predictors still work.

Why is personality a relatively poor predictor of future job performance? Personality is a rather complex variable, as outlined in the discussion above on the Big Five personality model. While personality overall is not a valid predictor, one particular trait or personality factor is highly correlated with job performance. Conscientiousness is the only personality factor which correlates across occupations and industries with job performance. Other personality traits are only occasionally found to correlate with some job performances with isolated job classifications. For instance, extraversion has been found to correlate with "outside sales" job success—but not even in all sales jobs. This sort of does make sense as extroverted salespersons are more likely to engage with potential clients.

Conscientious behaviors have been described as careful, reliable, hardworking, well organized, scrupulous, self-disciplined, neat, punctual, deliberate, ambitious, emotionally stable, businesslike, energetic, knowledgeable, persevering, intelligent, fair, perceptive, and cultured. Some might say that conscientiousness "is" job performance. What manager or coworker would not wish to work with such employees?

However, can you get an honest response about how hardworking an applicant is who is hoping to be selected for a job? Is a job applicant who is undirected—lazy, careless, disorganized, helpless, and/or aimless—going to admit to this at a job interview? Since we can reasonably expect applicants to not be completely honest when asked about their Conscientiousness in an employment situation, we may be unable to use this personality trait effectively in a pre-employment questionnaire.

Implications for Management

Just because we cannot practically use personality for hiring does not diminish its importance in managing people at work. Since personality traits can be defined as *behavior patterns that are relatively stable over time* these behaviors can be very important in one-on-one interactions, or even one-on-group interactions. The manager who is sensitive to the likely reaction of a subordinate can more carefully craft a communication approach which might be received more positively. For instance, a manager might ask a more introverted subordinate to read and think about an issue or write down input and bring it to a later meeting, rather than have that employee present it to a large group. The same manager might choose to have a verbal discussion with an extraverted subordinate. A manager might prepare for opposition on a new idea from a subordinate closed to new experiences while probing a subordinate for refinements on that new idea from a subordinate open to new experiences. And, a manager could potentially utilize the nitpicky skills of a neurotic employee to look through an intricate work-issue, as neurotic individuals tend to be very detail oriented.

Attitudes, Values, Competencies, and Abilities

Definition

Attitudes. These are predispositions to react to something or someone in either a positive or negative way. Attitudes are judgments such as "I like the new manager that was hired" or "I absolutely hate country music." Attitudes can be subdivided into C-A-B: cognition, affect, and behavior.

Affect is the emotional part of the attitude. Employees bring their whole self to work—their brains, their body, and their emotions. Positive and negative emotions can have great effect at the workplace. Managers are increasingly interested in developing their social intelligence so that they might take the emotional state of others into account. As an aside, affect is also one of the more commonly confused words in written documents—so, pay attention to when you're writing as to whether you're referring to affect or to effect.

Behavioral Intent is the intention to act in a certain way based upon the attitude. For instance, "I am going to apply for the new job where I will work closely with that new manager I like" or "I am not going to that restaurant because I dislike Chinese food."

Cognition is the intellectual processing of the beliefs, opinions, and other information that the person might have about the target (like the new manager or the new restaurant in the examples). While the acronym A–B–C might help a student learn the three components of attitudes, the attitude process really moves in a different order: C–A–B. Typically the thoughts come first (Cognition), then feelings occur (Affect), and these thoughts and feelings lead to intentions (Behavior).

Cognitive dissonance is when cognition and affect do not synchronize, with behavior. "This is a terrible place to work; I hate working here; but here I am again today" nicely illustrates cognitive dissonance. Managers who recognize a lack of balance or congruence in a subordinate's attitudes have an opportunity to improve one of the elements to help the subordinate harmonize his or her overall attitude. Astute managers could attempt to try to improve conditions in the workplace to reform subordinate's negative cognitive attitudes about the workplace.

Values. These are beliefs that guide actions, judgments, and decisions across many different situations. Values are deeply held beliefs that drive broad preferences concerning the "right" courses of action. Values help an individual in deciding what is right or wrong behavior.

Values may be divided into *terminal* values and *instrumental* values. Terminal values are focused upon the *ends* one might achieve during one's lifetime. Instrumental values are focused upon the *means* for achieving such *ends*. One worker might have the instrumental value of helpfulness while her coworker might be more focused upon something different like independence or imagination. There will be differences among employees in both their terminal and instrumental values. An excellent manager would be sensitive to value differences among employees.

Values combine into *value systems* that affect attitudes, perceptions, and the motivation behind job performance. Some observers have speculated that there has been a shift in values of workers in the U.S. over the past decades. This shift might be away from valuing economic rewards, organizational commitment, and toward valuing meaningful work and self-actualization.

Work ethic is a specific value system directly linked to the workplace. It is the relative belief that there is dignity in all work and that hard work will be rewarded, or is its own reward. Work ethic also includes the belief that idleness and laziness are negative behaviors and should be avoided. Benjamin Franklin's comment,

"Early to bed, early to rise, makes a man healthy, wealthy, and wise" illustrates the work ethic personality. Our values determine what work we are willing to do and for whom. These values determine the commitments we are willing to make to the organizations—our loyalties, our expectations, and what boundaries we will not cross. Values might determine how well we do our job and whether we can or will be cooperative in the workplace. The continued economic success of the U.S. has been attributed to a combination of capitalism and workers exhibiting this work ethic. However, many believe the work ethic may be changing in the U.S. (Malanga, 2009). The chapter on Generational Management in this book discussed the values people hold within different generations.

Competency. This term is used by human resource professionals to describe a workplace behavior that can be mastered. For instance, an employee might master a second language, computer statistical software, or maintenance of financial records. However, broader areas of expertise or mastery might include teamwork, adapting to change, or leadership. The term competency generally replaced the term "skill" at many workplaces since competency is something that can easily be demonstrated. Many employers maintain a Human Resource Information System (HRIS) which tracks the competencies completed by individual employees. These competencies might be tracked through job experience, training, education, or other experiences which have provided expertise to the employee. Each employee will have a unique set of competencies which will frame his or her understanding, approach, and interest.

Abilities. These are the mental and physical capacities of an individual. Physical abilities include the ability to lift, bend, walk, run, reach, and provide a physical foundation for other body-motion behaviors. The American's with Disabilities Act protects workers from negative discrimination as long as a person with disabilities (physical or mental) can perform the essential functions of the job. Mental abilities generally refer to such cognitive functions as memory, association, concept formation, language, attention, pattern recognition, and problem solving. Some employers seek to learn about the mental abilities of its employees, or applicants, by administering cognitive ability tests. Assessment centers are also used to track mental abilities particularly among managers and highly skilled professionals. Both cognitive ability tests and assessments are among the very best hiring approaches according to research on selection,

Competencies, abilities, skill levels, education levels, and other differences that might appear on a resume are yet another set of differences which have the capacity to make an organizational unit either stronger or more conflicted based upon the skill of the manager.

Outcomes of Attitudes, Values, Competencies, and Abilities

This section of the chapter has defined, illustrated, and discussed important workplace individual differences based upon values, attitudes, demographics, competencies, and abilities. These five differences can be added to differences based upon personality and individual perception as seven important workplace individual differences.

The values of leaders and individuals comprise the foundation on which the culture at the workplace is based. Research connects these values with organizational culture and then culture to important workplace outcomes like performance (Gregory, Harris, Armenakis, & Shook, 2009). It should be no surprise that attitudes differ from person to person and that employee attitudes matter. For instance, research finds that positive worker attitudes about human resource programs and policies are correlated with higher performance and other important workplace outcomes (Kehoe & Wright, 2010).

Competencies and abilities can be seen as one of two direct contributors to the important workplace outcome of job performance. Many suggest that the two components of performance are "can do" and "will do." While "will do" questions refer to motivation primarily, "can do" questions are focused upon the competencies and abilities of the individual. Managing those who have both experience and abilities is different from managing those who lack either or both.

Implications for Management

Managing individual differences based upon values, attitudes, demographics, competencies, and abilities can be as challenging and rewarding as managing differences based upon personality and perception. While it may be obvious that individuals are different, many of the numerous implications for managers may be less obvious. Since managers are focused primarily upon performance and a positive organizational culture, the challenge is to manage either through or around individual differences. The first step in doing so is to realize intellectually some of the ways in which we differ one from another. Acknowledging stereotypes and biases about "types" of individuals can help managers avoid unnecessary misunderstandings and conflicts.

However, simply acknowledging that each individual is unique does not necessarily equip a manager to be effective at managing a diverse workforce. The appreciation and acceptance of what individual differences offer to a workforce is the next step. Research has found that those companies who have training programs about, and management policies encouraging, both individual and group differences report better business performance than their competitors. Also, companies with training to better enable acceptance of individual and group differences are most likely to have employees who believe procedures for determining promotions are fair.

It fact, it seems that it is the management of differences, not differences themselves, which creates the best opportunity for positive organizational outcomes. For instance, research suggests that racial diversity often correlates negatively with organizational performance. However, when moderated by appropriate management policies and practices, racial diversity correlates positively with organizational performance (Choi & Rainey, 2009). The effective understanding and managing of differences can take a negative situation and turn it into a positive outcome.

Perception

While personality differences between employees are often obvious, the unique way each individual perceives the world creates another difference important to managers who wish to motivate and lead employees effectively.

Definition

Perception is a process through which individuals sense, select, and organize stimuli they receive in order to give meaning to their environment.

"Where you stand depends on where you sit." This statement gets at the heart of the importance of understanding people's perceptions. Several individuals may look at the same thing but perceive it differently. Police report that witnesses to a car accident often report very different versions of the same accident. An illustration of perception within a work setting is that an employee may be viewed by one colleague as a hard worker who puts forth sincere effort, but viewed by another colleague as a lazy worker who expends no effort at all.

Therefore, viewpoint or perception is a key individual difference. Another simple example to illustrate this is to consider that two individuals may perceive the same movie differently, one may like the film and the other may dislike the film. Perceptions vary!

Perceptual Process

Perception can best be viewed as a multi-step process. The steps of the human perception process are sensation, selection, and organization.

Sensation. This is the first step in perception. Stimuli in the external environment are observed by our human senses. We observe sensations by hearing, seeing, touching, smelling, and tasting. Workplaces are filled with people, events, and objects which are observed through these five senses. The environment produces an overload of sensations. This stimuli overload sets up the need for the next step in the perception process; selection.

Selection. This is the step in perception at which the human brain focuses upon certain stimuli and ignores others. We notice how fast a car drives past us on the freeway but we fail to notice the color of the car or the gender of the driver. Why we select to pay attention to only certain stimuli is very interesting and complex. One way to analyze perceptual selection is to divide the factors driving this selection into external and internal factors.

Internal factors. These factors influencing the selection step in perception would include things about us as individuals. One view of perception is that we don't hear or see things as they are but rather as *we* are. Aspects about us as individuals would include our motivation or needs, our prior learning, and our personality. For instance, when we are hungry and need to eat we pay attention to the food court if we are in a shopping mall. However, we will pay less attention to restaurants, food commercials, and food fragrances if we are not motivated by hunger at the moment. We are also more likely to pay attention to things we have learned about, or studied, before. Our personality also influences our attention selection. For instance, a person who is "open to new experiences" will be more inclined to investigate the new coffee shop in the office building than someone who is "closed to new experiences."

External factors. These factors influencing selection include aspects of the stimulus such as motion, size, intensity, contrast, novelty, and repetition of the sensation. For instance, something that is moving is more likely to "catch our eye" than something sitting still. Something large moving toward us is more likely to attract our attention than something very small. We are more likely to hear a loud sound than a very quiet one. We are more likely to notice or attend to something that sounds or tastes very different or is repeated again and again.

Organization. This is the third step in the process of perception. This is the stage at which the individual tries to make sense of stimuli being observed and interpret it. This step in perception is also complex. Two of the factors which help individuals to assemble, organize and categorize information are the *figure-ground differentiation* and *perceptual grouping* effects. We are more likely to pay attention to the figure that is perceived as being the primary image in the foreground rather than the image in the background. This natural tendency to focus upon the figure or "subject" rather than the "ground" or background is well understood by those in many occupations. For instance, the marketing professional wants the observer to see the advertiser's product and so the product will be presented as the figure in contrast to a background. However, what is the figure and what is the ground depends upon the organization being conducted in the mind of the observer at the moment. For instance, in the classic drawing (see Figure 1) an individual can see a black goblet in front of a white background, or two white faces, looking at each other, in front of a black background. Another example of differing perception is the dress which was perceived differently by different individuals—some saw it as being blue and black, whereas others saw it as being gold and white.

Figure 1
Figure–Ground Differentiation

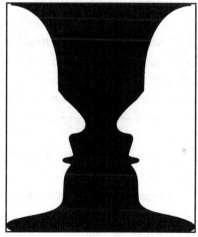

Perceptual grouping is the brain's activity of grouping several individual stimuli into a pattern that is meaningful. We see certain stars in the sky at night and we can perceive the Big Dipper. We see a group of cars driving closely together at a slow speed and we interpret the group of cars as a funeral procession. We have seen a funeral procession before and we group the cars in our mind as a procession rather than individual cars. Therefore we have given meaning to what we see.

In summary, the mind is active at dealing with all of the stimuli it receives through a process called perception. Through the steps of sensation, selection, and organization the world is taken in, given focus, and then organized into meaning. Of course, all of this is going on at the workplace all of the time.

Perceptual Errors. It would be interesting if everyone perceived things exactly the same. It would also be very dull if we did not have differences between individuals. Differences define us as individuals but can also lead to errors in perception.

Selective perception. People are bombarded with thousands of pieces of information daily. As stated before, individuals perceive information through their five senses in the sensation step of perception. The term "information overload" is popular because the amount of information available keeps increasing. Because individuals cannot focus upon all they observe, they engage in selective perception. Individuals select pieces of information on the basis of their own interests, background, experience, and attitudes. At the workplace, manager A is focused upon employees being well-dressed and walks into a meeting paying particular attention to what employees are wearing. Manager B is focused upon teamwork and walks into that same meeting and observes the amount of interaction between the members of the meeting and noticing little about the clothing of the employees. The perspective of these managers is different which causes their minds to perceive "reality" in different ways based upon selection. Often employees with low self-esteem over-select cues that imply that they are failing and under-select cues that would tell them that they are doing a good job. Managers must be aware of these differences in their employees, so as to be fair in their assessments of employees.

Contrast principle. People may view something due to its contrast with another object. This even affects our perception of objective values such as the weight of an object. For example, if a person lifts a light book, and then a heavier book, they will estimate the weight of the second book to be greater than if they lifted it without lifting the lighter book first.

Consider car buyers who are thrifty but are willing to spend $900 extra on a sound system upgrade that they haven't even heard. When could this happen? Right after they spend $43,000 on a new luxury sedan and the salesman during the closing mentions available upgrades. The same customer who would never spend $900 on a home stereo decides to spend $900 on a sound system upgrade because he or she just spent $43,000 on a new car. Car dealers have learned that after a person spends thousands on a new car, a few hundred for an upgrade by contrast doesn't appear to be as extravagant, and thus they wait until after the price of the vehicle has been agreed upon to offer a series of upgrades. Similar examples could be drawn from the real estate profession where buyers end up sometimes going beyond their comfortable mortgage limits.

Projection. Individuals often assume that others are similar to themselves. The tendency for people to attribute their own feelings or characteristics onto others is called projection. For example, if a particular manager is status conscious or has a strong desire of power, then he or she may extend these traits to other managers. This perception disorder can even lead one to project one's own traits or characteristics when evaluating others. "He seemed very aggressive to me," is translated to "I am sure he seemed very aggressive to you too (since I believe you react like me)." Managers often tend to hire people like themselves because they project their own success onto others who are similar in some aspects. Of course hiring individuals who are truly just like the others at work can lead to a lack of diversity within a workplace. However, many aspects of another employee that seem similar to the observer are merely projections.

Expectation bias. Expectation bias (or availability bias) occurs when individuals expect a certain outcome because it is easy for them to imagine—because it is readily available. In fact, it is generally normal for emotionally charged possibilities to be perceived as more likely than other outcomes (Thompson, Neale, & Sinaceur, 2004). Consider an actual zoning case in which neighbors who heard about a proposed new multiple-unit housing development in their quiet, single family house neighborhood. They quickly formed an "opposition group" to appear before the city zoning commission and spoke out against the proposal. Why? They had expected to see a proposal for unsightly, low-cost housing which would lower their property values, because those were the televised images they were familiar with from other neighborhood zoning battles. In reality the proposal was for an upscale, expensive retirement living project which the neighbors eventually embraced. Initial expectations can be quite powerful.

Stereotyping. Stereotyping is the process of judging people based on superficial qualities rather than essential characteristics. It can also be the process of judging people on the basis of what the observer perceives about the group to which they belong. For example, an individual might have encountered people identified by their race, ethnic background, age, or occupation. In observing these individuals, an assumption is made that the individuals observed possess certain traits. Next, a perception is formed that everyone in this category possesses these common traits. For example, suppose Juan observes several engineers during his lifetime *all* of whom are bad at communication. Juan forms the stereotype that *all* engineers are bad communicators. When a new engineer joins the team at work Juan believes that the new engineer is going to be bad at communication also. Actually the new engineer might or might not be good or bad at communication. Stereotypes strip an individual of his/her individual characteristics, and instead provide an individual with perceived group characteristics.

Halo effect. A halo effect occurs when a person uses only one characteristic of an individual to form their overall impression of the individual. For example, one trusted employee is always punctual and arrives at work early and opens up for business each day. Their manager, due to this punctuality factor, gives the employee high evaluation on *all* areas of their work. This high evaluation includes factors such as customer service along with quality and quantity of work. However, in reality the employee is only an average performer in those non-punctuality areas. The high and accurate rating—on punctuality—was biasing the other parts of the evaluation! You can notice this in a college scenario as well, and perhaps use it to your advantage at times—a student who is always present in class, and looks attentive, will foster a halo effect upon his/her professor, and perhaps reap the rewards of a favorable perception.

Halo effects may occur from something that is either favorable or unfavorable that influences how the individual is perceived. A negative halo, also called the "devil's horns effect," can also occur. Consider the sales manager who is routinely slow at returning calls from her supervisor and thus receives poor evaluations from that supervisor—when in reality the quality and quantity of his or her sales should be rated as excellent. Perhaps, the reason the sales manager is slow in returning calls is because he or she is busy making successful sales pitches.

Self-fulfilling prophecy. A self-fulfilling prophecy occurs when a person's expectations of another individual's abilities determine his or her behavior and performance, thus making the expectations come true. Research in this area could be summarized to say that when managers' expectations are raised for individuals performing a wide variety of tasks, higher levels of performance and achievement have been obtained. A related self-fulfilling prophecy phenomenon, the *Galatea Effect*, occurs when high self-expectations lead to high performance. The theory is that people's behaviors are consistent with their own expectation, and those behaviors, in turn, influence their outcomes. People gain information from a variety of sources to formulate judgments about their own ability to perform a certain job at a given level. That judgment then influences the effort and persistence they expend in performing their job. This effort ultimately influences their actual job performance (McNatt & Judge, 2004). Unfortunately, it is possible for self-fulfilling prophecy to also lead to negative outcomes. The opposite of the *Galatea Effect* is the *Golem Effect*, where job performance deteriorates due to low expectations.

Fundamental attribution error. *Attribution* is the process in which one person assigns *causes or motives* to the behavior of another person. This generally results in attributing credit or blame. This theory has important implications for managers. Fundamental attribution error is when the manager blames poor performance upon the worker for "internal causes"—either lack of effort or skill. Conversely, this error is also found when the manager credits good performance by the employee to external reasons—good coworkers, excellent support, or luck. This means that when an employee's performance is poor the manager's perceptual lens does not cue her/him to see external causes as the likely blame.

Self-serving bias. Fundamental attribution error and self-serving bias are in some way two sides of the same coin. If the fundamental attribution is harsh with *others*, the self-serving bias is lenient with one's *self*. People often exhibit the tendency to take credit for positive outcomes of their own behavior, but deny the blame for negative outcomes of their behavior. For example, if a marketing vice president champions a product that becomes successful, he or she might attribute success to his or her understanding of the customers and the marketplace. However, if the same product is unsuccessful, the marketing vice president might attribute this poor performance to external causes like the marketing research firm that provided the sales estimates or perhaps blame it on the poor economy.

Outcomes of Perception

As discussed, each of these perceptual problems increases the opportunity for miscommunication, misunderstanding, conflict, and other negative workplace outcomes. When individuals see or hear the same message differently they are likely to have trouble communicating about that message. If the manager makes comments in a meeting that some individuals perceived as communicating that there will be job stability for the next year, but others perceived the comments to signal possible layoffs there are likely to be communication problems in the near future. Further, many, if not most, conflicts arise from difference in points of view or how individuals differently frame their understanding. Differences in communication can escalate to conflicts. An effective workplace should seek to minimize conflicts and misunderstandings so that better focus can be given to the tasks at hand.

Implications for Management

It is important for managers and workers to recognize that others may view the same ideas, concepts or facts very differently due to any of the perceptual distortions that we talk about in this chapter. Thus, an employee who strongly disagrees with another on an issue may not have a personal disliking of the other person, but instead just have a different viewpoint due to a perception distortion. An inexperienced manager could believe that the dissenting employee does not like that individual. This manager may even misinterpret differences in perception as insubordination. The situation would then become potentially fraught with conflict.

Self-regulation, training, and education can help solve problems based upon issues of perception. Managers must self-regulate their own behavior by consciously examining their own understanding so as to be aware of the perception process and to avoid common errors in perception. However, self-regulation must be based upon a sound foundation. To enable the manager to better understand perception, organizations need to provide training and development. For instance, training managers about the fundamental attribution error can enable supervisors to avoid being quick to blame subordinates for lack of effort when something goes wrong. Education and educative travel can also be encouraged, as education and travel can both provide one with a better understanding of how perceptions differ, and are prone to faulty attributions. Jobs today require higher levels of education than ever before. Understanding perception is a key component in courses in psychology, sociology, business, and other degree programs. Organizational support of education can help managers obtain a baseline of knowledge on many issues, including the perception process.

Questions for Students

1. Why is the concept of individual differences important to managers?
2. What is personality and how is this concept different from a mood?
3. What are the personality traits which comprise the Big Five Model of personality and where do you believe you rate on each of them? Complete the scale in the appendix for further illumination.
4. Discuss the following personality traits and how differences on these might impact a work team: Locus of Control, Type A, B, and D personalities.
5. What are the three steps included in the process of perception? Describe how a difference in perception at the workplace between a manager and a subordinate could cause problems.
6. Discuss how the following perceptual distortions—selective perception, halo effect, self-fulfilling prophecy, and the fundamental attribution error – can cause a manager to do a poor job of assessing the true performance of a subordinate.
7. What is the difference between Terminal and Instrumental values? Which is more important to a front-line and/or junior employee?
8. How has the Work Ethic of US workers changed over the past generations? Interview an older person that you know to learn more about this trend.
9. What is an attitude? Explain is the A–B–C model of attitudes.
10. How does racial diversity affect the management of a department of employees?
11. List some physical abilities that might be important at the workplace. How can an employer best screen for these where hiring?

Exercise: Perceptions of Personality
in Public Figures

Divide the class into groups (3–5 members) and have the groups discuss how the big 5 personality traits are perceived by people. Each group should select two individuals, one that the group admires, and one that the group dislikes. Then, the students should discuss their perceptions of the personalities of those two individuals, and compare the two personalities with each other. For instance, students could pick Dalai Lama and compare his personality profile with that of Kim Jong Un—many other individuals can be compared along these lines. Students should discuss specific examples of how they think certain personality traits affected their judgments of the individuals. Which trait was most instrumental in their admiring someone, and which trait was most instrumental in their disliking someone?

Have one member from each group report after the team has finished its discussion.

1. Which of these five personality traits was viewed as most helpful in terms of creating a positive image for an individual? Is that trait also linked with performance?
2. Which of these five personality traits was viewed as least helpful in terms of creating a positive image for an individual? Is that trait also linked with performance?
3. Is there a "perfect" personality that every individual should aspire to possess, that would be linked with good performance?

Case: Employee Development Opportunity: A tale of two perspectives

You are looking for someone to send to a national industry conference on your behalf. As Vice-President of your division you are invited to many conferences each year, but you cannot attend them all. You know that it can be useful to develop a promising junior employee by sending him or her to attend a conference on your behalf. There will be two days of sessions at the upcoming conference and it is being held in a location near a popular beach. The conference was obviously picked based upon the attractiveness of the location. It is also relatively near so the flight time is only two hours.

You have a manager, Kim Henderson that reports directly to you that would be a natural selection for send to the conference. However, Kim has applied for retirement in the upcoming year. You have asked her for a recommendation for this assignment.

Kim has average to above-average results in her department. You have heard some of her employees joking about how Kim is a stickler for punctuality.

She arrives about one-hour prior to the start of the workday each day. She also is viewed as being harsh with employees who occasionally come in a few minutes late.

Kim is recommending the only other person in her department who also arrives very early each morning, Melanie Fitzpatrick. You can see in the department data that Melanie's outcomes are only average but Kim defends her as the best worker. "She is always ready to go at the beginning of the day," according to Kim. "She works hard and that is why she performs so well."

You assume that Melanie will also be Kim's recommendation as her replacement once Kim retires. You wonder if her assessment is biased or unfair because she is so focused upon one element of performance—punctuality.

Jorge Borge easily has the best outcomes in the department according to the official records. However, Kim frequently has something bad to say about Jorge. You do not know a whole lot about Jorge personally. You do know that Jorge has five young children. You know that Kim complains that "Jorge never arrives even 15 minutes early!" You also know he also never arrives late because you checked his attendance records. Kim has said on several occasions that Jorge's "numbers"—the productivity reports available to you—are high only because his work is "easier" than that of others (like Melanie). She has also said that Jorge is "lucky."

You are inclined to ask Jorge to attend the conference on your behalf since you are impressed with his "numbers" However, you do not want to disregard the recommendation of your manger, Kim. Kim seemed somewhat angry when you asked whether it might be a good idea to send Jorge to the meeting instead of Melanie.

Exercise: The Big Five Personality

The exercise on the Big Five asks students to discuss the five personality traits of OCEAN—Openness, Conscientiousness, Extraversion, Agreeableness, and Neuroticism.

Question 1. The trait most likely to create a positive image for individuals is agreeableness—but results may vary, and if so, that would be very much context driven. Depending on which traits various groups talk about, class discussion will be fostered. For the second part of the question, one answer could be conscientiousness. There is a good deal of confusion about the relative importance of personality when focused upon job performance. In general personality is not a good predictor of future performance. However, some studies discuss higher correlations between personality and performance. These are almost entirely based upon the single personality trait of Conscientiousness –which can not accurately be determined during hiring. This is because applicants will engage in impression-management (they will lie) about questions on Conscientiousness on a hiring questionnaire.

Instructors ask how and why applicants might lie on such questions during interviews. Other implicit theories about how personality can be important for hiring can be rational but have not been supported despite decades of research. Instructors should keep the learning on the link between personality and performance based in reality.

On the other hand, we all have personal preferences about personalities around which we like to be. One question might be, "Do we date and/or marry individuals who are like us, or different from us, on personality?" Do we seek the congruence and expectations of someone with a similar personality to our own, or the excitement and unexpected qualities of someone with a different personality? Do opposites really attract?

Question 2. The trait most likely to create a negative image for individuals is neuroticism—but results may vary, and if so, that would be very much context driven. Depending on which traits various groups talk about, class discussion will be fostered. There is no link in terms of "least useful" personality for performance. However it can be fun identifying personalities with whom students have had trouble. There is a whole literature out there about working with, and managing, "difficult people." In doing this exercise in the past we have seen "Closed" (opposite of Open) and Neuroticism (opposite of Emotionally Stable) as unappealing personalities. However, most everyone has known people with these sometimes unappealing traits who have been excellent employees.

Question 3. This questions returns students to a preference for a variety of personalities. This is a practical approach since this is what any employee is likely to experience at the workplace, as long as the number of the members of the group is not small. Having everyone in the group as an Introvert or as Closed could make meetings very difficult.

Case: Manager's Retirement

This realistic case study places the student in the position of deciding on someone to send to a conference. This selection is important because a manager (Kim Henderson) will soon retire and this could be seen as an early indicator of preference for an internal candidate. It would also help develop or train the person selected.

The facts make Kim "guilty" of having a preference for "coming to work early" behavior. This preference seems to create a "Halo Effect" perceptual bias that may create more distortions—like selective perception (and perhaps Fundamental Attribution Error).

The manager (student) also has a bias perhaps—to the performance records which themselves may not tell the whole story at work. Bias toward printed records is also a common bias at work.

Question 1. The "Perception Distortions" might include selective perception, projection, stereotyping, halo effect (this is probably the primary one), and fundamental attribution error. Haloing is what we know or suspect and the other distortions are likely outcomes.

Question 2. The student may be inclined to select Jorge based upon the records. However, the records might be very incomplete and so this also might be a halo effect distortion ("bias toward the numbers"). For instance, if you had an employee working in a shoe store the only record you might have is the number of shoes sold. However, you might be lacking data on other aspects important to the job. For instance, what about stocking and restocking shoes, dealing appropriately with customer complaints, etc.

Question 3. Halo effect distortion can lead to Fundamental Attribution Error (and other distortions). If Kim cherishes coming in extra-early above almost all other behaviors then one could argue this could lead to blaming Jorge for internal weakness to do this behavior. Any poor performances on Melanie's part could be excused (self-serving bias) for external causes.

Question 4. The Vice President is left with imperfect information and yet still needs to make a decision. It is important for students to realize that the answer to every management decision cannot be to make no decision and "wait until you have more information." Managers cannot maximize every decision.

It might show a lack of emotional or social intelligence in working with your manager Kim if you decide to send Jorge. Kim has shown emotion on this issue of conference selection and someone high on social intelligence would take this into account.

On the other hand, this might be an excellent opportunity to learn whether Jorge is a legitimate candidate to replace Kim once Kim retires.

Appendix—Big 5 Scale

Instructions: How well do the following statements describe your personality? For each statement below, use the following scale to indicate which is most descriptive of your personality:

1 = Strongly Disagree
2 = Disagree
3 = Slightly Disagree
4 = Neither agree nor disagree
5 = Slightly agree
6 = Agree
7 = Strongly agree

1. I see myself as someone who is reserved.
2. I see myself as someone who is generally trusting.
3. I see myself as someone who tends to be lazy.
4. I see myself as someone who is relaxed, handles stress well.
5. I see myself as someone who has few artistic interests.
6. I see myself as someone who is outgoing, sociable.
7. I see myself as someone who tends to find fault with others.
8. I see myself as someone who does a thorough job.
9. I see myself as someone who gets nervous easily.
10. I see myself as someone who has an active imagination.
11. I see myself as someone who is considerate and kind to almost everyone.

R indicates reversed items (so, the scores reverse here—7 becomes 1, 6 becomes 2, 5 becomes 3, 4 remains 4, 3 becomes 5, 2 becomes 6, and 1 becomes 7)

Extraversion: 1R, 6
Agreeableness: 2, 7R
Conscientiousness: 3R, 8
Neuroticism: 4R, 9
Openness to Experience: 5R, 10, 11

Higher scores on dimensions reveal that your personality is shaped more by those dimensions.

Suggestions for Further Reading

Boyle, G. J., Matthews, G., & Saklofske, D. H. (2008). The SAGE handbook of personality: Theory and assessment of personality theories and models (Vol. 1). Thousand Oaks, CA: Sage.

Gibson, C. B., Cooper, C. D., & Conger, J. A. (2009). Do you see what we see? The complex effects of perceptual distance between leaders and teams. *Journal of Applied Psychology, 94,* 62–76.

Poropat, A. E. (2009). A meta-analysis of the five-factor model of personality and academic performance. *Psychological Bulletin, 135,* 322–338.

References

Baron, R. A. (1989). Personality and organizational conflict: The Type A behavior pattern and self-monitoring. *Organizational Behavior and Human Decision Processes, 44,* 281–297.

Choi, S. & Rainey, H.G. (2009). Managing diversity in U.S. federal agencies: Effects of diversity and diversity management on employee perceptions of organizational performance. *Public Administration Review, 70(1),* 109–121.

Friedman, M., & Rosenman, R. H. (1974). *Type A behavior and your heart.* New York: Knopf.

Gregory, B. T., Harris, S. G., Armenakis, A. A., & Shook, C. L. (2009). Organizational culture and effectiveness: A study of values, attitudes, and organizational outcomes. Journal of Business Research, 62, 673–679.

Kehoe, R. R. & Wright, P. M. (2010). The impact of high performance human resource practices on employees' attitudes and behaviors. *Journal of Management, 36,* 1–26.

Kunze, F., Boehm, S. A., & Bruch, H. (2011). Age diversity, age discrimination climate and performance consequences—a cross organizational study. *Journal of Organizational Behavior, 32,* 1099–1379.

Lefcourt, H. M. (Ed.). (2014). *Locus of control: Current trends in theory & research.* Psychology Press.

Malanga, S. (2009). Whatever happened to the work ethic? *City Journal of the Manhattan Institute, 19* (3), 3–8.

McCrae, R. R., Costa, P.T. Jr. (1987). Validation of the five-factor model of personality across instruments and observers. *Journal of Personality and Social Psychology, 52,* 81–90.

McNatt, D. B. & Judge, T. A. (2004). Boundary conditions of the Galetta Effect: A field experiment. *Academy of Management Journal, 47,* 550–565.

Rushton, J. P., & Irwing, P. (2008). A General Factor of Personality (GFP) from two meta-analyses of the Big Five: and. *Personality and Individual Differences, 45*(7), 679–683.

Spector, P. E. (1982). Behavior in organizations as a function of employee's locus of control. *Psychological Bulletin, 91,* 482–497.

Thompson, L., Neale, M. & Sinaceur, M., (2004). The evolution of cognition and biases. In M. J. Gelfand & J. M. Brett (Eds.), *The handbook of negotiation and culture* (pp. 7–44). Stanford, CA: Stanford Business Books.

Versteeg, H., Spek, V., Pedersen, S., & Denollet, J., (2011). Type D personality and health status in cardiovascular disease populations: A meta-analysis of prospective studies. *European Journal of Cardiovascular Prevention & Rehabilitation, 30,* 1741–8267.

2. Generational Management

Dana Burr Bradley
Western Kentucky University

Organizations are facing a more diverse group of employees characterized by age, gender, race, and educational level. One of the most challenging issues for managers to face is that large numbers of workers will retire while a new generation of employees enters the job market. This rapidly changing landscape requires organizations to seek out resources to help them understand generational differences, and for managers to adapt to these differences by adjusting leadership styles, workplace culture, and human resource management skills. With four generations currently in the job market, organizations have never been as tested as they are today when it comes to managing a generationally diverse workforce. While it is important not to stereotype, each generation has some differences in their preferences, communication, learning and working styles. The ability to identify and respond to these differences and design a common working environment that supports these differences calls for creative management strategies in many organizations.

Nature of Generational Management

Definition

Generational management is associated with understanding the differences, and facilitating, and optimizing these differences among the four generations of employees working alongside each other. Managers do this by incorporating differences in expectations from an employer, work-life balance, communication, and learning styles into their management strategies.

Generational Theory

A generational cohort is a group of individuals similar in age who have experienced the same historical events within the same time period. The term "generation" as it is used in this chapter should not be confused with members of different familial generations (i.e., child, parent, and grandparent). Generations are not self elective groups; individuals do not choose to be a part of their generation, or are they necessarily self aware of their membership. Instead, generation membership is based on the shared position of an age-group in historical time. A generation not only shares birth years, but also considerable life events at critical developmental stages, usually occurring during the childhood and adolescent years (Carpenter & Charon, 2014). These shared experiences may create similar points of view, principles, methods of communication, and standards, which are reflected in the workplace.

Today's workforce employs up to four generations within an organization, which can partially be attributed to increased longevity and individuals remaining employed past retirement years. Spanning more than 60 years, these current workforce generations display individual traits, values, and perspectives that set them apart. This leads to a workplace where there are multiple sets of personal values, attitudes and personal preferences. These diverse characteristics can create challenges for human capital management. Multi-generations impact human resource issues including retention and compensation, along with management issues such as leadership, motivation, communication, and teamwork. Solving problems of conflicting attitudes, miscommunication, and motivational differences helps engage each generation and bridges the organizational generation gap.

Generational Taxonomy. In this chapter, the taxonomy developed by Howe and Strauss (2000) is used. The authors used rich historical data to define U.S. generations: Traditionalists (born before 1946), Baby Boomers (born during 1946–1964), Generation X (born during 1965–1980), and Generation Y or Millennials (born during 1981–1994).

Generational Overview. Each generation possesses a general set of traits which are delineated in individual perspectives of employment creating a managerial challenge for organizations. Traits such as values, attitudes, motivators, communication style, and technological knowledge may differ among the four generations and factor into management of the organization's culture.

Traditionalists. This is also known as the "Greatest Generation," were born between 1922 and 1944. This generation grew up during the depression era in conservative, structured homes with strong nuclear families and parents modeling traditional roles. Central influences for the Traditionalists include two world wars, Disney's first animated film, the Japanese attack on Pearl Harbor, and the beginning of the Korean War. The wake of the Great Depression and the world wars instilled values of self-sacrifice, loyalty, patriotism, and duty. Traditionalists often have a strong work ethic and value and seek respect. Though traditionalists only make up five to six percent of the workforce, they continue to be important members of the workplace. Traditionalists' sense of loyalty and the value of delayed gratification commonly kept them at one company for their entire career (Carpenter & Charon, 2014). Their dominant values are benevolence, loyalty, and conformity. They prefer direct, face-to-face communication, and need-to-know information. Traditionalists who remain in the workforce are past the retirement age, but linger because of economic hardship or boredom. At this point in their career they are motivated not by promotion or other extrinsic rewards, but by their value and work being connected to the overall good of the organization (Carpenter & Charon, 2014)).

Baby Boomers. This generation was born between 1945 and 1964. This generation grew up with post-World War II financial affluence and security, with an emphasis on the nuclear family and stay-at-home moms. Major influences of the Baby Boomer generation include the introduction of television into homes, the assassinations of John F. Kennedy and Martin Luther King, Jr., the Cold War, the Korean and Vietnam Wars, Woodstock, and Watergate. Raised to be creative and inquiring by their parents, Boomers entered the workforce questioning and lacking respect for authority (Wesner & Miller 2008). Also known as the "Me" generation, Boomers are described as confident, driven, career-oriented, and competitive.

Baby Boomers' dominant values include tolerance, authority, achievement, and determination (Amayah & Gedro, 2014). Their aspirations for success make them career ladder-climbers, often at the expense of the organizations they work for. They are more likely to change jobs or companies than the generations before them and do not consider job security a critical part of job satisfaction (Wesner & Miller, 2008). They are motivated by status, promotions, extrinsic rewards, and recognition for achievement (Lyons & Kuron, 2014). Boomers are excellent networkers and focus on relation-based interactions with co-workers and managers. In the workplace, Boomers utilize email and instant messaging; however, face-to-face, telephone, and one-on-one interactions with colleagues is preferable (Amayah & Gedro, 2014). Having been introduced to television at an early age, Boomers are no strangers to technology and have experienced great technological advancement in their lifetime.

Generation X. This often referred to as the "lost" generation, is the generation born between 1965 and 1980. This generation came of age during a sharp economic downturn in the early 1990's, which was fraught with institutional scandal and corporate layoffs which affected their parents. Early Generation Xers entered the workforce during this same economy. Many Gen Xers did not have the security of the nuclear family, having experienced parental divorce and mothers entering the workforce. As a result, Gen Xers tend to be independent, adaptable, and autonomous. Major influences on Generation X include the Challenger disaster, the Berlin Wall, Tiananmen Square, the Clinton sex scandal, and the prosperous economy of the late 1980's (Fountain, 2014). Generation Xers are described as skeptical of authority, suspicious of Boomer values, and will question anything static or status quo (Amayah & Gedro, 2014)

Generation Xers value stimulation, self-direction, self-gratification, and, like Baby Boomers, achievement (Amayah & Gedro, 2014). Reflecting the Boomer mentality, Xers are less committed to the organization in which they work, focusing instead on personal careers. Rather than a career ladder, Gen Xers are willing to move laterally for job satisfaction and are likely to change jobs and even careers multiple times. Generation Xers are generally comfortable with diversity, work well within a multi-cultural environment, and are more accepting of alternative lifestyles than the Boomer generation (Fountain, 2014). Rather than status or monetary compensation, Gen Xers are motivated by jobs offering flextime or telecommuting, independence, and organizations valuing a work–life balance. Despite the autonomy this generation seeks, Xers appreciate constant feedback with a direct approach to communication (Amayah & Gedro, 2014). Xers' main form of communication is through email, voicemail, and cell phones,

Generation Y. This generation more commonly known as *Millennials,* is possibly the largest generation currently in the workforce (Amayah & Gedro, 2014). Born between 1981 and 2000, they are the children of Baby Boomers. Major influences on this generation include the Oklahoma City bombing, Columbine High School, Y2K, 9/11, corporate scandals such as Enron, the Internet, instant messaging, and texting (Fountain, 2014). This is an extremely self-confident group, almost to the point of appearing arrogant, reflecting their parents' "Me" generation attitude. Millennials have carried their self-confident "me" attitude into the workplace earning them a reputation for holding an attitude of entitlement and high, if not unreasonable, expectation. Having been immersed in technology since birth, Millennials are more than at ease with technology. This generation is adept at using cell phones, computers, and the Internet, often simultaneously; thus, they have become proficient at multi-tasking on the job.

Millennials closely mirror Gen Xers in their dominant values, which include stimulation, self-direction, and self-gratification. Some studies Millennials value work/life balance, career development, mentoring, and training (Lyons & Kuron, 2014). They are naturally team oriented having participated in team activities including sports, study groups, and playgroups from a very young age. They work well in groups and understand the concept of collaborating to better accomplish tasks. Millennials primarily communicate through cell phones, instant messaging, and text messaging.

Generational Shift

The workplace is undergoing a generational shift and this is challenging how we think about managing people. Although the recent economic recession has allowed the retirement of Baby Boomers and Traditionalists from the job market, this is a temporary state of affairs. These generations are still aging and may simply exit the job market in even larger numbers faster when the economy turns around. At the same time, the Millennials are slowly entering into the workforce. The changing dynamics of the generational mix creates yet another management challenge.

Mass departure of the Baby Boomers, the transition of Generation X into leadership positions, and the influx of Millennials into the workforce are creating dramatic changes in organizational climate, including a dwindling labor force and an increased demand for high-skilled labor. Generation X is just over half the size of the Baby Boom and this means that there will likely be fewer members of that generation will be available to move into management roles. Not only is Gen X smaller in numbers than Baby Boomers, many women in this generation are not returning to work after having children. This decrease dramatically impacts the labor pool and the ability for organizations to draw from and develop the next set of leaders from this generation. Organizations will have to do more in order to recruit and retain talent, primarily within the Millennial generation.

Millennials have been the subject of best management practices over the last five years, which is largely due to the concern over the looming workforce gap. Many organizations are seeking to attract and retain Millennials. According to a report released jointly by the Department of Defense and the White House, the federal government is experiencing pressure to bolster its growing IT sector, which is dependent on Millennial skills. Managers are finding that they have to make adjustments in management models to meet the demands of this genera-tion which include providing more flexibility during the workday and providing opportunities for Millennials to learn on the job. (Napoli, 2015).

Outcomes of Generational Differences

Work Related Values

The Society for Human Resource Management (SHRM, 2004) surveyed 258 human resource (HR) professionals in the United States. The managers generally thought that there were positive relations between the generations. However, al-most half of the HR professionals observed conflict among employees as a result of generational differences largely due to differing perceptions of work ethic and work/life balance. Forty-two percent of the SHRM survey respondents reported that their organization has lost employees who are members of the two youngest generations because they felt that the members in the organization from the two older generations held top positions and they would not advance fast enough. The change in perceptions of work values may be one of the major contributors of generational conflicts in the workplace. Generational differences in work values may be linked to changes in the meaning of work. These changes are due to increasing expectations for work/life balance by the growing number of dual-career and single parent families and to the increased use of electronic media and continuous learning of new skills.

Values have been found to impact one's behavior and to shape how we see ourselves. Attitudes are evaluative statements and the attitudes developed by a generation influence how a person views the world, which includes how the person is motivated and wants to be managed. The common key values for each generation are:

- **Traditionalists:** Loyal, hardworking, financially conservative and faithful to institutions.
- **Baby Boomers:** Hardworking, have a sense of entitlement, optimistic, cynical toward institutions, and believe in endless youth.
- **Generation X:** Work hard, prefer "hands off" supervision, seek immediate gratification, and want their need for a work/life balance respected.
- **Millennials:** Adaptable to change, technologically advanced, seek challenging and motivating tasks, are flexible, and seek opportunities for growth including training.

The different values of the various generations may lead to conflict and loss of organizational effectiveness and efficiency. Communication and a positive organizational culture can help to resolve friction between the generations as well as meeting each generation's desire for different rewards.

Work Related Attitudes

The popular press often highlights generational difference in attitudes. Generally defined, work attitudes are evaluative or emotional reactions to various aspects of work. Despite the popular press' accounts, findings from empirical research on generations' work attitudes are mixed. Cross-sectional research have found that Boomers exhibit lower job involvement or commitment due to feelings of obligations, but higher commitment due to the perceived costs of leaving then their Gen X counterparts. Millennials exhibit a higher voluntary turnover rate than Boomers and Gen Xers, and Millennials and Gen Xers reported a higher desire to leave their current place of employment (Lyons & King, 2014).

The traits characterizing each generation are elements that can create barriers in workplace relations between managers and colleagues, influence training and team building, and determine the overall culture and climate of an organization. It is easy to imagine that working with people who seem to approach their professional obligations differently can create the appearance of conflict; these problems can manifest themselves in methods of management, reactions to authority, communication styles, approaches to work, and workplace expectations.

Implications for Management

Generational diversity creates a greater need for strong leadership skills to effectively manage individuals who bring their differences into the workforce. There are several things that managers can do to develop a more cohesive workplace. The first step for managers is to raise awareness of generational differences by acknowledging the presences of generational diversity within the workplace, and to leverage generational commonalities. The second step is for managers to recognize and move past their own generational preferences so they can develop an organizational culture that promotes diversity (Hernaus & Vokic, 2014).

Managers can model bias-free language, both written and spoken, and demonstrate a genuine acceptance of different methods and manners, which can create a work environment that will nurture and profit from diversity. Finding solutions to create a solid intergenerational workplace requires developing value-creating strategies and does not include a one-size-fits-all approach. This means creating multiple options for training and communication. Strategies will vary between organizations, but can be accomplished by identifying the core needs of each generation, providing training for generational diversity, and creating forums for open communication on generational values and viewpoints.

Continuity in management and supervisory practice are important for success in supporting multiple generations for several reasons. There are similarities as well as differences among the different generations. Furthermore, many of those differences are not ingrained within individuals, but are context dependent. Individuals within generations also constitute a diverse group and as such, preferences associated with a particular generation are not necessarily true of all its members. Finally, intergenerational conflict often appears to stem from errors of attribution and perception rather than from valid differences. Therefore, it appears that effective conflict management is essential for good management of a multiple generational workforce.

Retention

Boomers hold the majority of management and leadership positions and lean towards a bureaucratic method of management that does not resonate with Gen Xers or Millennials. Since Gen Xers are naturally skeptical of authority and resist status quo, they will not respond favorably to a routine management style. Given their tendency towards autonomy and independence, many Gen Xers also have adverse reactions to Boomer's collaborative, team player approach. Conversely, Gen Xer's style of management, inclusive of direct communication only when necessary, does not agree with a Millennials' need for instant approval and praise (Amayah & Gedro, 2014).

Training

Many organizations are now taking into account generational differences organizations train and develop employees. Most adults have a fundamental learning style and habits reflective of how they were taught when they were young (Hernaus & Vokic, 2014). Traditionalists and Baby Boomers are comfortable in a learning environment that includes lecture and printed text, and are familiar with a strict and structured format. As trainers and designers of trainings, Baby Boomers will lean towards creating a training environment reflective of their learning style and an environment they are comfortable in; however, younger generations often find Boomer training techniques slow, over laden with lecture, and lacking interactivity and technology. Younger workers identified different training needs than their older counterparts. For instance, older generations like skills training in their areas of expertise, whereas younger workers prefer leadership training. Since training needs differ, employers and HR managers should match training to specific needs (Mencl & Lester, 2014).

Management

One important implication for management is that managers need to be educated about and inform their employees about actual generational differences as well as generational similarities rather than making assumptions solely about differences. Strategies include accommodating employee differences by for instance, learning about their unique needs and serving them accordingly;

creating workplace choices such as allowing the workplace to shape itself around the work being done or decreasing bureaucracy; and operating from a sophisticated management style which would involve adapting leadership style to context or balancing concerns for task and concerns for people for instance. Managers should make sure that they do not assume all employees within a generational cohort value the same things. Managers still need to pay attention to individual differences such as personality, gender, and motivational needs when determining the best response in interpersonal situations. Other management strategies include respecting competence and initiative and nourishing retention by using such strategies as diverse ways of training, including one-on-one coaching opportunities, interactive computer-based training and classroom courses.

Communication and Respect

How technology is utilized in the work environment may both attenuate generational conflict and diminish outright disagreements. Often conflict is more likely to arise from errors of attribution and perception, than from valid differences. Therefore, effective communication is critical in dealing with generational conflict. Hageger & Lingham (2014) suggest paying more attention to how employees use technology to manage work and life domains. This has important ramifications for how employees communicate with each other and manage other life domains.

For example, employees and employers alike need to figure out why people are asking questions, as opposed to assuming that employees asking questions are causing trouble, being disrespectful or trying to make the person in authority look bad or a combination of these (Mencl & Lester, 2014). Managers and other employees should identify possible reasons why someone might be asking questions rather than jumping to the wrong conclusions. For example, younger workers tend to value building job skills and retaining marketability on the job market, which older managers may view as disloyalty. However, younger workers are more likely to stay with an employer willing to make an investment in his or her personal skills and who maximizes the use of their unique contribution as the first generation to grow up in the Internet era

Scripps Health in San Diego implemented a system-wide approach for attracting and retaining workers from all generations (AARP, 2007). As a result of systematic changes in their organization, employee satisfaction has increased as well as retention. Their efforts included:

- Conducting training for all leaders about generations. They learned about communication styles for each of the generations, studied workplace motivation and committed to a specific leadership strategy.
- Developed a life cycle employment and benefits program based on what employees need at certain stages of life and work.
- Created work/life and wellness programs including health assessments, concierge services, and on-site massage services.
- Implemented training and re-skilling scholarships, career pathways, and coaching.
- Revamped their employee orientation program to reflect their commitment to a multigenerational workforce.

Scripps Health understood the importance of managing from a perspective that values generational differences and incorporated these insights into their corporate culture.

Having an awareness of generational diversity is particularly important in light of the changes taking place in the workforce including the flattening of the hierarchy and involvement of employees in decision making which has heightened the interaction of employees from different generations. There is a real demographic change of fewer available workers over time and the demand for Baby Boomers to stay in the workplace longer due to necessity or personal choice.

Managers that acknowledge the experience of older workers, and respect the talents and contribution of new workers may experience a more cohesive organizational culture. Employers who accommodate their employees' desire to balance work and personal goals may also have stronger cohesion across the workplace. In conclusion, the dynamics of the workplace have changed and will continue to change. Managers that are pro-active in managing these changing dynamics will be the employers of choice in the future.

Questions for Students

1. What are some of the generational characteristics and traits that you can identify within yourself?
2. Why is it important to understand your own generational traits and preferences?

3. What are some benefits to having multiple generations in an organization?
4. What are some of the dangers when we label people or over-generalize generational characteristics and preferences?

Exercise

Overview: This activity encourages participants to think critically about the stereotypes they have of other generations.

Objectives: Help participants identify and think critically about stereotypes that are commonly held for younger and older people.

Steps

1. Write out each of the statements listed below on a blackboard or large sheet of paper. They could also be typed up and handed out.
2. Read out loud each of the statements listed below and have participants vote (show of hands) whether they think the target is young people, older people, or perhaps both young and older people.

- They always stick together and keep their distance from other age groups.
- I hate the way they drive. They're a menace on the road.
- They're always taking and never giving. They think the world owes them a living.
- They're so opinionated. They think they know everything.
- They're never satisfied, always complaining about something.
- Don't hire them, you can't depend on them.
- Don't they have anything better to do than hang around the parks and shopping malls?
- Why are they always so forgetful?
- I wish I had as much freedom as they have.
- Why don't they act their age?

Note those statements that call to mind common stereotypes of young people and older people.

3. Discuss using the following themes: Has anyone ever heard any of these statements? Stereotypes are the basis for prejudice and discrimination. Note how such statements express common stereotypes about groups of people only defined as "they." As a youth or an adult, have you ever experienced or known anyone who has experienced prejudice or discrimination based on their age (for example, when applying for a job, renting an apartment, or trying to participate in some activity of another age group)? Can both younger and older people be the victims of prejudice and discrimination based on age? Are there any other ways in which "growing up" is similar to "growing old"? What are they?

Case: Hiring and Retention in an Intergenerational Marketplace

Askers Equipment Company, a high technology manufacturing company has over 5000 employees in 10 different states. The corporation is experiencing a lot of Baby Boomers retiring and exiting the organization. This means that Askers is losing their knowledge, skills and insights. At the same time, many young workers were leaving Askers for other hi-tech companies (especially in their Silicon Valley location). The Human Resources Department in conjunction with senior leadership at Askers has convened a working group to identify possible solutions *before* the company experiences major adverse consequences.

The group came up with two strategic arrangements. Askers developed arrangements with exiting employees so they can come back as consultants or on emergency basis. By utilizing "alumni" networks, Askers can continue to leverage the strengths and relationships of many willing retirees. They can keep the specialized knowledge of Boomer employees and help them document and coach other high-potential replacements.

Askers also created the Early in Career" ERG for Millennials and "Experienced Influencers" group for Boomers and other maturing workers. These groups are self directed and meet regularly to create a culture around multi-generational collaboration and teamwork. The desired outcome: Lower turnover.

Suggestions for Further Reading

DelCampo, M. R. G., Haney, M. J., Haggerty, L. A., & Knippel, L. A. (2012). *Managing the multi-generational workforce: From the GI generation to the millennials.* Gower Publishing.

Ng, E., Lyons, S. T., & Schweitzer, L. (Eds.). (2012). *Managing the new workforce: International perspectives on the millennial generation.* Edward Elgar Publishing.

Parry, E., & Urwin, P (2011). Generational differences in work values: A review of theory and evidence. *International Journal of Management Reviews, 13*, 79–96.

References

AARP, (2007). *Leading a multigenerational workforce valuing the generations: A study of scripps health.* Washington, DC: AARP

Amayah, A. T., & Gedro, J. (2014). Understanding generational diversity: Strategic human resource management and development across the generational "divide." *New Horizons in Adult Education and Human Resource Development, 26*(2), 36–48.

Carpenter, M. J., & Charon, L. C. (2014). Mitigating multigenerational conflict and attracting, motivating, and retaining millennial employees by changing the organizational culture: A theoretical model. *Journal of Psychological Issues in Organizational Culture, 5*(3), 68–84

Fountain, J. M. (2014). *Differences in generational work values in America and their implications for educational leadership: A longitudinal test of Twenge's model.* University of Louisiana at Lafayette.

Haeger, D. L., & Lingham, T. (2014). A trend toward Work–Life Fusion: A multi-generational shift in technology use at work. *Technological Forecasting and Social Change, 89*, 316–325.

Hernaus, T., & Pološki Vokic, N. (2014). Work design for different generational cohorts: Determining common and idiosyncratic job characteristics. *Journal of Organizational Change Management, 27*(4), 615–641.

Howe, N., & Strauss, W. (2000). *Millennials rising: The next great generation.* New York: Vintage Books.

Lyons, S., & Kuron, L. (2014). Generational differences in the workplace: A review of the evidence and directions for future research. *Journal of Organizational Behavior, 35*(S1), S139-S157.

Mencl, J., & Lester, S. W. (2014). More alike than different what generations value and how the values affect employee workplace perceptions. *Journal of Leadership & Organizational Studies, 21*(3), 257–272.

Napoli, J. (2015, January). The Net Generation: An Analysis of Lifestyles, Attitudes and Media Habits. In *Proceedings of the 2000 Academy of Marketing Science (AMS) Annual Conference* (pp. 362–362). Springer International Publishing.

Society for Human Resource Management (SHRM) (2004) *2004 generational differences survey.* Alexandria, VA: Society for Human Resource Management.

Wesner, M. S., & Miller, T. (2008). Boomers and millennials have much in common. *Organization Development Journal, 26,* 89–96

PART II
Managing Communication, Conflict, and Stress

3. Communication

Deloris McGee Wanguri
University of Houston–Downtown

Communication is prerequisite for the effective management of personnel in the workplace. Communication is ubiquitous in organizations. It occurs within a variety of settings, including interactions between supervisors and workers, discussions within teams and committees, and interfaces with the community. It also encompasses all levels of management, frequently originating, for example, at the top management level of the organization and extending downward to lower-level employees, and sometimes originating at lower levels of the organization and extending upward to supervisory or middle management. Successful communication is essential to the operations of all organizations.

Nature of Organizational Communication

Defining Communication

In any communication interaction, regardless of the setting or the number of people involved, you can expect to find these 10 elements:

- *sender*, the originator of the message.
- *receiver*, the destination of the message.
- *message*, the actual signal that is transmitted from the sender to the receiver.
- *noise*, anything that interferes with the channel of communication.
- *channel*, the means by which we convey the message.
- *encoding*, the process of converting ideas into a message.
- *decoding*, the process of attaching meaning to a message.
- *context*, the setting in which communication occurs.
- *feedback*, the response of a receiver to a sender's message.
- *field of experience,* the total makeup of each participant in the communication situation.

Communication therefore is a process that occurs when *senders* and *receivers* with overlapping *fields of experience encode* and *decode* respectively to exchange *messages* in a particular *context* by the use of verbal and/or nonverbal *channels* of communication and react to each other's messages through verbal and/or nonverbal *feedback*. The effectiveness of this communication process can be diminished by semantic, physical, physiological, or psychological *noise*.

Levels of Communication

Communication within an individual and between and among people occurs in various types of interactions. These are as follows.

Intrapersonal. Some communication is intrapersonal, occurring within the individual. This level of communication can include one's self-perception, self-worth, self-concept, and self-esteem.

Interpersonal. A second level of communication is interpersonal, occurring between two people. This level can occur in face-to-face settings or it can involve two people who are in different settings interacting.

Small Group. A third level of communication is small group, generally involving five-to-seven people with a common goal who interact to achieve that goal. People meeting to share information or to solve problems can represent this level.

Public Speaking. A fourth level of communication is public speaking, involving one person talking to many people. This level can occur in a multitude of organizational settings: one person conducting an orientation session for 50 new employees, one person leading a training session for 10 workers to introduce new software, or one person delivering a presentation to 25 managers on organizational policies.

Mass Communication. A fifth and final level of communication is *mass communication*, involving the use of media to convey a message.

These levels of communication actually correspond to levels of communication you can expect to find in various types of organizations. At the intrapersonal level are organizational members and their self-images. At the interpersonal level is superior–subordinate communication between supervisors and the workers who report to them. At the small group level are dynamics that occur within teams and committees. At the public level, which encompasses public speaking and mass communication, are internal and external public communication.

Defining Organizational Communication

Organizational communication specifically can be defined as *all communication that occurs within the boundaries of organizations and between organizations and their environments.* Organizational communication ranges in scope from communication between supervisors and workers to communication between interviewers and job applicants and from communication within training sessions and quality circles to risk and crisis communication in the workplace. Consider the following scenario:

> *Sunnyside–Up Inc. is a local property management company. At Sunnyside–Up whenever an employee breaks the rules, management discusses the problem with the employee. If no changes are made to improve the behavior, management writes up the employee and gives demerits. After three write-ups, the president of the company terminates the employee with the approval of the board of*

directors. Management explains to employees that one reason for such stringent policies is the interdependency of various functions and responsibilities. If for example the accountant misses countless days of work or does not perform her job duties, the bills will not get paid. This will result in termination of the utilities at all properties, which will anger the tenants. At the same time, management has an open-door policy that allows any employee to talk with the president of the company about family or personal issues and about how to perform effectively on the job. When it comes to its tenants, the company goes the extra mile every October by hosting its annual Fall Harvest for all tenants at a particular property to get to know their neighbors. Face painting, moonwalks, and snacks are for the kids as well as the parents to enjoy.

In this scenario we can see multiple examples of organizational communication.

Classical Approach. The stringent policies regarding inappropriate behavior, resulting in write-ups and ultimately termination, reflect a very classical approach to managing workers, in which formal rules, roles, and relationships are communicated to workers. Communication with this approach is task-oriented, downward, usually written, and formal. This approach is frequently evident in the emphasis on fitting the right person to the right job (Lawler & Finegold, 2000).

Social Systems Approach. The focus on the interdependency of various functions, responsibilities, and operations reflects the social systems approach to managing workers, in which all parts interact and each part influences every other part. This approach is often reflected in discussions of the interdependency of organizational approaches and specific environments (Weick & Sutcliffe, 2001).

Human Relations Approach. The communication to workers regarding the open-door policy of management reflects the *human relations approach* to managing workers, in which the feelings, attitudes, capabilities, and perceptions of workers are viewed as important. Communication with this approach is task and social-oriented, vertical and horizontal, often face-to-face, and informal. This approach is apparent in observations of tensions between the "non-actualized masses and the actualized few," in which Maslow's presentation of self-actualization as a natural human condition that is open to all, contrasts with the more elitist premise that some people are more likely to achieve self-actualization than others (Cooke, Mills, & Kelley, 2005).

Cultural Approach. Finally the Fall Harvest reflects the cultural approach, in which slogans, rituals, ceremonies, and events help propel the organization. This approach is evident in the use of metaphors, rituals, stories, artifacts, and performances as communicative devices in organizations (Hoffman & Medlock-Klyukovski, 2004; Scheibel, 2003; Smith & Keyton, 2001).

Communicative-Cultural Elements in Organizations

It is the latter category on the use of communicative devices—metaphors, rituals, stories, artifacts, and performances—as symbolic expressions and cultural elements (Eisenberg, Goodall, & Trethewey, 2010) that will form the focal point of the remainder of this chapter. In reality these five communicative devices are not independent and exclusive of one another; in fact they frequently overlap and coexist in organizations. More specifically this section will examine how organizations and their members use verbal, behavioral, and physical symbolism to communicate their culture internally within the organization and externally to outside audiences.

Metaphors. As verbal symbols of organizational culture, metaphors define "an unfamiliar experience in terms of another more familiar one" (Eisenberg, Goodall, & Trethewey, 2010, p. 105). An interesting example of this device is how Disneyland has used such metaphors as "drama", "casting", "on-stage", "back-stage", "family", and "guests" to create the image of an organization with strong concern for its customers and widely shared core values and beliefs. Another example involves metaphors that describe the invisible barrier women who are seeking to move up organizational hierarchies often face. It is thought this phenomenon may be responsible for the relative shortage of women holding leadership and senior management positions in some organizations. While "glass ceiling" has become a popular term, other metaphors for this phenomenon include "labyrinth", "firewall", "gossamer ceiling", "glass escalator", "glass floor", "glass walls", "glass door", and "concrete ceiling." Interestingly, metaphors have even emerged that emphasize gender inequality in specific occupational areas, such as "perspex ceiling", focusing attention on women in manufacturing industries, and "grass ceiling", focusing on the scarcity of women in agricultural organizations (Smith, Caputi, & Crittenden, 2012, pp. 437–438).

Rituals. As behavioral symbols of organizational culture, rituals are frequently occurring organizational events that communicate and reinforce the institution's values and can include meetings, celebrations, and conferences. Rituals may actually be *personal*, which are routinely done at the workplace each day; *task*, which are associated with a particular job in the workplace; *social*, which involve relationships with others in the workplace; and *organizational*, which pertain to the organization overall (West & Turner, 2010). An example of the power of rituals involves three communities of Benedictine women who were able to resist church-imposed identities of women as being rightly excluded, subordinate, and disempowered. More specifically, "Benedictine women adapted the Eucharist and other rituals in three primary ways: (1) by enacting leadership roles in liturgy; (2) by using inclusive symbols; and (3) by honoring the contributions of women" (Hoffman & Medlock-Klyukovski, 2004, p. 399). In this way, "Sisters [were able to] reinforce the transformation of their own culture; and by doing so in the presence of outsiders, they [were able to] make an argument for the transformation of the larger culture of the church" (Hoffman & Medlock-Klyukovski, 2004, p. 389). Another type of organizational ritual is the *tournament* ritual, which is a social mechanism that determines an organization's social standing and signals commonalities among participants (Patterson, Cavazos, & Washington, 2014, p. 74). These specific rituals serve to reinforce shared meanings, support the legitimacy of participants, distribute status among those who are judged as worthy of participation, emphasize social order, communicate values, provide meaning, and highlight peer recognition. Examples of such rituals include the Academy Awards, which honor cinematic achievements in the film industry, the Grammy Awards, which recognize outstanding achievement in the music industry, and the Tony Awards, which recognize achievement in live Broadway theatre (Patterson, Cavazos, & Washington, 2014, p. 79).

Stories. As verbal symbols of organizational culture, stories communicate to organizational members "what and who the culture values, how things are to be done, and the consequences for cultural compliance or deviation" (Eisenberg, Goodall, & Trethewey, 2010). These stories can be used broadly to capture organizational culture and values, to unite organizational members, to link members to their organizations, to provide evidence of organizational members' competing discourses, to entertain organizational members, and to maintain control within an organization (Smith & Keyton, 2001). Examples of storytelling abound and occur in all types of organizations, ranging from the entertainment industry, with the Disney Corporation, to the television production industry, with Mozark Productions. In a recent article Bartlett (2011) wrote the following about the power of storytelling in her profession:

> *Organizational storytelling is an emerging management technique that can help librarians improve their organizations through the power of narrative. Organizational storytelling may be very loosely defined as the skills of delivering a meaningful story in order to communicate, connect and influence. Stories can be used to teach people in organizations about the corporate culture (i.e., how to navigate the organizational environment), to help people with workplace anxiety and uncertainty, and of course to entertain and build morale....As librarians, we understand the power of story to change others' lives. What better way to change our own organizational culture than by beginning to tell our own stories?* (pp. 1–2)

Artifacts. As physical symbols of organizational culture, artifacts can include art, design, logos, buildings, spatial arrangements, décor, material objects, dress codes, and even websites. These act as nonverbal markers of organizational culture. These nonverbal markers are so important that they can even influence employee attitudes toward changes within organizations. For this reason organizational leaders need to be aware that employees identify with various artifacts in the organization and that individuals who identify with artifacts are cognitively and behaviorally supportive of change. Kovoor-Misra and Smith (2011) offer the following advice:

> *During mergers and acquisitions organizational artifacts may become the target of change. Managers would be wise to pay attention to organizational artifacts as they can be important to their employees. Artifacts provide a means for individuals to connect with their workplaces, and new or modified artifacts can attract identification during the change process and influence support for change.* (p. 601)

In addition it should be noted that innovative organizations such as Pixar, Google, Red Bull, and IDEO use their unconventional workplaces to embrace openness, transparency, spontaneity, creativity, playfulness, teamwork, and collaboration. Instead of the traditional offices and cubicles, these workplaces are more open environments, which include in some cases hammocks, recliners, and slide-downs.

Performances. As behavioral symbols of organizational culture, performances suggest that organizational life is like a theatrical production. Performances may be *ritual*, which are regular and recurring presentations in the workplace; *passion*, which are organizational stories that employees share with one another; *social*, which are organizational behaviors intended to demonstrate cooperation and politeness with others; *political*, which are organizational behaviors that demonstrate power or control; and *enculturation*, which are organizational behaviors that assist employees in discovering what it means to be a member of an organization (West & Turner, 2010).

Outcomes of Organizational Communication

The outcomes of organizational communication are well-documented. Indeed research has indicated a positive relationship between various facets of organizational life and employee satisfaction. Encouraging employee participation in decision-making, increasing involvement in organizational activities, crafting opportunities for personal growth, and creating perceptions of fairness, for example, are certainly strategies that will enhance job satisfaction for employees.

However, it is also possible to affect employee satisfaction and commitment through the use of communicative-cultural elements. For example, stories in the workplace can help organizational members to understand and make sense of organizational events (Ricketts & Seiling, 2003) and can enhance employee commitment (McCarthy, 2008). As a mechanism for clarifying key values and demonstrating how things are done in an organization, organizational commitment and storytelling have been found to be strongly correlated. In fact, based on a study of managers and employees at a major Scandinavian-based global ocean transport shipping company:

> *Organizational commitment and storytelling were found to be highly interrelated. When members told more stories, especially stories with a positive tone, they were far more likely to exhibit heightened commitment to the organization;*

when stories were more value laden, storytellers separately
expressed much higher levels of organizational commitment.
(McCarthy, 2008, p. 178)

As an example McCarthy provided the following story excerpt from a corporate storyteller who exhibited very high organizational commitment and whose story expressed a positive perspective of how the merger process was well handled and very effective.

Even [after] the merger we had [*sic*] very good, nice experience, from [the new CEO] coming over, seeing us quite a lot—especially [he] was here quite often [and] had meetings with every group. Really, I think he got to know everybody.

> *I think he knows everybody by name, which makes it [feel*
> *like] he really showed an interest in us. And I think that was*
> *important that it came from the top. That part was better, at*
> *least, I feel [that's] better now than it was [before. ...] So,*
> *it was a surprise from the beginning, yes, and it had to go*
> *fast. I think the announcement was sometime in the end of*
> *March and [by] the beginning of May like 6, 7—less than two*
> *months afterwards—everybody should have a fixed position.*
> *It was a very, very fast procedure. ... It did happen more*
> *or less [as scheduled] , I think, so that was an enormous*
> *job, I think, from those involved because there were very few*
> *people who knew about the merger in advance.* (McCarthy,
> 2008, p. 180)

Implications for Management

What can leaders do to improve communication within their organizations? Organizational communication is a multilevel, multidimensional process that can be enhanced in many ways.

In interpersonal interactions, for example, the following skills are important. Managers should remember to be nonjudgmental; to be approachable, open, and willing listeners; to ask or persuade, rather than demanding or telling; to be sensitive to the needs and feelings of workers; and to be open in communicating job-related information whenever possible.

In group interactions, on the other hand, the following skills are important. Managers should prepare for group participation by reviewing relevant materials before meetings and formulating ideas; value diverse opinions and people by encouraging broad participation; contribute ideas and seek information by asking for opinions; stress group productivity by identifying group strengths; ease tensions by stressing cooperation; support leadership by helping leaders accomplish goals; and produce results by encouraging responsibility from team members.

In addition however, managers should look beyond the preceding rather standard recommendations to the implications of metaphors, rituals, stories, artifacts, and performances as strategies for increasing employee satisfaction and commitment. It is clear that employees prefer supervisors who are approachable and considerate, but it is also important to think "outside the box" about ways to increase employee satisfaction and commitment by using communicative-cultural elements. Whether managers choose to use metaphors and to tell organizational stories, to create a departmental slogan and an organizational logo, or to create rituals to celebrate individual success and accomplishments, all, when used judiciously and in the case of celebrations, consistently, have positive outcomes.

Communication in organizations can be oral, written, visual, and audio. It is ongoing and everywhere in the workplace. It is an essential component in establishing positive rapport, cultivating mutual respect, developing high productivity, influencing goodwill, improving organizational performance, building trust and confidence, achieving organizational goals, and increasing employee satisfaction and commitment.

Questions for Students

1. The traditional top-down decision-making style in which management communicates policies to lower-level employees represents which approach to organizational communication: classical, human relations, social systems, or cultural?
2. Metaphors and stories are communicative-cultural elements that represent what type of symbolism in the workplace: verbal, behavioral, or physical?
3. Think about a past or current workplace. Which type of symbolism—verbal, behavioral, physical—is most dominant in that setting?

Exercise

In groups of 5–7 students, discuss each of the following four examples of organizational communication and characterize each in terms of whether it reflects the classical, human relations, social systems, or cultural approach:

- A restaurant manager explains the dress code to her employees during orientation. Afterwards, if an employee shows up for work with missing apparel, he or she is sent home and suspended for the shift.
- Often Human Resources is the place in an organization where everyone is caring and helpful toward others. In this office everyone is cooperative and understanding towards others' issues. The communication amongst supervisors and employees is key to success in this office.
- The Ford assembly line workers are interdependent. If one employee does not put the window brackets in properly, the next employee cannot put in the window.
- Walmart's slogan is "Save money. Live better." The company guarantees to match the lower advertised price on an identical item.

As a group generate one example of each of the four approaches to organizational communication and present them to the class.

Case: Studying the Culture of Meetings

As a student of organizational communication and a member of an organization (your class, college, sorority or fraternity, or place of employment), you are likely intrigued by the idea that meetings hold important clues to organizational cultures. For this case study, you will immerse yourself in a culture to understand, analyze, and write about it in the form of an ethnography. You will collect the data to be analyzed and then write about it using what you have learned in this chapter. Here are some guidelines for conducting your cultural study.

1. Record and transcribe the exchanges between members of the group, team, or organization at one or more of its meetings. Use the following questions and illustrations to guide your work:

a. Who opens the meeting? Who takes notes? Answering these questions should tell you something about the leadership of the meeting, as well as the role of one of more of the group members.

b. In general, who says what to whom and with what effect? Answering this question may help you isolate particular relationships and power structures.

c. Pay close attention to exchanges of conversation—both on-topic and off-topic—that occur during the meeting. What are the exchanges about? What do they say about the role and relative power of the group members? What is the role of silence in the group? Is anyone excluded from the talk?

d. What is the function of humor in the group, if any?

e. What clothing do the group members wear to the meeting? Is there a relationship between their clothing and the conduct of the meeting (e.g., formal, informal)?

f. Does the group use a particular style of language? For example, is it highly technical? Does it contain a lot of jargon or slang? Can you tell "who is in the know" just by listening? Can you tell who isn't? Is there any attempt to mentor new group members? Are there any metaphors that recur in the group and seem to suggest a common understanding?

g. What other affiliations or associations can you assume characterize these group members' lives outside of this meeting? How much of those extra-meeting cultures are brought into the culture of the meeting?

h. How do the meetings end? Are assignments made? Are they equitably apportioned? How much does expertise play a role in the assignments? How about friendship?

2. Decide how you will analyze the data based on your reading in this chapter. For example,

a. What communication approach (e.g., classical, human relations, social systems, cultural) best characterizes the meeting)?

b. Does the group operate like a system? If so, how? If not, why not?

c. What is the role of leadership in the group?

d. How are power relations established and maintained? How are they challenged?

e. What is the role of gender, race, class, or sexual orientation in the group? How do you know?

3. Perform your analysis.

a. Write a narrative account (i.e., a story) about the group meeting. Be sure to include as much detail about the conversations and your impressions as you can. Make sure your story has an identifiable beginning, middle, and ending.

b. Where possible, apply material from this chapter to the story. When you are finished with a draft, add an introduction that theoretically frames the story and a conclusion that attempts to "sum up" what you have learned about this culture from the study.

4   Share your ethnography with your class.

Adapted from:

Eisenberg, E. M., Goodall, Jr., H. L., & Trethewey, A. (2010). Organizational *communication: Balancing creativity and constraint* (6th ed.). Boston: Bedford/St. Martins. ISBN–10: 0–312–57486–X

Suggestions for Further Reading

Ahmed, Z., Shields, F., White, R., & Wilbert, J. (2010). Managerial communication: The link between frontline leadership and organizational performance. *Journal of Organizational Culture, Communication and Conflict, 14* (1), 107–120.

Bisel, R. S., Messersmith, A. S., & Keyton, J. (2010). Understanding organizational culture and communication through a gyroscope metaphor. *Journal of Management Education, 34*, 342–366.

References

Bartlett, J.A. (2011). New and noteworthy: A natural fit: Organizational storytelling in the library. *Library Leadership & Management, 25* (4), 1–3.

Cooke, B., Mills, A., & Kelley, E. (2005). Situating Maslow in Cold War America: A recontextualization of management theory. *Group and Organization Management, 30*, 129–152.

Eisenberg, E. M., Goodall, Jr., H. L., & Trethewey, A. (2010). *Organizational communication: Balancing creativity and constraint* (6th ed.). Boston: Bedford/St. Martins.

Hoffman, M. F., & Medlock-Klyukovski, A. (2004). "Our creator who art in heaven": Paradox, ritual, and cultural transformation. *Western Journal of Communication, 68*, 389–410.

Kovoor-Misra, S. & Smith, M.A. (2011). Artifacts, identification and support for change after an acquisition. *Leadership & Organization Development Journal, 32* (6), 584–604.

Lawler, E., III, & Finegold, D. (2000). Individualizing the organization: Past, present, and future. *Organizational Dynamics, 29* (1), 1–15.

McCarthy, J. F. (2008). Short stories at work: Storytelling as an indicator of organizational commitment. *Group and Organization Management, 33,* 163–193.

Patterson, K.D.W., Cavazos, D.E., & Washington, M. (2014). It does matter how you get to the top: Differentiating status from reputation. *Administrative Sciences, 4* (2), 73–86.

Ricketts, M., & Seiling, J. G. (2003). Language, metaphors and stories: Catalysts for meaning making in organizations. *Organization Development Journal, 21* (4), 33–43.

Scheibel, D. (2003). "Reality ends here": Graffiti as an artifact. In R. Clair (Ed.), *Expressions of ethnography: Novel approaches to qualitative methods* (pp. 219–230). Albany: SUNY Press.

Smith, F., & Keyton, J. (2001). Organizational storytelling: Metaphors for relational power and identity struggles. *Management Communication Quarterly, 15,* 149–182.

Smith, P., Caputi, P., & Crittenden, N. (2012). A maze of metaphors around glass ceilings. *Gender in Management, 27* (7), 436–448.

Weick, K., & Sutcliff, K. (2001). Managing *the unexpected: Assuring high performance in an age of complexity.* San Francisco: Jossey-Bass.

West, R., & Turner, L. H. (2010). *Introducing communication theory: Analysis and application* (4th ed.). Boston: McGraw Hill.

4. Conflict

Afzal Rahim
Center for Advanced Studies in Management

Conflict is inevitable in contemporary organizations. As the organizations learn and change in order to improve their competitive position, conflict will take place. Change is associated with conflict and learning how to deal with conflict effectively is essential for realizing the benefits of change. High performing learning organizations like Honda, Motorola, Dow Corning, and General Electric have developed the kind of leadership, culture, and organizational design needed to manage conflict effectively. But many organizations are still handling conflict ineffectively. Managers and administrators attempt not so much to understand and deal with conflict functionally as to find ways of reducing, avoiding, or terminating it. It appears that this state of affairs has remained unchanged. As a result, scarce and valuable resources are wasted as employees engage in dysfunctional conflict and miss the opportunity of utilizing conflict to improve their individual, group, and organizational effectiveness.

Nature of Conflict Management

Definition

Conflict is defined as an *interactive process manifested in incompatibility, disagreement, or dissonance within or between social entities* (*i.e., individual, group, organization, etc.*) (Rahim, 2011. Calling conflict an interactive state does not preclude the possibilities of intraindividual conflict, for it is known that a person often interacts with himself or herself. Obviously, one also interacts with others. According to Roloff (1987), "organizational conflict occurs when members engage in activities that are incompatible with those of colleagues within their network, members of other collectivities, or unaffiliated individuals who utilize the services or products of the organization" (p. 496). This definition is consistent with the one just presented. Some of the manifestations of conflict behavior are expressing disagreement with the opponent, yelling, verbal abuse, interference, and so on.

Foundations of Conflict Management

The presence of conflict among employees can have both negative and positive consequences for organizations. Perhaps most evident are the negative consequences, which include dysfunctional behaviors (e.g., absenteeism, tardiness) stemming from poor interpersonal relations between the conflicting employees. Possible positive consequences include enhanced creativity and innovation, higher quality decision making, and improved mutual understanding (cf. Pelled, Eisenhardt, & Xin, 1999; Rahim, 2011). Management of organizational conflict requires that its negative consequences be minimized and its positive consequences maximized. Literature on conflict management provides no clear set of guidelines to suggest *how* different types of conflicts should be handled to increase individual, group, or organizational effectiveness.

Criteria for Conflict Management. In order for conflict management strategies to be effective, they should satisfy certain criteria. These have been derived from the diverse literature on organization theory and organizational behavior. The following criteria are particularly useful for conflict management, but in general, they may be useful for decision making in management:

Organizational learning and effectiveness. Conflict management strategies should be designed to enhance organizational learning (see chapter on organizational learning). It is expected that organizational learning will lead to long-term effectiveness. In order to attain this objective, conflict management strategies should be designed to enhance critical and innovative thinking to learn the process of diagnosis and intervention in the right problems.

Needs of stakeholders. Conflict management strategies should be designed to satisfy the needs and expectations of the strategic constituencies (stakeholders) and to attain a balance among them. Mitroff (1998) strongly suggests picking the right stakeholders to solve the right problems. Sometimes multiple parties are involved in a conflict in an organization and the challenge of conflict management would be to involve these parties in a problem solving process that will lead to collective learning and organizational effectiveness. It is expected that this process will lead to satisfaction of the relevant stakeholders.

Ethics. Mitroff (1998) is a strong advocate of ethical management. He concluded that "if we can't define a problem so that it leads to ethical actions that benefit humankind, then either we haven't defined or are currently unable to define the problem properly.

To manage conflicts ethically, organizations should institutionalize the positions of employee advocate, customer and supplier advocate, as well as environmental and stockholder advocates. Only if these advocates are heard by decision-makers in organizations may we hope for an improved record of ethically managed organizational conflict (Rahim, Garrett, & Buntzman, 1992). The disastrous outcomes in Enron and Worldcom probably could be avoided if this process was legitimized in these organizations.

Conflict Types. Managing conflict requires a good understanding of various conflict types that can occur in organizations. Literature shows that the following types may have significant impact on an organization's effectiveness and therefore, they should be properly dealt with.

The classification of conflict is often made on the basis of the antecedent conditions that lead to conflict. Conflict may originate from a number of sources, such as tasks, values, goals, and so on. It has been found appropriate to classify conflict on the basis of these sources for proper understanding of its nature and implications. Following is a brief description of this classification.

1. Substantive conflict. This is caused by difference of opinion regarding task, policies, procedures, and other business-related or content issues. Substantive conflict is intellectual opposition to the ideas and is an essential step to problem solving. Engaging in substantive conflict involves evaluating opinions and ideas on the basis of evidence, logic, and critical and innovative thinking. This type of conflict has also been labeled *task conflict, cognitive conflict*, or *issue conflict*.

2. Affective conflict. This occurs when two or more interacting social entities, while trying to solve a problem together, become aware that their emotions and feelings regarding some or all the issues are incompatible. These emotions and feelings are associated with personal attacks and criticisms that lead to hostility, distrust, and cynicism. Affective conflict is also created by personality clashes, sarcasm, and making fun of one's ideas.

3. Other forms of substantive–affective conflict. The preceding discussion suggests that theorists have traditionally suggested that organizational conflict has two dimensions: one consisting of disagreements about the task and one consisting of socio-emotional or interpersonal disputes. While these prior investigations provide important clues about the nature of conflict, considerably more investigations should be conducted before scholars and practitioners have a solid grasp of the phenomenon. In particular, there is a need to look beyond these traditional dimensions of task and emotional conflict, investigating other dimensions that may be influential. The traditional dichotomy may be extended by adding two other kinds of conflict to it that can be classified as transforming and masquerading conflicts. For example, alluding to the idea of transforming conflict, Eisenhardt et al. (1997) have noted, "A comment meant as a substantive remark can be interpreted as a personal attack. ... Personalities frequently become intertwined with issues" (p. 78). Alluding to the idea of masquerading conflict, Pelled (1996) observed that "individuals may express hostility by manufacturing useless criticisms of each other's task-related ideas" (p. 620).

Transforming Conflict. This occurs when substantive conflict degenerates to affective conflict. This happens when people involved in a substantive conflict start attacking each other personally and disagreements on business issues drift to emotional conflicts. In many cases a group discussion starts with a focus on business-related issues, but if the disagreement among members becomes intense, they may become involved in personality clashes and attack each other personally.

Masquerading Conflict. This refers to disagreements when members have emotional conflicts with each other, but disguise them as substantive conflicts. This conflict appears to be task-related on the surface but that is actually emotional in nature. Here group members who don't get along on a personal level disguise their relationship issues as criticisms of each other's business-related ideas.

4. Process conflict. This type of conflict is associated with how different tasks should be performed, responsibility to complete specific tasks, delegation of duties and responsibilities, and deadlines and is distinct from substantive and affective conflicts (see Jehn, 1997). Process conflict can be defined as "disagreements about logistical and delegation issues such as how task accomplishment should proceed and in the work unit, who's responsible for what, and how things should be delegated" (Jehn, Greer, Levine, & Szulaqnski, 2008, p. 467).

Conflict-handling styles. One factor that has an important impact on the constructive management of organizational conflict is the style employees use to handle conflicts they are involved in. There are various styles of behavior by which interpersonal conflict may be handled.

Rahim and Bonoma (1979) differentiated the styles of handling conflict on two basic dimensions: concern for self and concern for others. The first dimension explains the degree (high or low) to which a person attempts to satisfy his or her own concern. The second dimension explains the degree (high or low) to which a person attempts to satisfy the concern of others. Combination of the two dimensions results in five specific styles of handling interpersonal conflict, as shown in Figure 1 (Rahim & Bonoma, 1979, p. 1327).

1. Integrating (high concern for self and others) style is associated with problem solving, i.e., the diagnosis of and intervention in the right problems. The use of this style involves openness, exchanging information, looking for alternatives, and examination of differences to reach an effective solution

Figure 1
The Dual-Concern Model of the Styles of
Handling Interpersonal Conflict

Concern for Self

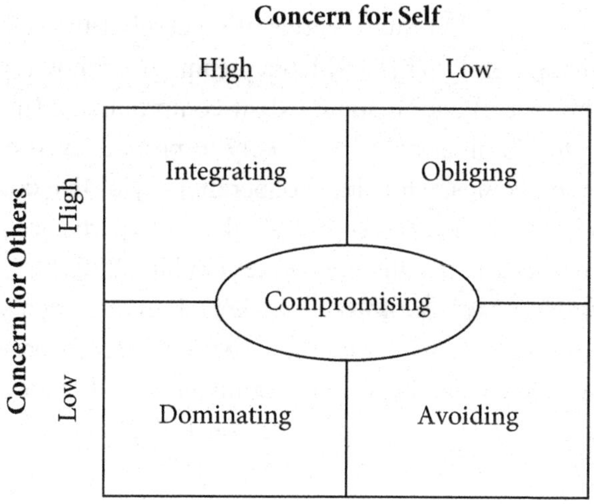

acceptable to both parties. This style is often described as a win–win style of handling interpersonal conflict that satisfies the concern of both parties and is associated with functional outcomes.

2. Obliging (low concern for self and high concern for others) style is associated with attempting to play down the differences and emphasizing commonalities to satisfy the concern of the other party. An obliging person neglects his or her own concern to satisfy the concern of the other party. This style is often described as a lose–win style of handling interpersonal conflict that satisfies the concern of the other party and is associated with functional outcomes.

3. Compromising (intermediate in concern for self and others) style involves give-and-take whereby both parties give up something to make a mutually acceptable decision. It may mean splitting the difference, exchanging concession, or seeking a quick, middle-ground position and it is associated with functional outcomes.

4. Dominating (high concern for self and low concern for others) style has been identified with win–lose orientation or with forcing behavior to win one's position. A dominating or competing person goes all out to win his or her objective and, as a result, often ignores the needs and expectations of the other party. This style of handling interpersonal conflict that does not satisfy the concern of the other party and is generally associated with dysfunctional outcomes.

5. Avoiding (low concern for self and others) style has been associated with withdrawal, buckpassing, or sidestepping situations. An avoiding person fails to satisfy his or her own concern as well as the concern of the other party. This style is often described as a lose–lose style of handling interpersonal conflict that does not satisfy the concern of either party and is generally associated with dysfunctional outcomes.

The literature indicates that more cooperative conflict management styles, such as integrating and obliging (in which a meaningful amount of concern is shown for the other party) and to some extent compromising (in which some concern is shown to the other party) are likely to produce positive individual and organizational outcomes, while less cooperative styles like dominating and avoiding (in which little concern is shown for the other party) frequently result in escalation of conflict and negative outcomes (Rahim, 2002).

Problem solving and bargaining dimensions. Further insights into the five styles of handling interpersonal conflict may be obtained by organizing them according to the integrative and distributive dimensions of labor–management bargaining suggested by Walton and McKersie (1965). Figure 2 shows the

Figure 2

The Dual-Concern Model: Problem Solving and Bargaining
Strategies for Handling Interpersonal Conflict

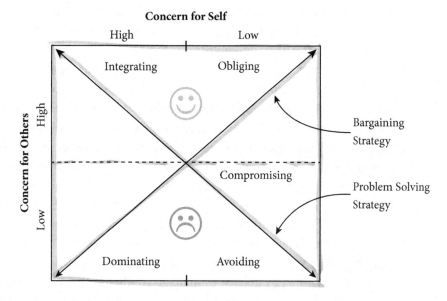

five styles of handling interpersonal conflict and their reclassifications into the
integrative and distributive dimensions.

The integrative dimension—Integrating style *minus* Avoiding style represents
a party's concern (high–low) for self and others. The distributive dimension—
Dominating style *minus* Obliging style—represents a party's concern (high–
low) for self or others. These two dimensions represent the *problem solving*
and *bargaining* strategies for handling conflict, respectively. A problem solving
strategy represents a party's pursuit of own *and* others' concerns, whereas the
bargaining strategy represents a party's pursuit of own *or* others' concerns. A
High–High use of the problem solving strategy indicates attempts to increase
the satisfaction of concerns of both parties by finding unique solutions to the
problems acceptable to them. A Low–Low use of this strategy indicates reduction of satisfaction of the concerns of both parties as a result of their failure to
confront and solve their problems. A High–Low use of the bargaining strategy
indicates attempts to obtain high satisfaction of concerns of self and providing
low satisfaction of concerns of others. A Low–High use of this strategy indicates
attempts to obtain the opposite. Compromising is the point of intersection of the
two strategies, that is, a middle ground position where a party has an intermediate level of concerns for own and others.

A positive score on the problem solving strategy (high concern for self and others) indicates that an employee is handling his/her conflict with supervisor, subordinates, or peers with relatively more integrating than avoiding style. A negative score on bargaining strategy (low concern for self and high concern for others) indicates that an employee is handling his/her conflict with supervisor, subordinates, and peers with relatively more obliging than dominating. A positive score on problem solving strategy *plus* a negative score on bargaining strategy indicate that an employee is handling conflict to satisfy the concerns of both parties or the other party (supervisor) which should lead to positive outcomes. This is a functional strategy for managing conflict. A negative score on the problem solving strategy and positive score in the bargaining strategy indicate that an employee is handling conflict not to satisfy the concern of both parties or satisfy the concerns of self only which will lead to negative outcomes. Functional and dysfunctional strategies are portrayed in Figure 2—above or below the broken line, respectively.

Conflict management strategy. Existing literature on conflict management is deficient on strategies needed to manage conflict at the macro-level, which can satisfy the above criteria. An effective conflict management strategy should:

1. *Minimize Affective and Process Conflicts at Various Levels.* Evidence indicates that affective conflict impedes group performance. It affects group performance by limiting information processing ability and cognitive functioning of group members and antagonistic attributions of group members' behavior. Affective conflict diminishes group loyalty, workgroup commitment, intent to stay in the present organization, and job satisfaction (Amason, 1996; Jehn, 1995, 1997; Jehn et al., 1999). These result from higher levels of stress and anxiety, and conflict escalation. Process conflict is also negatively associated with group performance, satisfaction, and group commitment and it should be reduced (Jehn & Mannix, 2001; Behfar, Peterson, Mannix, & Trochin, 2008).

2. *Attain and Maintain a Moderate Amount of Substantive Conflict.* A study by Jehn (1995) suggests that a moderate level of substantive conflict is beneficial as it stimulates discussion and debate, which help groups to attain higher level of performance. "Groups with an absence of task conflict may miss new ways to enhance their performance, while very high levels of task conflict may interfere with task completion" (Jehn, 1997, p. 532). Groups that report substantive conflict are able to make better decisions than those that do not (Amason, 1996).

Groups that report substantive conflict generally have higher performance. This conflict can improve group performance through better understanding of various viewpoints and alternative solutions (Eisenhardt & Schoonhoven,

1990). It should be noted that the beneficial effects of substantive conflict on performance were found only in groups performing nonroutine tasks, but not groups performing standardized or routine tasks.

Although substantive conflict enhances group performance, like affective conflict, it can diminish group loyalty, workgroup commitment, intent to stay in the present organization, and job satisfaction (Jehn et al., 1999). As a result, interventions for conflict management should be designed to develop cultural norms to support disagreement among group members in connection with tasks and other related management issues without generating affective conflict.

3. *Select and Use Appropriate Conflict Management Strategies.* As discussed before, there are various styles of behavior, such as integrating, obliging, dominating, avoiding, and compromising, which can be used to deal with conflict. Organizational members would require training and on-the-job experience

Table 1

Styles of Handling Interpersonal Conflict and
Situations Where They Are Appropriate or Inappropriate

Conflict Style	Situations Where Appropriate	Situations Where Inappropriate
Integrating	1. Issues are complex.	1. Task or problem is simple.
	2. Synthesis of ideas is needed to come up with better solutions.	2. Immediate decision is required.
	3. Commitment is needed from other parties for successful implementation.	3. Other parties are unconcerned about outcome.
	4. Time is available for problem-solving.	4. Other parties do not have problem-solving skills.
	5. One party alone cannot solve the problem.	
	6. Resources possessed by different parties are needed to solve their common problems.	
Obliging	1. You believe that you may be wrong.	1. Issue is important to you.
	2. Issue is more important to the other party.	2. You believe that you are right.
	3. You are willing to give up something exchange for something from the other party in the future.	3. The other party is wrong or unethical.
	4. You are dealing from a position of weakness	
	5. Preserving relationship is important.	

Dominating	1. Issue is trivial.	1. Issue is complex.
	2. Speedy decision is needed.	2. Issue is not important to you.
	3. Unpopular course of action is implemented.	3. Both parties are equally powerful.
	4. Necessary to overcome assertive subordinates.	4. Decision does not have to be made quickly.
	5. Unfavorable decision by the other party may be costly to you.	5. Subordinates possess high degree of competence.
	6. Subordinates lack expertise to make technical decisions.	
	7. Issue is important to you.	
Avoiding	1. Issue is trivial.	1. Issue is important to you.
	2. Potential dysfunctional effect of confronting the other party outweighs benefits of resolution.	2. It is your responsibility to make decision.
	3. Cooling off period is needed.	3. Parties are unwilling to defer, issue must be resolved.
		4. Prompt attention is needed.
Compromising	1. Goals of parties are mutually exclusive.	1. One party is more powerful.
	2. Parties are equally powerful.	2. Problem is complex enough needing problem-solving approach.
	3. Consensus cannot be reached.	
	4. Integrating or dominating style is not successful.	
	5. Temporary solution to a complex problem is needed.	

to select and use the styles of handling interpersonal conflict so that various conflict situations can be appropriately dealt with. The styles of handling conflict that are appropriate in various situations are presented in Table 1.

Outcomes of Conflict Management

The preceding section discussed the effects of the three types of conflict on job performance, satisfaction, and commitment of group members. This section discusses the effect of handling these conflicts with problem solving styles. One would expect the outcomes of conflict that satisfy the concerns of both parties to be functional for an organization. Previous studies generally indicate that a collaborative or integrating style by the members of an organization leads to greater satisfaction and effectiveness of the organizational members. A study by Behfar et al. (2008) concluded that affective, substantive, and process conflict should be handled with appropriate conflict-management strategies. Their study found support for the "existing conclusions about the benefits of integrative and collaborative approaches to managing conflict and the drawbacks of contending and avoiding approaches" (p. 182).

A study that tested a structural equations model of power bases, conflict-management styles, and job performance shows, among others, that problem solving strategy (i.e., using more integrating and less avoiding styles), not bargaining strategy (i.e., using more dominating and less obliging styles), positively influences job performance at the group level (Rahim, Antonioni, & Psenicka, 2001).

Lawrence and Lorsch (1967) indicated that a confrontation (integrating) style was used to deal with intergroup conflict to a significantly greater degree in higher- than lower-performing organizations. Likert and Likert (1976) strongly argued, and provided some evidence to suggest, that an organization that encourages participation and problem-solving behaviors attains higher level of effectiveness.

Misquita (1998) reported that when subordinates perceived that their supervisors were handling conflict with an integrating style, their organizational commitment increased. If the subordinates perceived that their supervisors were using avoiding and dominating styles, their organizational commitment reduced. Several studies on conflict management show consistent results. The use of the integrating style results in high joint benefit for the parties, better decisions, and greater satisfaction of the partner (Tutzauer & Roloff, 1988; Korbanik, Baril, & Watson, 1993).

Implications for Management

The implication of this review is that supervisors can encourage employees to enhance their problem solving conflict-management strategy and reduce their bargaining conflict-management strategy through education and training. The challenge for a contemporary organization is to enhance the conflict-management skills of their members through appropriate training that will involve survey feedback, lecture, case studies, and exercises (see Rahim, 2011). Training should be made available to both management and nonmanagement employees.

Organization members should also be encouraged to enhance their conflict-management skills through continuous self-learning. Organizations should provide appropriate reinforcements for learning and improving employees' conflict-management skills so that they can handle various situations effectively. Recent literature shows that learning organizations are providing ample opportunities to managers for continuous learning that should help to improve their conflict-management skills. To attain this goal, appropriate changes in organization design and culture would be needed (Rahim, 2002). Changes in organization design would require creating flatter, decentralized, and less complex structures. Also there should be appropriate changes in organizational culture that provides rewards for learning new behaviors. These changes will encourage employees to acquire conflict-management competencies needed for improving their job performance, behavior, and job-related attitudes.

Questions for Students

1. What is the difference between substantive and affective conflicts?
2. What are the problem solving and bargaining dimensions of conflict-management styles?
3. What are the criteria for conflict management?
4. What are the strategies for managing conflict?
5. What are the outcomes of conflict management?

Exercise: Effective Conflict-Handling

Premeeting Preparation

Complete the ROCI–II (Form A), to be supplied by the teacher, and construct the indices of your styles of handling interpersonal conflict with superior. After completing the instrument, read this chapter. Additional readings may be assigned by the teacher.

Procedure

The teacher discusses the chapter and the scoring of the ROCI-II and asks you to do the following:

1. Break into subgroups of five or six members.
2. Elect a leader for your subgroup.
3. Write on the newsprint at least three situations where each of the five styles are appropriate.
4. Post on the walls the newsprint listings of the situations where each style is appropriate.
5. The subgroup leaders present the situations identified by their subgroups.
6. The subgroup leaders prepare the final list of situations where each style is appropriate.

The teacher asks the participants to make comments on the exercise and the new behavior learnt from it.

Case: How to Silence a Noisy Crowd

On January 7, 2010 Yum! Brands Inc., owner of the Kentucky Fried Chicken released an ad in Australia titled, "How to Silence a Noisy Crowd" in Australia. The ad shows a white man in a crowd of cheering black cricket fans asks, "Need a tip when you're stuck in an awkward situation?" He then holds up a bucket of KFC chicken to the black fans to calm the situation and the fried chicken will do the trick. The commercial attracted international attention after it was posted on the video-sharing website YouTube. A large number of Americans saw the ad and described it as racist. The commercial was deemed as racist because a Caucasian male was passing around a bucket of fried chicken to a group of Black people, to ease an "awkward situation." In America, there has always been a stereotype that African Americans like to eat fried chicken. But this is not the case in Australia. A representative for the Kentucky Fried Chicken in Australia said, "It is a light-hearted reference to the West Indies cricket team. The ad was reproduced online in the U.S. without KFC's permission, where we are told a culturally-based stereotype exists, leading to the incorrect assertion of racism."

The commercial attracted media attention in the U.S. The New York Daily News and Baltimore Sun both ran online polls asking their viewer to decide if the commercial was racist in content. In an effort to avoid any further controversy and negative press toward the brand, KFC issued an official announcement on their Australian website, "KFC Australia apologizes unreservedly for any offence caused which of course was wholly unintended." KFC also said, "We unequivocally condemn discrimination of any type and have a proud history as one of the world's leading employers for diversity."

The pulling of the commercial by KFC may have satisfied the U.S. viewers but the responses from other areas of the world were quite different—people outside the U.S. understood that this was not an ad about African Americans or even black people. It was a satire about the rivalry between Australia and the West Indies in cricket, a game played all over the world.

References

Amason, A. C. (1996). Distinguishing the effects of functional and dysfunctional conflict on strategic decision making: Resolving a paradox for top management teams. *Academy of Management Journal, 39,* 123–148.

Behfar, K. J., Peterson, R. S., Mannix, E. A., & Trochim, W. M. K. (2008). The critical role of conflict resolution in teams: A close look at the links between conflict type, conflict management strategies, and team outcomes. *Journal of Applied Psychology, 93,* 170–188.

Eisenhardt, K. M., Kahwajy, J. L., & Bourgeois, L. J. (1997). Conflict and strategic choice: How top management teams disagree. *California Management Review, 39* (2), 42–62.

Eisenhardt, K., & Schoonhoven, C. (1990). Organizational growth: Linking founding team, strategy, environment, and growth among U.S. semiconductor ventures, 1878–1988. *Administrative Science Quarterly, 35,* 504–529.

Jehn, K. A. (1995). A multimethod examination of the benefits and determinants of intragroup conflict. *Administrative Science Quarterly, 40,* 256–282.

Jehn, K. A. (1997). A qualitative analysis of conflict types and dimensions in organizational groups. *Administrative Science Quarterly, 42,* 530–557.

Jehn, K. A., Greer, L., Levine, S., & Szulanski, G. (2008). The effects of conflict types, dimensions, and emergent states on group outcomes. *Group Decision and Negotiation, 17,* 465–495.

Jehn, K. A., & Mannix, E. A. (2001). The dynamic nature of conflict: A longitudinal study of intragroup conflict and group performance. *Academy of Management Journal, 44,* 238–251.

Jehn, K. A., Northcraft, G. B., & Neale, M. A. (1999). Why differences make a difference: A field study of diversity, conflict, and performance in workgroup. *Administrative Science Quarterly, 44,* 741–763.

Korbanik, K., Baril, G. L., & Watson, C. (1993). Managers' conflict management style and leadership performance: The moderating effects of gender. *Sex Roles, 29,* 405–420.

Lawrence, P. R., & Lorsch, J. W. (1967). Differentiation and integration in complex organizations. *Administrative Science Quarterly, 12,* 1–47.

Likert, R., & Likert, J. G. (1976). *New ways of managing conflict.* New York: McGraw-Hill.

Misquita, V. C. (1998). *Exploration of factors leading to organizational commitment of the subordinate in unionized environment.* Unpublished doctoral dissertation, Illinois Institute of Technology, Chicago.

Mitroff, I. I. (1998). *Smart thinking for crazy times: The art of solving the right problems.* San Francisco: Berrett-Koehler.

Pelled, L. H. (1996). Demographic diversity, conflict, and work group outcomes: An intervening process theory. *Organization Science, 7,* 615–631.

Pelled, L. H., Eisenhardt, K. M., & Xin, K. R. (1999). Exploring the black box: An analysis of work group diversity, conflict, and performance. *Administrative Science Quarterly, 44,* 1–28.

Rahim, M. A. (2002). Toward a theory of managing organizational conflict. *International Journal of Conflict Management, 13,* 206-235.

Rahim, M. A. (2011). *Managing conflict in organizations* (4th ed.). New Brunswick, NJ: Transaction.

Rahim, M. A., Antonioni, D., Psenicka, C. (2001). A structural equations model of leader power, subordinates' styles of handling conflict and job performance. *International Journal of Conflict Management, 12,* 191–211.

Rahim, M. A., & Bonoma, T. V. (1979). Managing organizational conflict: A model for diagnosis and intervention. *Psychological Reports, 44,* 1323–1344.

Roloff, M. E. (1987). Communication and conflict. In C. R. Berger & S. H. Chaffee (Eds.), *Handbook of communication science* (pp. 484–534). Newbury Park, CA: Sage.

Tutzauer, F., & Roloff, M. E. (1988). Communication processes leading to integrative agreements: Three paths to joint benefits. *Communication Research, 15,* 360–380.

Walton, R. E., & McKersie, R. B. (1965). *A behavioral theory of labor negotiations: An analysis of a social interaction system.* New York: McGraw-Hill.

5. Stress

Sharon Davis
Open University, United Kingdom

Afzal Rahim
Center for Advanced Studies Management

Don G. Schley
Colorado Technical University

Stress is usually understood as negative, but that is not the case. Stress can actually be broken down into two forms—good stress or *eustress* and bad stress or *distress*. Most persons understand stress as distress. High levels of organizational and individual dis-stress can lead to burnout, and thus lead to the loss of human capital, which directly impacts the organization's bottom-line. Since the cost of replacing a productive worker runs between one and-a-half and two and-a-half times annual salary, such stress-induced attrition is very expensive for organizations. Not only are good people lost, but those who stay may be switched-off or demotivated, and the consequent costs in healthcare expenses, absenteeism, poor quality of work, industrial sabotage, and in extreme cases, litigation, add up. Thus it makes sense for organizations to protect their staff from excessive stress, particularly dis-stress, as human capital is often the most costly part of their operating budget. The cost of putting stress management strategies in place will be off-set by the returns in increased productivity, improved labor relations, lowered absenteeism and greater retention of key employees.

Nature of Stress

Definition

Stress can be defined as the reaction individuals have to the demands being placed on their minds and bodies, affecting their capacity for coping and resulting in changes in their physical, psychological, and behavioral performance. Another definition of job stress is the work attributes that pose threats or risk to an employee, results from a poor person–environment fit.

Stress in Everyday Life

Stress is an everyday term used by individuals when discussing their workdays: "My day has been so stressful" or "I am so stressed out!" So most individuals have some notion of what stress is and what causes their stress. However, when two people are sharing these thoughts, each one's idea of a "stressful" experience can be quite different. This is where the notion of stress becomes complex. Stress, real or implied, is subject to the psychological and or physiological experience of the individual. Individual differences can be traced to experiences, both while growing up and in adult life, and to genetic predispositions and to a person's state of physical and mental health. When individuals attend work, these experiences come with them, and, combined with the experiences had while at work, will affect their responses to situations.

It is impossible to lead a stress-free life, and no one would want a workforce so relaxed (under-stressed) that productivity was low. However, work-related stress has been described by the World Health Organization a worldwide epidemic (Avey, Luthans, & Jensen, 2009). Organizations and their managers need to understand the *subjective nature* of stress—*what stress is*, and what its *causes* and *effects* are, both with respect to individual employees and to their organizations. Workers and managers need to be able to find the balance for the right amount of stress for performance optimization (eustress) and *how to deal with stress* in order to keep both workers and organizations healthy and productive.

The *subjective nature* of stress means that people may view the same situation differently, and that what is stressful to one person may not be to another. What might be exhilarating and even beneficial to one might be beyond acceptability to another. For instance, some would find a roller-coaster ride exciting while another person might vomit at the thought of such an experience. A professional athlete, if not psyched up (under stress) at the start of his game, might perform poorly. These examples give the participants some control over their experiences: a person can choose to go on the roller coaster or not; the professional athlete is paid to perform, and that athlete must respond positively to stress in performance. The athlete's stress would be classed as beneficial—in other words, *eustress*. The fact that most people go to work because they must reduce the element of choice in how they spend their time and increases their stress.

Within the workplace, many experiences lie outside the employees' control. Someone directed to give a presentation in front of a group will naturally be under stress to perform. Whether this stress is experienced as good (eustress) or bad (distress) will depend on the individual. One who enjoys giving presentations will thrive on the challenge, do a good job and gain a lot of positives from the experience. Someone unprepared or fearful who dislikes presenting will experience a high level of distress, which will be counterproductive to the performance. This chapter focuses mostly on the experience, causes, and effects of *distress*.

Components of Stress

Stress has three main components: the stressor, the appraisal of the stressor, and the stress response.

Stressors. A stressor is a stimulus in the environment that leads to the appraisal of the stressor, and a stress response. It can include the following elements:

Physical. Stressors can be physical in the form of trauma or injury (professional athlete), excessive physical exertion (building and construction), excessive time on the job leading to fatigue, and so on.

Environmental. These factors include noise, overcrowding, excessive heat or cold, or conditions of extreme air pollution such as carbon monoxide poisoning, coal dust, cotton dust, chemical fumes, and other threats.

Psychosocial. This form of stress includes major negative life events (divorce or death of spouse), minor events such as daily hassles in family/home life (childcare issues), and workplace impacts (poor management).

Stress involves a stressor and a response, the initial response being physiological. The stressor and stress response are connected by how the situation or information is appraised, and they vary between individuals and situations.

Appraising a Stressor. People respond differently to stressors. Individuals appraise a situation and decide whether it is threatening or non-threatening, e.g. the presentation scenario, although the appraisal is not always conscious. At that point, a decision is made: can they cope physiologically and psychologically with the challenge? This decision influences how well an individual adapts to similar situations later. If the presentation was dreaded and did not go very well, the next time will be far more stressful than the last one, producing a lot of negative neuro-chemicals. If, on the other hand, the performance was successful and even enjoyable, the next time around will most likely improve, and the amount of (negative) neuro-chemicals produced will decline.

Response to Stress. The response to stress has to do with how one deals with stress. This response can be influenced by individual differences in the form of intellect, personality, and motivation. Because human beings' behavior is driven by the way the brain works, a quick overview of the biology of stress is necessary.

Stress is a physiological response to an event (stressor, e.g. giving a presentation) or the environment, often in the form of anxiety. This response activates the autonomic nervous system. If the situation is appraised as a threat (either consciously or subconsciously) several things happen. First, the body and mind become highly aroused—by how much is often based on past experiences affecting both behavior and how the brain reacts. Two responses occur quite quickly:

- an extremely rapid one for an emergency, triggering a release of hormones (most notably cortisol), noradrenalin, and adrenalin, to increase alertness,
- an increase in heart rate in order to prepare more oxygen and nutrients to be used very quickly.

This first sequence involves the body going into a high state of *flight–fight* readiness. Why? Because humans are hard-wired that way. If our ancestors were out hunting and were confronted by a serious predator, such as a saber-toothed tiger or cave bear, they could respond to such life threatening events. The *flight–fight* reaction associated with meeting such a creature was accompanied by an increased physiological arousal to allow escape—the body producing the neuro-chemicals and nutrients that would make escape possible. Although necessary for our evolutionary survival, our autonomic nervous system continues to respond to pressures at work the same way.

If we are exposed to stressors every time we go to work, we receive a daily fix of these neuro-chemicals. Our bodies learn to adapt, with the result that our resting heart rate and blood pressure remain higher than they should. Thus our physical systems are bombarded with surplus adrenalin, cortisol, hormones, and nutrients possibly leading to (a) an inefficient immune system (lots of colds and flu), (b) low energy reserves (poor concentration, fatigue), (c) poor health (excessive sick days), (d) damage to brain tissue (difficulty in appraising situations rationally), (e) poor attention and decision-making, and (f) burnout and potential death. New technologies such as magnetic resonance imaging (MRI) have allowed researchers to look directly at the biological effects of stress on the brain.

Causes of Stress

Job stress results from the interaction of workers with the conditions in which they experience work. There are two schools of thought on the causes of stress.

Individual Differences. One school posits that individuals appraise situations differently. The individual personalities and coping styles are the most important factors in predicting whether certain job conditions will result in dis-stress.

Stressors in the workplace take many forms. If an individual's capacities to cope when confronted by high work demands are mismatched, stress can occur. Indeed, four main factors determine the degree to which a person will feel stressed, or how he or she will appraise a situation: *control, predictability, expectations,* and *support* (Kowske, 2009). In order for there to be low levels of work stress, individual workers need to feel that they have *control* in their working lives; their work experiences are *predictable*; their *expectations* are met; and that they feel *supported* at work. If any of these conditions are not met, then work stress will occur. Organizations that give *control* to the workforce, that enable the workforce to *predict* their futures via communication, that allow an alignment between workers' *expectations* and work demands, and that provide *support* mechanisms for work/life balance for workers, bear the hallmark of a healthy organization.

Working Conditions. The second school of thought posits that *working conditions* cause stress and will be stressful to all workers. Such working conditions could be in the form of excessive workload, conflicting workplace expectations, and poor working conditions (including health and safety considerations and job security issues). And different jobs and different industries have characteristics that bring their own job stress factors.

1. Physical environment. This can create high levels of stress through heat, cold, lighting or the sheer physicality of the job. The physical environment is a big factor in the construction industry. Extremes of hot and cold, rain and snow, high winds and other weather-related factors are beyond the control of management and workers alike. In addition, the requisite physical strength for lifting and carrying tools and materials has an effect. The worker may find the physical aspects unpleasant—wet, cold, heat, dust, noise, and heavy loads. The managers, on the other hand, will be affected differently—perhaps in the way the physical environment retards the project schedule and leads to financial losses.

2. Task characteristics. These also come into play: long work hours and shiftwork, and routine tasks where little skill or initiative is required. Both result in a low sense of control. A heavy workload with few rest breaks is also direct cause of workers stress. Unclear and non-specific *work roles* may be seen as unfair, and these, too, increase stress.

Identifying task characteristics is important for the individual carrying out that particular job. Workers presented with *work-demands* and *expectations* that do not match their knowledge, skills or abilities (either physically and/or mentally), can be challenged beyond their ability to cope. This situation is called a *mismatch* or poor *person–environment fit* and may result in stress. A high pace of work with conflicting demands, or an environment where workers have little *control* over how and when they work, particularly if there is low social *support*, will create serious stressors, with potential outcomes of dysfunctional conflict and unacceptable behavior.

Work roles. One of the problems in contemporary organizations is role overload that can be classified as *quantitative* and *qualitative.* The former refers to situations in which role occupants are required to perform more work than they can within a specific time period. The latter refers to situations in which role occupants believe they do not possess the skills or competence necessary to perform an assignment.

While role overload is a significant problem in contemporary organizations, role underload is also another problem that organizations have to deal with. Two types of role underload are *quantitative* and *qualitative*. Quantitative underload refers to a situation where employees do not have much work to do, and, as a result, they spend part of their time doing very little work. Qualitative underload refers to a situation where an employee's training and experience are inadequately used at work. This happens in many routine repetitive jobs. The work roles discussed here can create stress.

3. Organizational culture and management style. These can have a direct impact on workers' stress. If the organization has poor communications, policies that are not family-friendly, authoritarian, top-down decision-making with little worker input, or a culture of blame and fear, political climate, stress will be high.

Coping with Stress

Individuals who develop strategies such as positive thinking cope better than those who do not (Hede, 2010). Other strategies include developing commitment to the organization, gaining a sense of control and challenge in their work, and being involved in events and gaining influence over them, rather than sitting on the sidelines feeling powerless. Employees who are recognized for their achievements and have skills to both give and receive positive feedback, are better able to deal with the effects of stress. Managers who sincerely implement such strategies improve worker self-esteem and their workers' ability to cope, bringing about improved workplace well-being and performance.

Effects of Stress

The consequences of poorly managed stress are wide-ranging and can have long lasting health implications for the individuals and their organizations. Some early warning signs of stress for individuals are frequent headaches, short temper, job dissatisfaction, poor concentration, gastro-intestinal issues and poor sleep patterns. When stress becomes chronic, poor physical and mental health are potential outcomes, including cardiovascular disease, increased likelihood of workplace injury, psychological disorders, and an increased possibility of cancers, ulcers and an impaired immune system. The effects of stress are many and can be grouped into five broad areas: Cognitive, affective, behavioral, physiological, and organizational (see Table 1).

Table 1

Effects of Stress

Cognitive Effect
  Inability to make sound
    decisions
  Poor concentration
  Mental blocks
  Short attention span
  Reduced situational
    awareness
  Hypersensitivity to
    criticism

Emotional Effect
  Loss of temper
  Boredom and apathy
  Cynicism and resentfulness
  Feeling unable to cope with
    failure
  Aggression and conflict
  Anxiety
  Low self-esteem
  Feeling of hopelessness
  Nervousness
  Angry

Behavioral Effect
  Accident proneness
  Counterproductive work
    behaviors
  Self-damaging behaviors:
    smoking, alcohol, drugs,
    and reckless driving
  Impulsivity and irritation

Presenteeism (attending
    work when feeling sick or
    fear of losing job)

Physiological Effect
  Dryness of mouth
  Sweating
  Dilation of pupils
  Increase blood glucose
    levels
  Increased heart rate
  Chronic fatigue
  Sleep disorders
  Ulcers
  Headaches
  Depression
  Cardiovascular disease
    particularly heart attacks
    and stroke
  High Blood pressure
  Reduced immune system
    functioning

Organizational Effect
  High absenteeism
  Poor health and safety
    record
  Lower productivity
  Reduced job performance
  High turnover
  Increased conflict, violence,
    bullying, and harassment

Managing Stress at Work

Regardless of how good an organization has been at implementing stress reduction strategies, it is very unlikely to eliminate stress for all workers. The most efficient way of reducing stress is by organizational change to improve working conditions and ensure that effective policies and procedures are in place. In order to manage stress effectively at work, a combination of both organizational change and stress management strategies need to be implemented.

Organizational Interventions

Any model of work-stress intervention needs to differentiate between workplace stressors and stress responses. Unless managers are aware of how employees behave in times of stress and what causes them stress, they will have difficulty managing stress in the workplace. A sole focus on the individual employees' personalities and lifestyle in exclusion of employment facts is ineffective and often counterproductive. Such approaches lead to a culture of blame, where employees are less likely to admit to stress or an inability to cope. A good protector against this kind of situation is for the organization to create jobs with a high level of intrinsic reward (Malach-Pines & Keinan, 2006). Further organizational changes that can be implemented to prevent job stress are as follows:

1. Job design was discussed in the chapter on organization design. The job design approach developed by Hackman and Oldham (1975) attempts to make jobs more meaningful by increasing or adding certain job characteristics, such as skill variety, task identity, task significance, autonomy, and feedback. This type of comprehensive job design is able to reduce employees' perception of job stress.

2. Roles and responsibilities of the employees should be clearly defined to ensure that the workload is consistent with the employees' abilities to cope. Also providing work schedules that provide a balance to work-home life (telecommuting, comp-time, and flex-time are important here).

3. Other initiatives by organizations include the following:
- giving workers a voice and allowing them to participate in the decision-making processes (this approach is traditionally called "employee empowerment"),
- ensuring career development opportunities and future employment prospects,
- providing training in conflict management and time management.
- providing managers with the same training and additional training in effective performance appraisals.
- If employees are exposed to emotionally difficult and stressful experiences at work, organizations should be able to offer supervision and counseling services to protect their mental health and wellbeing.

Individual Interventions

Individuals must understand how they respond in person to stress and what signals their bodies give. They must also learn what their triggers are, and which ones can be dealt with and which ones cannot. Self-management of stress at the individual level can cover a wide range of strategies including:

1. **Knowing the sources** of personal stress, taking note of them, and identifying the feelings and behaviors engendered by stress.
2. **Learning to relax,** taking up yoga and/or meditation, having regular massages, and taking time off from work.
3. **Making regular exercise** a lifestyle choice. Regular exercise rids the body of surplus neurochemicals and glucose and releases endorphins, and leads to greater physical fitness,
4. **Eating a balanced diet**, including fresh fruit and vegetables, and keeping oneself well hydrated leads to greater physical fitness.
5. **Social support** is the availability of help in times of need from supervisors, coworkers, family members, and friends. Social support has positive effects on the physical and mental health of employees.

Implications for Managers

A comprehensive approach to stress management needs to include both personal stress management training for employees and organizational interventions. Golembiewski (2003) has provided the most advanced and detailed approach, using an eight-stage phased model of job burnout which can be used for stress management. Sustained management support for workers is important, providing the best possible outcomes for individuals as well as organizations (Chandola, 2012). Stress levels change according to hierarchical structures and positioning, with lower-level employees experiencing stress in different ways and potentially for different reasons. So how does a manager know what needs to be done? Before any process of dealing with stress can be implemented, a risk assessment needs to be carried out at an organizational level using a *Risk Assessment Cycle*. There are five phases:

1. **Identify** the stress risk factors in all areas of the workplace by undertaking audits and charting stressors.

2. **Gather data** decide who might be harmed and then use existing evidence: such as sickness absences information, productivity data, staff turnover, performance appraisals, and team meetings. Undertake surveys to ask staff opinion, take focus groups, have informal chats with staff. So use all sources of evidence to gain full information.
3. **Evaluate the risks** based on the information gathered, interpret, evaluate and formulate a statement of current good practice. Identify areas of concern and develop appropriate actions for both good and not so good. Extend good practice and target bench mark areas for improvement. Communicate the findings to employees.
4. **Record the findings** through consultation with staff, formulate an overall action plan and consider all factors identified.
5. **Monitor and review** undertake regular reviews of the action plans; assess how effective the practices are, then reappraise the action plan. Repeat the cycle again and regularly update.

Dealing with the stressors that an individual brings to work is difficult; controlling for and removing identifiable negative workplace stressors is far easier. Thus, good stress management by organizations can be effective, efficient, and productive. Employees need to have balance (work/life balance) with the organization's support for achievement of career goals. Equity and fairness issues create stress if employees appraise their situations as being either unfair or unequal. Thus, if employees regard pay and division of work among team members as equitable, less stress is likely. In addition, individuals need clarity as to how they have contributed to organizational goals. Organizations need enough team members to get the job done and must provide team members with clearly defined job responsibilities that do no conflict with other roles. Excelling on the job is related to less stress. In an economic downturn, actively managing job reassignments and solving workflow and workforce problems is essential. Conflicts need to be managed, and where dysfunctional, they need to be resolved effectively (Rahim, 2011). The overall ethos of the organization with respect to such factors as equity and conflict is therefore an important factor of successful stress management.

In short, unmitigated stress in the workplace has significant negative impacts on both soft factors, such as employee morale, and quantifiable factors such as productivity and cost. Accordingly, stress management is a critical management function, and one that, applied correctly, can yield surprising dividends in organizational performance.

Questions for Students

1. Why is dealing with stress in the workplace so important?
2. What are the main sources of stress in a workplace?
3. How would you go about identifying the levels of stress within your workplace?
4. How does stress affect the behavior of an individual at work?
5. What effect does stress have on the body?
6. What can an organization do to mitigate work-place stress?

Exercise

You have been given a new appointment to deal with stress. Your boss has approached you out of concern with a colleague who works alongside you. Your colleague has started complaining that she is feeling really stressed out and is not coping very well with her job, which she had previously done well. Your boss has asked you to see if you can identify what is really going on here. Your colleague has been taking quite a few days off work, complaining of headaches. She is also unable to finish assigned tasks given and generally never seems to be on top of her job. You suspect she is suffering from stress but you not sure what might be causing this. You need to find out if there is anything that you can do to support your colleague in order to get her back on track. (In the exercise, you may replace the term "boss" with tutor, and the term "colleague" with friend or fellow student, and "workplace with college/university).

Requirements

You will need some paper and pens or a laptop to jot down some thoughts and ideas.

Procedure

Based on the chapter and the risk assessment procedure in the chapter, see if you can:

1. **Identify** the stress risk factors in all areas of your colleague's workplace by undertaking audits and charting stressors within her work environment and job.
2. **Gather data** using existing evidence such as sickness, absence information and productivity data; you may also ask her opinion, or discussion the situation in an informal chat.
3. **Evaluate the risks** based on the information gathered, interpret, evaluate and formulate a statement of what areas are working well for your colleague, identify areas of concern and develop appropriate actions for both.
4. **Record the findings** through consultation with staff, formulate an overall action plan and consider all factors identified.
5. **Develop a risk monitoring and review plan** to determine if the situation has improved for your colleague or if not, why not?

Case: Organizational Stress Identification and Management in a Hospital

A hospital trust (a group of primary care hospitals) was experiencing an increase in stress-related illness in 2003 and the results of the annual staff survey placed them in the top 20% of trusts for work pressure experienced by staff. The Trust commissioned a survey and the results suggested problems with demands and control. In response to the survey, in autumn 2004, the Trust introduced a six-month "Valuing Staff" Campaign. The campaign had initiatives in nine areas including:

- Better training for managers
- Introducing a formula to enable managers to predict demand more accurately and to match staff to that demand
- Improving communications
- Introducing a system of absence management.

This campaign had measureable results that more than paid for the action taken. For example:

- Absences from illness were reduced from 6% in October 2003 to 3.85% in October 2005, yielding savings of £500,000 in the cost of agency cover.

- While absences from illness fell, the numbers of staff reporting to Occupational Health who were suffering from stress rose, suggesting a greater awareness on the part of staff for the need to seek help before taking sick leave.
- In 2003, the Trust had a range of unfilled vacancies; by 2005 there was a waiting list for applicants who had passed the selection system. This result suggested that the Hospital's image had improved.
- Productivity was substantially improved. Patient waiting times were reduced, while the number of patients in the system increased.

Reproduced with kind permission of the HSE (2007). Managing the causes of work-related stress: A step-by-step approach using the management standards. *Health and Safety Executive*, HSE Books.http://books.hse.gov.uk.

Suggestions for Further Reading

Chandola, T., & Marmot, M. (2012). *Handbook of stress science*. London: Springer.

Bowling, N. A., & Eschleman, K. J. (2010). Employee personality as a moderator of the relationship between work stressors and counterproductive work behavior. *Journal of Occupational Health Psychology*, 15, 91–103.

Srivastava, S. (2009). Locus of control as a moderator for relationship between organizational role stress and managerial effectiveness. *Vision: The Journal of Business Perspective*, 13, 49–61.

References

Avey, J. B., Luthans, F., & Jensen, S. M. (2009). Psychological capital: A positive resource for combating employee stress and turnover. *Human Resource Management, 48,*677–693.

Chandola, T. (2011). *Stress at work*. London: British Academy Policy Centre.

Golembiewski, R. T. (2003). *Ironies in organizational development*. Basel, Switzerland: Marcel Dekker.

Hackman, J. R., & Oldham, G. R. (1975). Development of the Job Diagnostic Survey. *Journal of Applied Psychology*, 60, 159–170

Hede, A. (2010). The dynamics of mindfulness in managing emotions and stress. *Journal of Management Development, 29,* 94–10.

Kowske, B. (2009). Economic crises equals work stress: How organizations can combat employee stress at work. In *Managing through turbulent times series*. Kenexa, UK: Research Institute.

Malach-Pines, A. & Keinan, C. (2006). Stress and burnout in Israeli border police. *International Journal of Stress Management, 13,* 519–540.

Maslach, C., & Jackson, S. E. (1986). *Maslach Burnout Inventory* (2nd ed.). Palo Alto, CA: Consulting Psychologists Press.

Rahim, M. A. (2011). *Managing conflict in organizations* (4th Ed.). New Brunswick, NJ: Transaction Publishers.

Toates, F. (1995). *Stress: Conceptual and biological aspects*. Chichester, UK. Wiley.

PART III
Leadership

6. Emotional Intelligence

Gita Gopaul Maharaja
Duquesne University

Afzal Rahim
Center for Advanced Studies in Management

The concept of emotional intelligence (EI) has attracted the attention of scholars and management practitioners around the world, in particular, its impact on job performance, satisfaction, and commitment of employees in organizations. It is now agreed that people need more than an intelligent quotient (IQ) to perform well in school and the workplace. Interest among behavioral scientists on emotions as a domain of intelligence has grown in recent years. Educators, business executives, psychologists, and human resource professionals are now interested in the phenomena of emotional intelligence to find how productivity can be enhanced. Business organizations are increasingly becoming aware of the importance of EI on the performance of both managers and other employees and of the need for training programs to improve the EI of its employees.

Nature of Emotional Intelligence

Definition

EI was first formally defined by Salovey and Mayer (1990) as "the ability to monitor one's own and other's feelings and emotions, to discriminate among them and to use this information to guide one's thinking and actions" (p. 189). This definition is still appropriate today. Goleman (1998) offers a complimentary definition which focuses on the abilities relating to organizing one's and others' feelings, motivating oneself, and managing one's emotions and in relationships. Davies, Stankov, and Roberts (1998) identify the following four EI dimensions, quite similar to Mayer and Salovey: appraisal and expression of emotion in oneself, appraisal and recognition of emotion in others, regulation of emotion in oneself and others, and using emotion to facilitate performance.

The different conceptualizations of EI presented above complement rather than contradict one another. The scholars assume that individual and groups attend to emotion in self and in others and that those who manage their and others' emotion appropriately have a higher probability of performing better at work. For the purpose of this book the definition and explanation of EI focuses on the following four components: (1) self-awareness, (2) regulating emotions in self and others, (3) understanding emotions of others, and (4) using emotions for productive processes (Davis et al., 1998; Goleman, 1998; Rahim et al., 2002; Law, Wong, & Song, 2004). These components of EI are discussed in the context of the relationship between managers and subordinates in an organization.

Components of EI

Self-awareness. This refers to the ability to perceive and understand one's emotions as well as to express emotions naturally (Mayer, Salovey, & Caruso, 2008). Individuals with this ability are aware of which emotions, feelings, moods, and impulses they are experiencing and why. Put it in another way, individual with this ability have the competence to recognize their strengths and weaknesses and can build on the strengths and improve on weaknesses.

Effective managers are able to recognize their own feelings and able to handle those feelings without being overwhelmed by them. Such ability allows an individual to use feelings to make decisions with confidence. Managers have to work with people, thus it is important that they identify and understand their own feelings, for example feeling tired, sad, happy, nervous, irritated, and anxious among others, while communicating with others. Accurate awareness of their own feelings helps managers to supervise their subordinates effectively.

Regulating Emotions in Self and Others. This component refers to the "ability to keep one's own emotions and impulses in check, to remain calm in potentially volatile situations, and to maintain composure irrespective of one's emotions" (Rahim et al., 2002, p. 305). This component of EI also includes one's awareness of the effects of his or her feelings on others. Individuals with this ability are less likely to lose their tamper and can return to a normal psychological state after an emotional encounter.

Managers who possess this ability maintain a positive outlook and do not give up in moments of set-back. Their focus is on end-results and how to get to there. They are able to motivate themselves and do not need instant gratification for their achievements. They also have the ability to handle stressful situations and are willing to take full responsibility for their actions. They are able to be flexible in their decision-making to achieve their goals successfully.

Understanding Others' Emotions. Understanding the emotions of others refers to one's ability to perceive and understand what others are feeling. The ability to identify how others feel in the organization enables managers to make good decisions and take appropriate actions. This ability enhances effectiveness of group leadership, conflict management, negotiations, individual and group interactions, customer service, and making deals.

Individuals with this ability are very sensitive to the emotions of others and are also able to predict others' emotional responses (Law, Wong, & Song, 2004). By understanding the emotions of subordinates, managers can persuade them to work towards the organization's goals, promote harmony, motivate others to learn, create a collaborative work environment, and encourage team-building. Furthermore, they are able to communicate effectively.

Using Emotions for Productive Purposes. This component of EI refers to one's ability to make use of emotions for constructive purposes and personal accomplishment. Individuals with this ability direct their emotions towards productive activities, positive outcomes, continuously motivate themselves, and strive to do better. Individuals with such ability positively impact their own and others' job performance. They are not only able to motivate themselves to do a better job but also serve as role models for others to follow with the intent of improving organizational performance (Davies et al., 1998).

Outcomes of Emotional Intelligence

Subordinates' Performance and Satisfaction

A number of measures of EI were used to assess its impact on job performance and satisfaction. Results were mixed, i.e. these studies found positive as well as non-significant relationship between EI and performance. In spite of the limitations of studies on the impact of EI on performance, existing evidence supports the notion that emotionally intelligent individuals have a higher chance of positively impacting the performance of followers (Walter, Cole, & Humphrey, 2011). A review of the four empirical studies on EI published in a special issue of the *International Journal of Organizational Analysis* concluded that they used an eclectic mix of methodologies and statistical techniques, but they all show positive relationships between supervisor's EI and behavior and attitudes in organizations (Svyantek & Rahim, 2002).

Leadership Effectiveness

A key question that is often asked in the literature about EI is how it impacts on leader effectiveness. Several studies have been conducted to find how leaders' EI influences the perception of leadership effectiveness in an organization. A study by Rahim et al. (2006) with triads found that subordinates' perceptions of leader EI were associated with transformational leadership behaviors across five countries (U.S., Greece, Portugal, South Korea, and Bangladesh).

It is important to point out that recent studies have raised questions about the role of EI for leadership (Walter et al., 2011). On one hand, practitioner-oriented publications about how EI differentiates high and low performers have led to the statement that "emotional intelligence is the sine qua non of leadership" (Goleman, 1998, p. 93) and on the other hand, other scholars suggest that the empirical evidence about the impact of EI is mixed, i.e. some studies have shown positive as well as non-significant relationship between EI and leadership effectiveness.

Subordinates' Behavioral Outcomes

Management studies suggest that supervisor and subordinate relationship is more effective when the former is sensitive to and recognizes the emotions of the latter which in turn improves organizational commitment, achievement of organizational goals, and conflict management. The literature review substantially covers ability-based studies on influence of leaders' EI on their relationship with and performance of subordinates (Ciarrochi, Forgas, & Mayer, 2001; Wong & Law, 2002). These studies suggest that leaders with a higher level of EI are able to motive others, gain trust of others, provide support for others and communicate the vision of the organization to others more effectively than those managers who lack EI. In their study, Wong and Law (2002) conclude that EI is positively associated job satisfaction and organizational citizen behavior of subordinates. Chang, Sy, and Choi (2012) suggest that "both average member EI and leader are positively associated with intrateam trust, which in turn positively relates to team performance" (p. 75).

The preceeding literature review points out the controversy about the effect of EI on leader effectiveness. Even though empirical evidence does not fully support arguments about the relevance of EI on leadership processes, there is adequate evidence to show that EI can potentially help to understand leadership emergence, leadership effectiveness, and leadership behaviors.

Sales Performance

Goleman (1998) suggests that EI is positively related to job performance of individuals working in sales and customer service and points out that positive outlook of the salesperson is associated with a high likelihood of success at work, for example, an optimistic salesperson would perform better than a pessimistic salesperson. Another study indicates that high-EI salespeople employ customer-oriented selling and influence customer decisions, thus generating higher revenues (Kidwell, Hardesty, Mutha, & Sheng, 2011).

Performance of Global Managers

Management literature indicates that the rise in global business is leading to a high demand for global managers who are able to adjust to different working environment in different countries. Studies suggest that global managers who have developed a higher level of EI competencies are able to better adjust in a foreign culture and perform more effectively in their overseas assignments than those who have a low level of EI competencies (Gabel, Dolan, & Cerdi, 2005).

Overall, the body of empirical research that contributes to a better understanding of EI suggests that there is a balanced picture of significant and non-significant findings. Although some scholars claim that EI has no effect on leadership and performance, others have reported significant relationships between EI and leadership effectiveness. Hence, it seems reasonable to suggest that EI has the potential to contribute to leadership effectiveness and its impact on subordinates' performance.

Implications for Management

Overall, it is reasonable to conclude that EI has a positive impact on management practices, ranging from follower and supervisor relationship, sales, cross-cultural adjustment of global managers, effectiveness of leaders to job commitment to marketing products. Based on the empirical evidence gained so far, it would seem that organizations should consider investing time and resources for EI training to enhance leadership and organizational effectiveness. Hopefully, this knowledge will assist educators, trainers, executives, and administrators in their efforts to create a better society where individuals are able to understand their and others' emotions.

The implication of this study is that by using their own emotional competencies managers can encourage subordinates to enhance their job satisfaction, organizational commitment, and conflict-management strategy. The perception of subordinates of their supervisors' use of these EI abilities may have compound positive impact on the subordinates' behavioral outcomes and probably job performance. Therefore, the challenge for a contemporary organization is to enhance the emotional intelligence of their managers. Managers may be trained to enhance their EQ (Cherniss & Golman, 2001) so that their subordinates are encouraged to improve their job performance and satisfaction.

Improving managers' EI would involve education and specific job-related training. Managers should also be encouraged to enhance their skills through continuous self-learning. Goleman (1998) suggests that managers need emotional competence training which should "focus on the competencies needed most for excellence in a given job or role" (p. 251). Organizations should provide appropriate reinforcements for learning and improving managers' essential emotional competencies needed for specific jobs.

Education and training may be of limited value when it comes to improving supervisors' EI. Organizations may have to adapt the policy of recruiting managers with vision and charisma who are likely to be high on EI. There should also be appropriate changes in the organization design which would require creating flatter, decentralized, and less complex structures. Also there should be appropriate changes in organizational culture that provides rewards for learning new behaviors. These changes in the organization design and culture will encourage managers and employees to acquire competencies needed for improving their job performance and satisfaction.

Exercise

In this section we are interested in your *opinion* about the way you do things in your organization. Please indicate by checking the appropriate box the extent to which you agree/disagree with each of the following statements.

		Strongly Agree				*Strongly Disagree*
1.	I am well aware of which emotions I am experiencing and why	☐	☐	☐	☐	☐
2.	I am conscious of my strengths and weaknesses.	☐	☐	☐	☐	☐
3.	I keep my distressing emotions in check.	☐	☐	☐	☐	☐
4.	I remain calm in potentially volatile situations.	☐	☐	☐	☐	☐
5.	I understand the feelings transmitted through nonverbal messages.	☐	☐	☐	☐	☐
6.	I operate from hope of success rather than fear of failure.	☐	☐	☐	☐	☐
7.	I stay focused on tasks at hand even under pressure.	☐	☐	☐	☐	☐
8.	If I accept a job, I would try to do my work in the best possible way.	☐	☐	☐	☐	☐

1. Score your responses to the four components of EI. A score of 2–6 represents a low component of EI and a score of 8–10 represents a high component of SI. Discuss the results with a team member in your class.
2. Discuss how your understanding of EI would improve your and subordinates' job performance?
3. Discuss different ways that managers in both domestic and international organizations can be trained to recognize the EI of their subordinates?
4. As a whole class, identify other abilities that a manger should possess to improve their effectiverness.

Source: The above 8 items were adapted from EQ Index designed by Rahim et al. (2002)

Case: Jeff, the Emotionally Intelligent Manager

Jeff was smiling. His teammates thought that was as it should be. After all, the board had just appropriated $6 million for his new product development team's efforts. Some of his fellow team members were openly shocked, believing that the project never had a chance. It would be the company's largest expenditure of this sort—ever. In addition, the project development schedule was aggressive, and the market for the product was quite different from the company's traditional core market.

Actually, Jeff was both thrilled and shocked. His smile was fixed on his face. His goal was to get the plan as far as the board, and if they approved the plan, he had expected that they would have provided only a small amount of funding, Now Jeff had to deliver, and he was worried.

Jeff was worried for an extremely good reason. The development team needed to find an original equipment manufacturer for the main component of the new product. After months of searching for a product to meet market requirements, engineering and purchasing had presented the options to the team. "It does it all.

In fact it's also twice as fast as what you are looking for." Purchasing claimed. Jeff looked at his product specification document and asked questions about other features. Engineering said there was no way to meet all the requirements. Jeff was very uncomfortable about the decision, as one key feature appeared not to meet his product specification, and this specification was part of the proposal to the board. But everyone else on the team thought it was great and, ultimately, product manager Jeff got caught up in the excitement. After all, it was just one feature out of many, and the team, had significantly upgraded the spec in order in other areas. And time was running out. He agreed to support the team and negotiations with the vendor began.

The next few months were anxious ones, as the team raced to meet the aggressive deadline for the product launch. There was a strong sense of excitement, and the team met the deadline. It was the fastest development project in the history of the company,

The team forgot Jeff's concerns regarding the missing product feature, although Jeff had lingering doubts. He did not allow these doubts to surface, however, and never discussed them. After all, he was one of the guys and part of the team. Everyone seemed so happy with the product that he thought it would be okay. He ignored his emotions and got caught up in the excitement of others.

But the product did not sell. At first, the team blamed sales. Sales blamed service. Service blamed the product.

Source: Cherniss, C. & Coleman, D. (2001). *The emotionally intelligent workplace*. San Francisco, CA: Jossey-Bass

Suggestions for Further Reading

Carmeli, A., & Josman, Z. E. (2006). The relanship among emotional intelligence, task performance, and organizational citizenship behaviors. *Human Performance, 19,* 403–419.

Mayer, J, D, Salovey, P., & Caruso, D. R. (2004). Emotional intelligence: Theory, findings and implications. *Psychological Inquiry, 15,* 3, 197–215.

Moon, T. W., & Hur, W-M. (2011). Emotional intelligence, emotional exhaustion, and job performance. *Social Behavior and Personality, 39,* 1087–1096.

References

Chang, J. W., Sy, T., & Choi, J. N. (2012). Team emotional intelligence and performance: Interactive dynamics between leaders and members. *Small Group Research, 43,* 75–104.

Cherniss, C., & Goleman, D. (2001). *The emotionally intelligent workplace.* San Francisco, CA: Jossey-Bass.

Ciarrochi, J., Forgas, J. P., & Mayer, J. D. (Eds). (2001). *Emotional intelligence in everyday life: A scientific inquiry.* Philadelphia: Psychological Press.

Davies, M., Stankov, L., & Roberts, R. D. (1998). Emotional intelligence: In search of an elusive construct. *Journal of Personality and Social Psychology, 75,* 989–1015

Gabel, R. A., Dolan S. L., & Cerdin, J. L. (2005). Emotional intelligence as predictor of cultural adjustment for success in global assignments. *Career Development International, 10,* 375–395.

Goleman, D. (1998). *Working with emotional intelligence.* New York: Bantam Books.

Kidwell, B., Hardesty, D.M., Mutha, B. R., & Sheng, S. (2011). Emotional intelligence in marketing exchanges. *Journal of Marketing, 75,* 78–95.

Law, K. S., Wong, C., & Song, L. J. (2004). The construct and criterion validity of emotional intelligence and its potential utility for management studies. *Journal of Applied Psychology, 89,* 483–496.

Rahim, M. A., Psenicka, C., Polychroniou, P., Zhao, J. H., Yu, C. S., Chan, K. A., Yee, K. W., Alves. M. G., Lee, C. W., Rahman, M. S., Ferdausy, S., & Wyk, R. V. (2002). A model of emotional intelligence and conflict management strategies: A study in seven countries. *International Journal of Organizational Analysis, 10,* 302–326.

Rahim, M. A., Psenicka, C., Oh, S-Y., Polychroniou, P., Dias, J. F., Rahman, M. S., & Ferdausy, S. (2006). Relationship between emotional intelligence and transformational leadership: A cross-cultural study. *Current Topics in Management, 11,* 223–236.

Salovey, P., & Mayer, J. D. (1990). Emotional intelligence. *Imagination, Cognition and Personality,* 9, 185–211.

Svyantek, D. J., & Rahim, M. A. (2002). Links between emotional intelligence aqnd behavior in organizationa: Findings from empirical studies. *International Journal of Organizational Analysis, 10,* 299–301.

Walter, F., Cole, M. S., & Humphrey, R. H. (2011, February). Emotional intelligence: Sine qua non of leadership or folderol? *Academy of Management Perspectives,* pp. 45–59.

Wong, C. S., & Law, K. S (2002). The effects of leader and follower emotional intelligence on performance and attitude: An exploratory study. *Leadership Quarterly,* 13, 243–274.

7. Social Intelligence

Afzal Rahim
Center for Advanced Studies in Management

There is great deal of interest in the study on intelligence that is evidenced by a steady stream of theoretical and empirical studies published in scholarly journals. Many scholars and leaders generally associate this construct with cognitive, academic, or analytical intelligence and they generally believe that IQ is the measure of intelligence. Hence, grade point average, Scholastic Aptitude Test, and other admission tests are used in academic institutions as surrogates of IQ. However, the literature on management shows that cognitive intelligence is inadequate to predict one's effective leadership or success throughout life. Is it possible that there are other types of intelligence that are necessary for successful leadership?

Scholars are now discussing other dimensions of intelligence: emotional intelligence, social intelligence, and cultural intelligence—what scholars refer to as "street smarts" (cf. Gardner, 1999; Mayer, Salovey, & Caruso, 2008; Sternberg, 2009; van Dyne, Ang, & Koh, 2009). This chapter discusses the components of social intelligence (SI) and how they relate to each other and to creative performance of leaders and subordinates' job performance and satisfaction.

Nature of Social Intelligence

Definition

John Dewey (1909) was the first educational psychologist to suggest that the "ultimate moral motives and forces are nothing more or less than *social intelligence*—the power of observing and comprehending social situations" (p. 43). It is generally recognized that Thorndike made a significant contribution by popularizing the construct through an article that appeared in *Harper's Magazine* in 1920. He suggested three components of intelligence: abstract (the ability to understand and manage ideas and symbols), mechanical (the ability to learn to understand and manage things), and social (the ability to manage and understand men and women, boys and girls, to act wisely in human relations) (p. 228). This definition of SI had both cognitive and behavioral components. Sternberg (2009) in his numerous studies provides empirical evidence that there are three types of intelligence—creative, analytical, and practical—that are needed for one's success. Sternberg's practical intelligence is very similar to social intelligence that is the subject of this chapter.

There are many definitions of intelligence. The APA Dictionary of Psychology defines intelligence as "the ability to derive information, learn from experience, adapt to the environment, understand, and correctly utilize thought and reason" (VandenBos, 2007, p. 488). Scholars agree that SI is different from cognitive intelligence. Most definitions of SI relate to one's social skills, but the definition should be expanded to include one's ability to interact with their relevant components of social environment and act effectively in various situations. A more comprehensive definition SI is the

> ability to be aware of relevant social situational contexts; to deal with the contexts or challenges effectively; to understand others' concerns, feelings, and emotional states; and to communicate and build and maintain positive relationships with others. (Rahim, 2014, p. 46)

This definition consists of four categories of *abilities*—situational awareness, situational response, cognitive empathy, and social skills. Situational awareness is associated with one's ability to collect information for the diagnosis and formulation of problem(s) and situational response is associated with one's ability to use this information to make effective decisions to attain desired results.

These are two basic abilities are needed for one's success i., life or effective leadership.

Cognitive empathy and social skills are secondary abilities that are needed for better understanding of people and to build and maintain relationships. These two abilities can help one to remain aware of various social situational contexts.

Components

The theoretical basis of the four SI components and interrelationships among them are described as follows.

Situational Awareness. This is associated with one's *competence or ability to comprehend or assess relevant social situational contexts*. Individuals with this ability are able to collect relevant information and make appropriate diagnosis of a situation(s) in a timely manner. This ability enables individuals to formulate a problem correctly. If they feel that they do not have adequate information on a problem or a potential business opportunity, they are likely to engage in internal and/or external environmental scanning behavior. If they do not understand a particular situation involving a technical problem, they may seek help from experts so that they have an overall understanding of the problem. For example, experts may bring different and even contradictory assessments of a problem, but it is the leader who decides which problem formulation reflects social reality and is to be accepted.

Bennis and Thomas (2002) describe this ability or competence as *contextual intelligence*. In their book on leadership, *In Their Time: The Greatest Business Leaders of the Twentieth Century*, Mayo and Nohira (2005) suggest that a leader's ability to understand as well as adapt to different situational contexts is associated with leadership effectiveness. This component should include, among others, the abilities to:

1. Formulate a problem correctly.
2. Read a complex situation quickly.
3. Understand the risks and gains present in a social situation.
4. Determine the root causes of a social problem.
5. Make realistic assessments of situations
6. Understand the real issues involved in a situation.

Situational awareness or the diagnosis of a problem is very important. If a problem is wrongly formulated, there is the possibility that one would solve a wrong problem. Leaders who possess this ability are able to collect necessary information and formulate a problem correctly. Situational awareness competence has been generally neglected in the contingency theories of leadership which implicitly assume that leaders have good understanding of the relevant situational variables and they are able to formulate their problems correctly. But leaders who are low on this competence may not be able to make an appropriate assessment of situational variables.

Situational Response. This is associated with one's *competence or ability to adapt to or deal with any social situation* effectively. This is essentially the decision making competence of leaders which was described by Bennis and Thomas (2002) as adaptive capacity. Mayo and Nohira (2005) do not distinguish between situational awareness and situational response abilities and lump them into situational awareness. In this chapter a distinction is made between the two abilities. This is because it is possible for one to recognize or diagnose a situation or problem correctly, but be unable to make decisions that are likely to lead to desirable outcomes.

In connection with organizational learning, Argyris and Schon (1996) in their numerous publications talk about *detection* and *correction* of error that are involved in organizational learning. In connection with the management or organizational conflict, Rahim and Bonoma (1979) present a model of diagnosis of and intervention in conflict and Schmidt and Tannenbaum (1960) describe these as abilities "to diagnose an issue and its causes" and "to decide on the best course of action" (p. 107). The two processes—diagnosis or detection of error and intervention or correction of error—correspond well with the two components of SI—assessment of and responses to situational contexts. These two components have overlaps, but are conceptually independent. In other words, it is possible for a leader to have high or low abilities associated with these two components. A high–high leader is more effective than a high–low, low–high, or low–low leader. In other words, these two abilities are essential for effective leadership.

Literature on leadership has generally done a better job of prescribing how to match leadership styles with situational variables for improving job performance and satisfaction of followers, unfortunately scholars were unable to capture the unique situations for which creative responses (leadership styles) would be needed for improving outcomes. Contingency theories of leadership generally suggest certain situational variables that should be adequately matched with appropriate leadership styles in order to enhance job performance and satisfaction of the subordinates. Unfortunately, leadership theories did not consider the need for leaders to possess the situational awareness and response competencies to define the situational variables and respond to them with appropriate styles. Even if a leader can diagnose a situation correctly, he or she may not possess the competence needed to make an effective decision to deal with it. Situational response component should include the abilities to:

1. Adapt appropriately to different situations
2. Respond to a crisis situation effectively.
3. Know how to adapt to a new work environment.
4. Make a decision that will lead to problem solving.

The preceding discussion made it clear that situational awareness and situational response competencies are essential for effective leadership. However, there are other abilities, such as cognitive empathy and social skills that can help leaders to improve their functions better. Following is a discussion of these abilities.

Cognitive Empathy. Another component of SI that has been discussed by scholars is empathy (cf. Goleman, 2005). Empathy refers to one's ability to understand others and taking active interest in them, recognizing and responding to changes in their emotional states, and understanding their feelings. Several components of empathy are cognitive, intellectual, affective, and behavioral. Cognitive empathy is associated with *one's ability to recognize the thinking, feelings, intentions, moods, and impulses of people inside and outside the organization* and is a component of SI. This component should include the abilities to:

1. Know how an individual is feeling.
2. Know what an individual is thinking.
3. Understand the moods of the people.
4. Understand people's feelings transmitted through nonverbal messages.
5. Know when people disguise their true feelings.

Cognitive empathy should help to improve a leader's awareness of the feelings and needs of subordinates, coworkers, and supervisors as well as people from outside the organization. This ability to connect with people should help to improve a leader's situational awareness.

Social Skills. Most of the definitions of SI include social skills which is associated with *one's ability or competence to speak in a clear and convincing manner that involves knowing what to say, when to say it, and how to say it.*

Social skills also involve building and maintaining positive relationships, to act *properly in human relations,* to deal with problems without demeaning those who work with him or her, and to manage conflict with tack and diplomacy. This component should include the abilities to:

1. Be comfortable among different people.
2. Manage with equal ability men, women, and children.
3. Interact appropriately with a variety of people.
4. Negotiate well to reach an agreement(s).
5. Build and maintain positive relationships.

Social skills competence enables a leader to continuously collect relevant information from internal and external environments which enhance their situational awareness. Social skills ability should help leaders to explain and justify their decisions to followers and motivate them so that leaders' decisions are effectively implemented. Studies by Baron and Markham (2000) and Baron and Tang's (2009) and suggest that entrepreneurs' social skills—specific competencies that help them to interact effectively with others—may also play a role in their success.

In the previous section it was indicated that cognitive empathy directly influences social skills, but indirectly influences situational awareness. In other words, social skills mediates the relationship between cognitive empathy and situational awareness. Also social skills is positively associated with situational awareness and indirectly associated with situational response. In other words, situational awareness mediates the social skills–situational response relationship.

Outcomes of Social Intelligence

Creative Performance of Supervisors

There is great interest among scholars in social sciences regarding the factors that encourage creative performance which is associated with the creation of new ideas regarding organizational processes, procedures, products, and services. This is different from routine performance that involves decisions leaders make to deal with day-to-day or routine operations.

There is a large literature on creativity which was discussed in the chapter on creativity. The present chapter discusses how a leader's SI influences his or her creative performance. The definition of creative performance, among others, should include the following behaviors:

1. Searching for new technologies, processes, and techniques to improve performance.
2. Suggesting new ways to increase quality of products/service.
3. Coming up with unique solutions to problems.
4. Promoting new ideas to achieve task objectives.
5. Developing plan for the implementation of new ideas.

Baron's (2008) literature review suggests that affect, which is associated with emotion and feelings (as distinguished from cognition and volition), exerts strong influence on individual, interpersonal, and organizational processes. His review also suggests that affect influences cognition involving creativity. In general, individuals experiencing positive affect tend to be more creative than those experiencing neutral or negative affect (Isen, 2002). An empirical study by Amabile, Barsade, Muller, and Staw (2005) reported that "affect relates positively to creativity in organizations and that the relationship is a simple linear one" (p. 367). SI which is associated more with affect than cognition is expected to be positively associated with creative performance of leaders.

Goleman (1998) suggests that leaders in business organizations who are high on emotional intelligence display creativity in their decision making and performance. Two studies have reported that the quality of a situational response (after controlling the effects of situational awareness, cognitive empathy, and social skills) is positively associated with creative performance (Rahim, 2014a; Rahim, Civelek, & Liang, in press).

The relationships of the four components of SI with each other and to creative performance are presented in Figure 1. The model shows that (a) cognitive empathy is positively associated with social skills. In other words, understanding another person's emotions, thinking, and feelings helps individuals to improve their use of social skills. The broken line connecting cognitive empathy and situational awareness indicates that cognitive empathy cannot directly influence situational awareness, but it has an indirect influence on situational awareness through social skills. (b) The broken line connecting social skills and situational response indicates that social skills cannot directly influence situational response. In other words, social skills has indirect influence on situational response through situational awareness. (c) The broken line connecting situational awareness and creative performance indicates that situational awareness cannot directly influence creative performance. In other words, situational awareness has indirect influence on creative performance through situational response.

Figure 1
A Model of Intelligent Leadership and Creative Performance

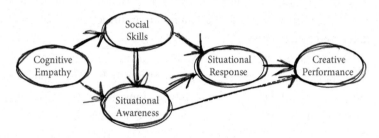

Job Performance, Satisfaction, and Other Outcomes of Subordinates

Several studies reported that job performance, satisfaction, and commitment of subordinates are positively associated with emotional intelligence (cf. Walter, Cole, & Humphrey, 2011). It is expected that similar relationships exist between social intelligence and job performance and satisfaction of subordinates. Other studies have reported that social intelligence is positively associated with interpersonal justice and negatively associated with turnover intention (Rahim, 1014b; Rahim, Civelek, & Liang, in press).

Implications for Management

The implications of this construct are that supervisors need to acquire the four components of SI to enhance their own creative performance and subordinates' job performance and satisfaction. Hopefully supervisor's SI will also positively influence employees' organizational commitment, and prosocial behavior, and negatively correlate with turnover intention, workplace incivlity, and other behavioral outcomes.

Appropriate interventions may be needed to enhance their SI competencies that would involve education and specific job-related training. Managers should also be encouraged to enhance their abilities through continuous self-learning. Organizations should provide positive reinforcements for learning and improving managers' essential SI competencies needed for specific jobs.

Even though education and training are useful for improving supervisors' SI, organizations may have to adapt the policy of recruiting managers with vision and charisma who are likely to be high on SI. This comment is based on the assumption that education and training may not be able to significantly change one's level of SI that may have a positive influence on leaders' creative performance and other outcomes.

Nevertheless, recent literature shows that learning organizations are providing ample opportunities to managers for continuous learning that should help to improve their use of SI. Learning organizations generally make appropriate changes in the organization design that involve creating flatter, decentralized, and less complex structures. Also there should be appropriate changes in organizational culture that provides rewards for risk-taking, learning new competencies, and for continuous questioning and inquiry. These changes in the organization design, culture, and positive reinforcements should encourage managers to acquire SI competencies needed for improving their own creative performance and subordinates' job performance, satisfaction, and other positive outcomes.

Exercise

Rank (5 = Very high, 4 = High, 3 = Moderate, 2 = Low, 1 = Very low) the following four U.S. presidents on the four components of social intelligence.

	Social Intelligence			
Professionals	Situational Awareness	Situational Response	Cognitive Empathy	Social Skills
1. Ronald Reagan	_____	_____	_____	_____
2. George W. Bush	_____	_____	_____	_____
3. Bill Clinton	_____	_____	_____	_____
4. Barack Obama	_____	_____	_____	_____

1. Form a group of three members and explain the reasons behind your rankings of these presidents.
2. After each group member explains his/her rankings to the group, the group as a whole will rank the presidents.
3. A representative from each group explains what they learnt from this exercise.
4. The instructor encourages the class to make further comments on what they learnt from the exercise.

Case: Joe Paterno

The Board of Trustees of Penn State informed the 84-year-old Joe Paterno, the iconic figure of a football program, on November 9, 2012, that he was being dismissed. This happened because of a sex-abuse scandal involving assistant coach Jerry Sandusky who was charged November 5, 2012 with molesting eight boys over a span of 15 years. The Board also fired the athletic director Tim Curley and the university president Graham Spanier.

Joe Paterno was accused of failing to notify authorities after being told about a 2002 incident by a graduate assistant Mike McQueary in which Sandusky was allegedly raping a boy in the showers of the football building. McQueary, now the Penn State assistant football coach is under fire for his reported lack of action in this alleged 2002 rape, said in an email to a former classmate that he stopped the assault in an athletic facility shower and discussed it with Joe Paterno. The New York Times reported that nearly 10 more people have come forward, alleging that they too were sexually abused by Sandusky.

While many people wondered what took the university so long in firing Joe Paterno, Penn State supporters wondered why Joe couldn't at least be allowed to say goodbye at the Nittany Lions' final home game of the season, against Nebraska.

Suggestions for Further Reading

Hedlund, J., Wilt, J. M., Nobel, K. R., Ashford, S. J., & Sternberg, R. J. (2006). Assessing practical intelligence in business school admissions: A supplement to the graduate management admission text. *Learning and Individual differences, 16,* 101–127.

Rahim, M. A. (2014). A structural equations model of leaders' social intelligence and creative performance. *Creativity and Innovation Management, 23* (1), 44–56.

van Dyne, L., Ang, S., & Koh, C.K.S. (2009). Cultural intelligence: Measurement and scale development. In M. A. Moodian (Ed.), Contemporary leadership and intercultural competence: Exploring the cross-cultural dynamics within organizations (pp. 233–254). Thousand Oaks: Sage.

References

Amabile, T. M., Barsade, S. G., Mueller, J. S., & Staw, B. M. (2005). Affect and creativity at work. *Administrative Science Quarterly, 50,* 367–403.

Argyris, C., & Schon, D. (1996). *Organizational learning–II.* Reading MA: Addison-Wesley.

Baron, R. A. (2008). The role of affect in the entrepreneurial process. *Academy of Management Review, 33,* 328–340.

Baron, R. A., & Markham, G. D. (2000). Beyond social capital: How social skills can enhance entrepreneurs' success. *Academy of Management Executive, 14,* 106–116.

Baron, R. A., & Tang, J. (2009). Entrepreneurs' social skills and new venture performance: Mediating mechanisms and cultural generality. *Journal of Management, 35,* 282–306.

Bennis, W. G., & Thomas, R. J. (2002). *Geeks and geezers*. Cambridge, MA: Harvard Business School Press.

Dewey, J. (1909). *Moral principles in education*. New York: McGraw-Hill.

Gardner, H. (1999). *Intelligence reframed*. New York: Basic Books.

Goleman, D. (1998). *Working with emotional intelligence*. New York: Bantum Books.

Goleman, D. (2005). *Social intelligence: The new science of human relationships*. New York: Bantum Books.

Isen, A. M. (2002). Missing in action in the AIM: Positive affect's facilitation of cognitive flexibility, innovation, and problem solving. *Psychological Inquiry, 13,* 57–65.

Mayer, J. D., Salovey, P., & Caruso, D. R. (2008). Emotional intelligence: New ability or eclectic traits? *American Psychologist, 63,* 503–517.

Mayo, A. J., & Nohria, N. (2005). *In their time: The greatest business leaders at the twentieth century*. Boston: Harvard Business School Press.

Rahim, M. A. (2014). A structural equations model of leaders' social intelligence and creative performance. *Creativity and Innovation Management, 23* (1), 44–56.

Rahim, M. A., & Bonoma, T. V. (1979). Managing organizational conflict: A model for diagnosis and intervention. *Psychological Reports, 44,* 1323–1344.

Rahim, M. A., Civelek, I., & Liang, H. (in press). Department chairs as leaders: A model of social intelligence and creative performance in a state university. *Business Creativity & The Creative Economy*.

Schmidt, W. H., & Tannenbaum, R. (1990, November–December). Management of differences. *Harvard Business Review,* pp. 107–115.

Sternberg, R. J. (2002). Successful intelligence: A new approach to leadership. In R. E. Riggio, S. E. Murphy, & F. J. Pirozzolo (Eds.), *Multiple intelligenecs and leadership* (pp. 9–28). Mahwah, NJ: Erlbaum.

Sternberg, R. J. (2009, Fall). Wisdom, intelligence, and creativity synthesized: A new model for liberal education. *Liberal Education,* pp. 10–15.

Thorndike, R. L. (1920). Intelligence and its uses. *Harper's Magazine, 140,* 227-235.

VandenBos, G. R. (Ed.). (2007). *APA dictionary of psychology*. Washington, DC: American Psychological Association.

Walter, F., Cole, M. S., & Humphrey, R. H. (2011). Emotional intelligence: Sin qua non of leadership or Folderol? *Academy of Management Perspectives, 25,* 45–59.

8. Power Bases

Afzal Rahim
Center for Advanced Studies Management

Power is one of the major areas of scientific studies in management and organizational behavior. Bertrand Russell (1938) described power as "the fundamental concept in social science ... in the same sense in which energy is the fundamental concept in physics" (p. 12). The phenomena of social power are all-pervasive in groups, organizations, and societies. In organizational settings, the process of exercising power serves as one of the characteristics which define dyadic relationships between supervisor and subordinates, between colleagues, and two unrelated employees. Acquisition, maintenance, and the use of the right types of power to attain desired goals are essential for effective leadership.

Nature of Power

Defining Power and Influence

Power is defined as the ability of one party to change or control the behavior, attitudes, opinions, objectives, needs, and values of another party (Rahim, 2009). This definition implies that the theory of power for this chapter is associated with the influence one has over another individual. *Power bases* differ from *influence attempt* as the former is associated with the ability to use power and the latter with the actual use of power.

Taxonomy of Power Bases

Several classifications of leader or supervisory power have been set forth, but the bases of power taxonomy suggested by French and Raven (1959) and Raven (1965)—coercive, reward, legitimate, information, expert, and referent—still appears to be fairly representative and popular in application.

Position Power Base. Coercive, reward, legitimate, and information power bases are associated with the position a person holds in an organization. That is, a person acquires these power bases by occupying a position in an organization. These power bases together constitute the position power of an organizational member.

Coercive Power. This power is based on subordinates' perception that their supervisor has the ability to punish them or withhold rewards if they fail to conform to the influence attempt. Firing, suspending, ridiculing, demoting, or reprimanding a subordinate constitute common ways of using coercive power by a subordinate. This power is essentially based on the subordinates' fear or perception that their supervisor can punish them for noncompliance.

Reward Power. This type of power is the opposite of coercive power and is based on the perception of subordinates that their supervisor can reward them for desired behavior. Supervisors often use financial rewards, such as pay raises and bonuses, and nonfinancial rewards, such as recognition, advancement, and pleasant work assignments to exert reward power over their subordinates.

Legitimate Power. This type of power gives a supervisor the right to prescribe and control the subordinates' behavior. This power is possibly the most complex of those presented here. It is based on the internalized values of the subordinates which dictate that the supervisor has the right to prescribe and control their behavior and they have the obligation to accept the influence. The power is vested in the rights, duties, and responsibilities of the position, not the person who holds position.

Information Power. This type of power is associated with one's access to information which is not public knowledge, but is needed by employees to perform their job effectively. A supervisor may have access to privileged salary, sales, net income, sales, and other data that can be used to influence the behavior of subordinates. This power also includes one's ability to acquire information that others want which is not presently available.

Personal Power Base. The remaining two power bases are associated with a person, not a position. Individuals acquire these power bases through their own efforts and together they constitute personal power. These power bases are described as follows.

Expert Power. It is based on subordinates' belief that their supervisor has adequate professional experience, training, special expertise, and access to knowledge. Accountants, marketing researchers, and engineers may exert significant influence on their subordinates because of their specialized skills. Expert power is also held by subordinates who are subject matter experts on whose technical expertise and judgment a superior must rely for successful work-related decisions and outcomes.

Referent Power. This type of power is based on the desire of a subordinate to identify and associate with his or her superior. Identification is the feeling of oneness of a subordinate with his superior. Here the control is dependent upon the supervisor's leadership style or charisma to attract subordinates so that they follow his or her leadership. Other variants of referent power are:

- *Affiliation or connection power* which is associated with one's connection with influential individuals.
- *Credibility power* which is associated with one's integrity, honesty, and reliability.
- *Persuasive power* which is associated with one's social skills needed to reason effectively and persuade others.
- *Prestige power* is associated with the status, social standing, and reputation of a leader.

Some examples of leaders who possess(ed) these power bases are in order. It is generally agreed that Bill Clinton has both expert and referent power bases, but President Regan had high referent power, but not expert power. In the private sector Lee Iacocca, the former CEO of Chrysler, had high expert and referent power bases, but the former CEO of General Electric—Jack Welch—had high expert but not referent power.

Interdependence of Power Bases

There are significant intercorrelations among the five power bases. These interrelationships should be explained so that practitioners can acquire and use appropriate power bases to influence their subordinates' conflict management strategies and propensity to leave a job. Greene and Podsakoff's (1981) field experiment indicates that a change in the perception of one power base may affect the perceptions of other power bases. For example, a change in the perception of reduced reward power may affect the perception of greater coercive power and the reduction of legitimate and referent powers, but not expert power. Knowing how power bases influence each other is important as each power base may influence outcomes, not only directly but also through the mediation of other power bases. It is possible that the position power base influences criterion variables through the mediation of the personal power base. Stated in another way, the position power base influences the personal power base, which in turn, influences criterion variables (see Carson, Carson, & Roe, 1993; Rahim, Antonioni, & Psenicka, 2001). These findings make sense, as supervisors who use a performance-contingent reward power base as well as their legitimate power base may be perceived by their subordinates as competent as well as friendly, considerate, and fair.

Several studies have found that the expert and referent power bases were significantly correlated. One possible explanation of this phenomenon is that subordinates like to identify and associate with a supervisor who possesses expert power. Furthermore, these studies reported that the reverse influence (i.e., referent power influencing expert power) is unlikely to happen. In other words, the perception of expert power positively influences the perception of referent power, but the reverse is not true.

Table 1
Levels of Leader Power Bases across
National Cultures

Power bases	U.S.		Bangladesh		S. Korea		
	M	Rank	M	Rank	M	Rank	
Coercive	3.81a	(2)	2.77b	(5)	2.54c	(5)	US, BA, SK
Reward	3.62a	(4)	3.40b	(4)	3.18c	(4)	US, BA, SK
Legitimate	4.03a	(1)	3.62b	(3)	3.50c	(1)	US, BA, SK
Expert	3.61b	(5)	3.73a	(1)	3.33c	(2)	BA, US, SK
Referent	3.66a	(3)	3.64a	(2)	3.20b	(3)	US & BA, SK

Note: U.S. = United States (*n* = 1, 474), BA = Bangladesh (*n* = 250), SK = S. Korea (*n* = 728). Means are adjusted for age, tenure, organizational level, and educational level. Means with different superscripts are significantly different (*p* < .05) from each other. Parenthetical figures indicate the ranking of each leader power base within each national culture on the basis of the adjusted means.

Comparing Leader Power Profiles across Cultures

Rahim and Magner's (1996) cross-cultural field study that compared the power profiles across three national cultures—the U.S., South Korea, and Bangladesh—suggests interesting patterns (see Table 1).

First, supervisors in individualistic cultures (such as the U.S.) appear to generally have higher levels of each power base than collectivistic cultures (such as S. Korea). Second, supervisors in individualistic cultures appear to place greater relative emphasis on coercive power than do those in collectivistic cultures, while supervisors in collectivistic cultures appear to place greater relative emphasis on expert power than those in individualistic cultures. There are important implications of these findings for expatriate managers.

Effectiveness of Power Bases

Oyster (1992) conducted an interesting study on women executives' perception of the power bases used by "best" and "worst" supervisors. Results show that male bosses were more likely than female bosses to be identified as the worst bosses, but males and females were equally likely to be identified as the best bosses. The best bosses used more reward, information, and expert, and referent and less coercive and legitimate power bases than worst bosses. Management literature generally suggests that personal power bases are more effective than position power bases for enhancing job performance, satisfaction of employees, and other positive outcomes. A number of studies have investigated the relationships of power bases to compliance, satisfaction with work and supervision, organizational commitment, styles of handling conflict, and job performance. The consensus among these studies has been that expert and referent power bases were generally associated with these criterion variables. Coercive power is ineffective in influencing these criterion variables and reward and legitimate power bases were considered by subordinates, but they showed no clear relationship with these criterion variables.

As discussed in the section on the interdependence of power bases, an alternative explanation of the weak relationship between position power and criterion variables is that position power base may influence criterion variables through the mediation of the personal power base. In other words, coercive, reward, legitimate, and information power bases influence expert and referent power bases; the expert power base influences the referent power base, and this, in turn, influences outcomes. In future studies, the relationships of the power bases to other criterion variables, such as motivation, creative behavior, and organizational citizenship behavior of employees may be investigated.

Implications for Management

What can leaders do to acquire and maintain the right types of power bases and learn how to use them to attain goals? Leaders can be more effective in enhancing functional outcomes and reducing dysfunctional outcomes of subordinates by enhancing their own personal and position power bases. Supervisors' use of reward, legitimate, information, expert, and referent power bases may have compound positive impacts on the subordinates' job performance, satisfaction, and other functional outcomes.

Personal Power Base

Enhancing managers' personal power bases is a challenge for organizations. In order to obtain desired results, there should be changes at the individual and organizational levels.

Expert Power. Basic education, job-related training, and on-the-training are essential for improving managers' expert power base. Managers should also be encouraged to enhance their skills through continuous self-learning. They will also need appropriate job experience to build on this power base.

Referent Power. Literature shows that **the** referent power base is more effective than other power bases in influencing criterion variables. Although this power base has the most potential, it is probably used the least. Supervisors who are deficient on this power base may be provided social intelligence training (see Chapter 3 for details) so that they learn to be empathetic to the subordinates' needs and feelings, to treat them ethically and with dignity, and to present their concerns to upper-level managers when there is a need to do so. These strategies should enhance a supervisor's base of referent power.

Appropriate reinforcement may be provided by organizations so that managers take initiative for enhancing their referent and expert power bases. Of course, training may be of limited value when it comes to improving the referent power base. Organizations may have to adopt the policy of recruiting managers with social skills and charisma who are likely to bring adequate referent power base.

Position Power. Appropriate training should help managers learn how to use **their** position power base to deal with certain social situations.

Coercive Power. Training may be provided to managers so that they use only performance-contingent coercive power to deal with appropriate situations. There is no need to enhance coercive power base of managers.

Reward Power. Training may be provided to managers so that they learn how to provide various kinds of performance-contingent rewards to subordinates for their contributions to the organization. Employees are more likely to follow a leader's instructions if he or she provides rewards to subordinates contingent upon performance.

Legitimate Power. Supervisors can enhance this power base if they provide instructions clearly, make sure that instructions are reasonable and appropriate, and explain **their** reasons for the instructions. Training can help supervisors to do just that, since subordinates may not carry out directives adequately if they believe the directives are unreasonable or unjustified.

Information Power. Managers can improve this power base if they provide appropriate and timely information to employees so that they can perform their jobs adequately. Supervisory training on what type of information is needed at what time by different subordinates should help to improve this power base.

Implications for Expatriate Managers

There are important implications for expatriate managers from the U.S. and other individualistic cultures who are assigned to work in collectivistic cultures. These managers may be well served by acquiring more education, training, and job experience so as to enhance their expert power base. On the other hand, coercive power, which they may have used extensively in dealing with subordinates in their own culture, is likely to be ineffective as a basis for leading employees in their new work setting.

Questions for Students

1. What is the difference between power and influence?
2. Why is the personal power base more effective in enhancing job performance and satisfaction of employees than position power?
3. How would you increase your own personal power base?

Exercise: Superiors' Power Bases

Rank (3 = High, 2 = Moderate, 1 = Low) the following four professionals on the six power bases.

	Power Bases					
Professionals	Coercive	Reward	Legitimate	Information	Expert	Referent
1. Your present supervisor	_____	_____	_____	_____	_____	_____
2. CEO of your company.	_____	_____	_____	_____	_____	_____
3. One of your management professors	_____	_____	_____	_____	_____	_____
4. President of your University	_____	_____	_____	_____	_____	_____

1. Form a group of three members and explain the reasons behind your rankings of these professionals.
2. After each group member explains his/her rankings to the group, the group as a whole will rank the professionals.
3. A representative from each group explains what they learnt from this exercise.
4. The instructor encourages the class to make further comments on what they learnt from the exercise.

Case: Misuse of Power

"It hardly seemed possible that the man had sway over politics and media for so long. Appearing before a parliamentary committee on July 19th [2011] to explain how phone-hacking had flourished in his British newspapers; why his company is alleged to have paid $160,000 in bribes to policemen; why two people in his pay have been jailed and several arrested; Rupert Murdoch paused alarmingly and fumbled his answers" ("Last of the moguls," 2011, p. 9). It is alleged that Rupert Mardoch's son, James Murdoch, himself authorized hush money to victims, but Rupert Mardoch denied any knowledge about these illegal activities and indicated that he should be held responsible for these acts committed by his employees.

Leaders in England are realizing that by destroying criminal evidence, threatening politicians, and hacking phones, and paying off police, Rupert Murdoch could intimidate opponents and make and break government officials. Fresh allegations of attempted phone hacking of Britain's royal family and illegally accessing medical and financial records of former prime minister Gordon Brown by Mardoch's *The Sun* and *Sunday Times* newspapers have caused further damage. It is alleged that Murdoch is known for dictating editorial positions to his papers. He could push politicians to back his ideas on political issues and destroying the careers of politicians with smear campaigns.

Rupert Murdock's father was Keith Murdock who was a war reporter in the early 1900's and his job it was to cover the first world war under strict guidelines from the military. Later Keith Murdock broke these guidelines while building his empire and influence the news. "Like Father—Like Son—and Like Grandson—The Murdock family has had their hands in political influence, money, media and power including infiltrating the halls of government and its secrets" ("Murdoch's dynasty," 2011).

Suggestions for Further Reading

Gupta, B., & Sharma, N. K. (2003). Bases of power as a function of organisation type and managerial level. *Behavioral Scientist, 4* (2), 73–78.

Raven, B. H. (2008). The bases of power and the power/interaction model of interpersonal influence. *Analysis of Social Issues and Public Policy, 8* (1), 1–122.

Tjosvold, D., & Wisse, B. (Eds.), *Power and interdependence in organizations*. Cambridge, UK: Cambridge University Press.

References

Carson, P. P., Carson, K. D., & Roe, W. (1993). Social power bases: A meta-analytic examination of interrelationships and outcomes. *Journal of Applied Social Psychology, 23,* 1150–1169.

French, J. R. P., Jr., & Raven, B. (1959). The bases of social power. In D. Cartwright (Ed.), *Studies in social power* (pp. 150–167). Ann Arbor, MI: Institute for Social Research.

Greene, C. N., & Podsakoff, P. M. (1981). Effects of withdrawal of a performance-contingent reward on supervisory influence and power. *Academy of Management Journal, 24,* 527–542.

Last of the moguls. (2011, July 23). *Economist,* p. 9.

Murdoch's dynasty of abuse of power. (2011). (http://www.politicolnews.com/sir-keith-murdochs-broken-rules, accessed on 7/22/11.

Oyster, C. K. (1992). Perceptions of power: Female executives' descriptions of power usage by "best" and "worst" bosses. *Psychology of Women Quarterly, 16,* 527–533.

Rahim, M. A. (2009). Bases of leader power and effectiveness. In D. Tjosvold & B. Wisse (Eds.), *Power and interdependence in organizations* (pp. 224–243). Cambridge, UK: Cambridge University Press.

Rahim, M. A., Antonioni, D., Psenicka, C. (2001). A structural equations model of leader power, subordinates' styles of handling conflict and job performance. *International Journal of Conflict Management, 12,* 191–211.

Raven, B. H. (1965). Social influence and power. In I. D. Steiner & M. Fishbein (Eds.), *Current studies in social psychology* (pp. 371–381). New York: Holt, Rinehart & Winston.

Rahim, M. A., & Magner, M. R. (1996). Confirmatory factor analysis of the bases of leader power: First-order factor model and its invariance across groups. *Multivariate Behavioral Research, 31*, 495–516.

Russell, B. (1938). *Power: A new social analysis.* New York: Norton.

PART IV
Creativity and Innovation

9. Creativity

Afzal Rahim
Center for Advanced Studies in Management

J. Krist Schell
Western Kentucky University

Powerful forces are now reshaping the business landscape faster than ever before. In the present fast-changing environments, all organizations are challenged in unprecedented ways to create value. Whatever advantages there ever were in knowing secrets is rapidly being replaced by the skill to turn information into the unique, the new, the profitable before all margin is lost. The force that powers this is creativity and those organizations which can harness its power will leave in the dust those that can't see new relationships, form new combinations, or better knit ideas together for revolutionary results.

Nature of Creativity

Definition

Sometimes the words creativity and innovation are used interchangeably, but each has a distinct meaning. Creativity is associated with generating novel and useful ideas, but innovation is associated with transforming these ideas into products, services, processes, and technology. Some of the synonyms of creativity are originality, imagination, ingenuity, and expressiveness. The APA Dictionary of Psychology defines creativity as "the ability to produce or develop original work, theories, techniques, or thoughts. A creative individual typically displays originality, imagination and expressiveness. Analyses have failed to ascertain why one individual is more creative than another, but creativity does appear to be a very durable trait" (VanderBos, 2007, p. 242).

Creativity as a Process

Creativity is first and foremost a process. A systems model of organizational creativity, presented in Figure 1, shows that leadership is essential to prepare the organization for generating creative ideas which lead to innovation (Puccio & Cabra, 2010). To make an organization creative, leaders need to recruit those with skills, experience, and intelligence; design a flat and flexible organizational

Figure 1
A Systems Model of Creativity in Organizations

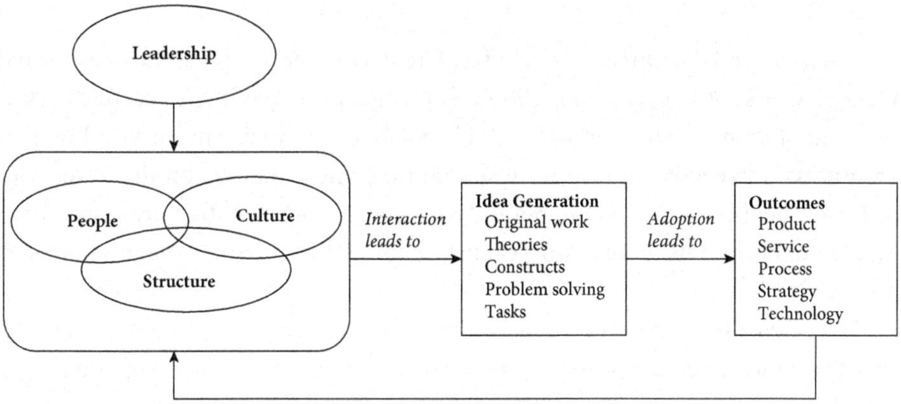

Source: Adapted **from Puccio & Cabra (2010, p. 148)**

structure; and foster an organizational culture that rewards risk-taking and experimentation. Interaction among people, structure, and culture is expected to have a positive impact on the generation of novel ideas relating to products, services, administrative processes, and technology. Figure 1 shows how these new ideas will lead to innovation.

Components of Creativity

It is generally accepted by scholars that creativity has two components—*novelty* and *utility*. Some scholars have suggested additional components of creativity, such as aesthetics and authenticity (Kharkhurin, 2014), genesis and elegance (Cropley & Cropley (2008), but there is no consensus among creativity researchers regarding the additional components. The following is an explanation of the novelty and utility components of the creativity construct.

1. **Novelty.** The standard definitions of creativity is linked to originality, ingenuity, or distinctiveness. Employees who generate ideas that are differentiated from others may be considered creative. Definitions of problems or their solution that do not follow standard operating procedures is generally considered as creative.

2. **Utility.** The standard definitions of creativity suggest that the outcomes of creative ideas must be useful to human beings. In other words, creative work can be put to some use.

Types of Creativity

Positive and Negative Creativity. Creativity can be positive or negative (James, Clark, & Cropanzano, 1999). The concept of usefulness carries with it the connotation of being either "good" (positive) or "bad" (negative). Positive creativity is expected to lead to desirable outcomes, such as product creation, reducing health costs, and adaptability to change, but negative creativity may lead to undermining goals and policies, exploitation, and sabotage (James et al., 1999).

We often think of a good idea as one that we can put into action, or one that has a clear, perceived likelihood of positive return. Leaders are constantly asked to evaluate many outputs of creative processes. It is very easy to discount and criticize new, creative ideas by trying to cram into the "useful" category. It is very hard, particularly in times of abnormal stress, to consistently be open-minded and see where and how new ideas could make your organization better, faster, richer. Perhaps we would be well to consider that though the idea may not have application immediately or to a particular task in question, but could in another context could be highly valuable.

Radical and Incremental Creativity. The theory of creativity was extended by the introduction of two additional types of creativity: radical and incremental (Madjar, Chen, Greenberg, 2011). Radical or divergent creativity is associated with ideas that are significantly different from the existing ones in an organization. Incremental or adaptive creativity is associated ideas that offer only minor modifications to existing products, processes, and service.

Individual Creativity. Musicians, writers, and dancers we all automatically consider creative. These individuals respond to their need to express themselves in ways that are new, compelling, and help us see and feel what we have not before. It is worth noting that we often respond most strongly to those forms of creativity borne by those with overwhelming dedication to perfecting their form of expression. Bach, Shakespeare, Dostoyevsky, or Picasso all achieved their recognition through single-minded dedication and intense commitment to become fluent in their modes of expression.

We also know scientists, mathematicians, or athletes to be creative, though perhaps differently than in the artistic sense noted above. Scientists are often charged with solving a problem through chemistry or biology; the insight occurring when a solution to a puzzling problem is often perceived as a creative event. Einstein reinterpreted previous thinkers' work in a new way to develop his theory of relativity; a noted cancer researcher was sitting in his synagogue when the realization that tumors in a body might communicate along chemical pathways suddenly came into his mind unbidden. Note that these two mental events, while seemingly prosaic, are nonetheless, new, special, and resulted in profoundly different outcomes in just the way we recognize a new painting, a new song, or a new creative events.

Organizational Creativity. At the macro-level an organization, like people, can be creative. This chapter discusses activities and suggestions that can help organizations respond productively to challenges in the world. Companies, for example, can learn to sense opportunities when the individuals that comprise them provide incentives for risk-taking, and even reward failure. A new car, for example, is clearly the result of prodigious teamwork, but at the core, it resulted from someone somewhere having an inspirational event when he or she responded to market desires.

Outcomes of Creativity

Some empirical studies have found a positive link between creativity and innovation. A literature review by Puccio and Cabra (2010) "support the important role of creativity plays in fostering innovation and the tangible benefits organizations derive from innovation" (p.148). It is no surprise by now that any Google search returns a lifetime of reading in only fractions of the second. Not only do you have this information, but so do your competitors. Given that you can be reasonably confident your organization faces competition from those now in its market or those about to be, any use of equally accessible data in ways that generate more revenue is incredibly valuable. More revenue can be a direct result of finding unique solutions that extend from current technology and processes used in new ways. You personally can develop your own competitive advantages by combining this information in unique fashion. The Web has become a great equalizer, but what it's really done is put a premium on those who can assemble thoughts, feelings, instincts, and all other physical resources for new, creative successes. So, here is the next logical question: what are the tangible benefits of improving creativity?

Creativity is essential to maintaining competitiveness in a global economy (Zhou & Shalley, 2008). The creative process leverages relationships, and leaders have an important role in encouraging employee creativity (Liao, Liu, & Loi, 2010) by removing barriers and providing resources. So, why should you as a leader pay attention to this? It's because there seems to be a clear positive link between the positive feelings you as a leader can help others to have and the degree of creative work that people produce (Amabile & Kramer, 2010). Creativity itself is a mood enhancer, improving feelings of self-worth (Simmons & Thompson, 2008). However, perhaps it's more functional to state it this way: seeing one's creativity become useful and make substantive progress leads to feeling better, and feeling better leads to even more creativity.

As it turns out, creativity is at the core of progress, and the feeling that one has made real progress has important effects upon job satisfaction and other workplace attitudes. As we will see below, leaders who consistently remove roadblocks and enhance their subordinates' ability to do meaningful, relevant work are highly rated. Humans view meaningful progress as a powerful indicator that their efforts are worth something. As a leader, removing roadblocks really means going beyond the common, the ordinary, the usual perception. Again, this means thinking and acting creatively.

If you are now in business school, you are training yourself to be a leader, and that means getting work done motivating others. It's important to know that it is the perception of meaningful progress that is likely the highest single motivator in creating positive feelings and efforts in the workplace, according to a study by Amabile and Kramer (2010). This same study found that six-hundred managers ranked progress as the least important motivator, while their employees ranked it as the most important motivator. In fact, feeling positive can have a huge effect upon creative output. In the aforementioned study, encompassing almost 12,000 individual work day diary entries, participants felt, and their entries corroborated, that their creative output was 50% higher when they felt their best (Amabile & Kramer, 2010). So, how do you help the people you lead to feel their best about work and be as creative as they can be?

Implications for Management

To encourage creativity among employees, there should be certain changes at the micro and macro levels in an organization. Recent literature shows that learning organizations are providing ample opportunities for employees to be creative. At the macro-level, learning organizations generally make appropriate changes in the organization design that involve creating flatter, decentralized, and less complex structures and culture which provides rewards for risk-taking and creativity. These changes require effective leadership. At the micro-level, between people, the following changes are worth considering.

Goal Setting. Set clear goals so people can effectively organize personal thinking and resources. It turns out that this is probably a leader's most important task, if for nothing else that the absence of clear goals seems so profoundly frustrating to people. This often means continually checking with other stakeholders in an organization to make sure your team's outputs match desired results.

Providing Support. Leaders need to provide resources, information, analysis, or assisting in any one of many possible activities that make up actual work processes. It means more than just asking how things are going, it means being actively engaged by listening to find out what team members need and then acting upon that knowledge yourself, personally.

Learn from Successes and Failures. This is vital to keep communication lines open. Assigning blame is rarely positive or helpful; instead, treating experiences as opportunities to learn will get you further in the long run. This means having lots of conversations that start with "So, what did we learn from this?" and "What would we do differently next time?"

It's worth observing here that the factors you are probably studying as the most important in creating positive workplace behavior are likely similar to the following: recognize good work, establish performance incentives, and support progress. The take away points for leaders are: set goals that don't change arbitrarily, be continually decisive, and provide needed resources (Amabile & Kramer, 2010). Here are other important considerations to take into account that you shape your behavior as a leader, again, all with the explicit intent to help improve creativity by helping people feel better about why and how they work.

Recognize that Some Activities may be Inherently More Complex. A team leader tries to match up those parts of the work process that he or she knows will need more creative energy with the time, physical resources, and people power to contribute to the best possible outcomes. This means recognizing that if an actual product that would meet client specifications would require much creative energy, the likelihood of success is much greater if team members you pick have shown creative ability, and you then stay out of the team's way (Seidel, Moeller, Weinbergen, & Rosemann, 2010). In short, anticipate the need for oversight, allow as much freedom as you can, and adjust your direction based on your instinct.

Listen to New Ideas. Note here the sense that a creative idea is not only new, but also useful and meaningful in some human context. However, it is well worth considering the effect these preconceptions have upon this common definition of creativity. In business, and business education, great stock is placed upon being useful, being able to measure and quantify the value of an idea: "what is its internal rate of return, its net present value?" There is a slang business phrase called "analysis paralysis" which refers to indecision (lost opportunity) caused by over-examination of a potential action. Sometimes one has to rely more on intuition than data, so while you are training yourself to use these analytical tools, always be conscious that the results from these tools are usually only pieces of the puzzle you must put together as a leader.

Since you are now part of an educational system, it is worth observing that the exams and papers you take and write ask you to find solutions that match with a preconceived outcome as a gauge for performance (Simmons & Thompson, 2008). You will keep communication channels open, if you develop the mindset that even if what your colleagues suggest might not work over here, it might work over there.

Be Fair in your Relationships with the Members of Your Team. Humans are a very social animal, and we place great importance on our interpersonal relationships. Individuals who make up the teams you manage will watch how you treat and interact with all members of the team. If you treat everyone equally and fairly with regard to distributing benefits, recognition, and workload, for example, you will help individuals feel good about contributing (Liao, Liu, & Loi, 2010).

Questions for Students:

1. Are your usually satisfied with the outcome of your organization meetings?
2. How often have you heard of a great idea that never came up in any discussion in your organization?
3. How often have your thought of a solution after a meeting, one that seemed to be better than anything the group developed? Do you think others felt the same way?
4. Have you considered solutions for these issues? What might work?

Exercise: Closer to Home: Personal Experience on Campus

Since meetings seem to be an inevitable part of being human, our task as leaders is to harness the efficiency of individual creativity, but guard against the group process that inhibits it. The following 20- to 50-minute, in-class exercise (adapted from Thompson, 2011) is intended to ensure much greater creative output and avoid much of the distracting and often destructive components of group interaction.

Step 1: Idea Generation

Pose a question in need of a solution to the class. Briefly discuss it only enough to make sure all members understand the issue, without comment or analyses. Examples could be: "What are the solutions to the lack of parking at our university?" or "What can we do to increase membership in our group?." Students then either in-class or outside of class write as many ideas for a solution as they can in 20 minutes, one idea per index card. Completing the cards outside of the meeting saves time; however it is useful to harness the competitive effect of seeing one's classmates complete after card in silence next to to spur more idea generation. It is also useful to practice simply being in a group environment without making idle conversation or gossip. Moreover, since members of any meeting rarely show up fully prepared with more than a few ideas, completing the cards in the meeting will likely increase overall output.

Step 2: Ranking and Analysis

With all the cards complete, divide the class into groups of four to six and ask all members to discuss and rank each individual's ideas. The ideas are then read aloud either by each author or a single member. The group then provides feed-back by each member providing a one through seven ranking, lowest to highest, for each idea. When all the ideas are read and ranked, the group averages the scores and the consensus appears through the highest averages. It's important that there be no criticism here, that every idea to get positively supported. The meeting facilitator should actively monitor and direct group comments to this purpose.

Step 3: Second Order Ideas

Now once the meeting has averages that indicate a consensus is forming, another technique, called "brainwriting" can capture key insights and allow members to express advanced options, extensions of ideas and solutions, and a host of other exceptional possibilities. Hand out additional cards, and again without commen-tary and in silence, group members once more provide out ideas and solutions to the central problem on index cards. The process gets repeated again though steps one and two above. The key intent here is to draw upon members' now greater familiarity with the context of the problem to enhances ideas for a solution. In particular, this third step draws upon the benefits of increased visualization and conception that can occur in people when their fear of public criticism fades. This is precisely why this exercise needs to be done in a climate where members of the group consistently highlight ways to make an idea work better

If this seems a little complicated for the first time, it probably is. But remember, we been brought up to believe that brainstorming is only "getting ideas out there" without any real understanding of whether or not positive outcomes typically occur. It's worth knowing that groups get better at doing this and report that the need for verbal distractions dramatically decreases over time.

In the end we are challenged to reexamine the habits and the misconceptions that have been ingrained into us from an early age. It is a challenge that is not easy to embrace: to fully accept we don't have to settle for mediocrity. One of the chief complaints voiced by talented undergraduate business students is the emphasis on group projects with the all too-often difficulty of group members who seem unmotivated. I would submit that is the group process, not the failing of innate creative ability that causes these complaints. Read this article, pass along its lessons in the form of purposeful leadership in your groups and their members, and always remember that you are worth more than you know, and know more than you think.

Case: Why Don't We Ever Get Anything Done?

Sarah Murdoch, Phi Rho house president, was thinking about the Sunday evening chapter meeting with a mixture of fear and frustration. Greek Week was less than three weeks away, and she felt her chapter was unlikely to have any great successes during one of the most important social events of the Greek calendar. As president, it was her responsibility to make sure that her chapter was well-supported and well-represented, and that the activities that the chapter promised to undertake for Campus Events would come off smoothly. But now, there seem to be so little time left before all the events had to be lined up that there didn't seem to be any way that it was going to be anything less than one of those last-minute-hurry-up-and-rush-kind of experiences that made everybody frustrated and would make a house look disorganized.

Phi Rho had signed up to lead the competitions between houses, which meant games had to be fun, but also had to show that Greek Week was something more than just a high school field day. Her house had sixty members, most of who lived on campus and were reasonably active. About two thirds were upperclassman, and most had participated in Greek week at least once. Greek week was one of the highlights of fraternity and sorority life on campus and was an important way for graduates to connect with current student members in the social functions that followed its daily events.

Sarah knew that she better prepare something for the meeting, so she thought of a few PowerPoints would be a start. She opened her laptop and started creating a few slides. The first one said, "What are we going to do for Game Day?" the second, "Here's what we did last year: Volleyball, Jell-O toss, Capture the Flag, Crazy Relay, and Tug-Of-War." The third slide listed the six hours in the weekend schedule that Phi Ro was responsible for hosting with time slots for people to sign up in. After staring at a blank fourth slide for a few moments, Sarah closed her laptop with a sigh and started chemistry homework that was due Monday morning.

The 8:30 evening meeting started pretty much on time. Sarah began by recognizing the achievements of the new freshmen members of the House and accepting the treasurer's report. She pulled up her first slide and started by saying "Okay guys, you'll know we signed up to do this. It's important that we look good and that everybody has a good time. Let's try a bit of a brainstorming session to figure out what we want to do.

Anyone have any thoughts about games for Game Day?" Silence greeted her question. She waited a few more moments. Still silence. More crickets. "Come on guys, I'm sure we can think of something. Here's what we did last year", and pulled up the second slide. "I don't like the tug-of-war, I got squished last year" was the first thing she heard. There were a few echoes of agreement throughout the fifty or so members. "Capture the Flag is just too hot most of the time", someone else said. This kind of reaction went on for another five minutes with various members raising similar and sometimes different objections, but without any substantively new suggestions. Sarah was growing increasingly frustrated. "Well, we figured out something to do last year. Is there anyone who would like to help me decide this time?" Three freshmen in the back row raised their hands together. "Okay, thank you. Would you three please see me right after the meeting, and we'll get some ideas on the table." The rest of the meeting was pretty typical, with a presentation from the National representative about fundraising ideas, a song, and a report from the membership vice president about attendance policy.

After the meeting, the three freshmen dutifully showed up and they made an appointment to meet Sarah Monday afternoon. The result of that Monday meeting was that the games Phi Rho hosted for Greek Week were exactly the same events it sponsored the year before.

Suggestions for Further Reading

Gabora, L. (2005). Creative thought as a non-Darwinian evolutionary process. *Journal of Creative Behavior, 39,* 65–87.

Sternberg, R. J. (Ed.). (1999). *Handbook of creativity.* New York: Cambridge University Press.

Rietzschel, E. F., Nijstad, B. A., Stroebe, W. (2010). The selection of creative ideas after individual idea generation: Choosing between creativity and impact. *British Journal of Psychology, 101,* 47–68.

References

Amabile, T. M., & Kramer, S. J. (2010). The power of small wins. *Harvard Business Review, 89* (5), 70–80.

Cropley, D., & Cropley, A. (2008). Elements of a universal aesthetic of creativity. *Psychology of Aesthetics, Creativity, and the Arts, 2,* 155–161.

James, K., Clark, K., & Cropanzano, R. (1999). Positive and negative creativity in groups, institutions, and organizations. *Creativity Research Journal. 12,* 211–226.

Kharkhurin, A. V. (2014). Creativity, 4in 1: Four-criterion construct of creativity. *Creativity Research Journal, 26,* 338–352.

Liao, H, Liu, D, & Loi, R. (2010). Looking at both sides of the social exchange coin: A social cognitive perspective on the joint effects of relationship quality and differentiation on creativity. *Academy of Management Journal, 53,* 1090–1109.

Madjar, N., Greenburg, E., & Chen, Z. (2011). Factors for radical creativity, incremental creativity, and routine, noncreative performance.

Nijstad, B. A., & De Dreu, C. D. W. (2002). Creativity and group innovation. *Applied Psychology,51,* 400–406.

Puccio, G. J., & Cabrea, J. F. (2010). Organizational creativity: A systems approach. In J. C. Kaufman & R. J. Sternberg (Eds.), *The Cambridge handbook of creativity* (pp. 145–173). New York: Cambridge University Press.

Seidel, S., Muller-Wienbergen, F., & Rosemann, M. (2010). Pockets of creativity in business processes. *Communications of the Association for Information Systems,* 27, 415–435.

Simmons, R., & Thompson, R. (2008). Creativity and perform activity: the case for further education. *British Educational Research Journal, 34,* 601–618.

VanderBos, G. R. (2007). *American psychological association dictionary of psychology.* Washington, DC: American Psychological Association.

Zhou, J., & Shelley, C. E. (2008). Expanding the scope and impact of organizational creativity research. In J. Zhoe & C. E. Sheeley (Eds.), *Handbook of organizational creativity* (pp. 347–368). New York: Taylor & Francis.

10. Innovation

Preeta M. Banerjee
Deloitte

If a company fails to innovate, it may die. Innovative firms—those that are able to generate and/or use innovation to improve processes, products, and services—outperform their competitors in market share, profitability, growth, and market capitalization. Not only does innovation enhance competitiveness but it can improve the quality of life for stakeholders such as the employees, the local community and the national economy. However, management of innovation is difficult and requires a different set of skills and knowledge from those of everyday business management.

Nature of Innovation

Definition

"Innovation is generally understood as the successful introduction of a new thing or method. Innovation is the embodiment, combination, or synthesis of knowledge in original, relevant, valued new products, processes, or services" (Luecke & Katz, 2003, p. 2). Innovation is also the ability to recombine existing elements, see connections, spot opportunities and make the best of resources on hand. Thus, innovation is not just about new products or markets, but also new ways of serving established or mature ones.

Types of Innovation

Managers of innovation refer to four broad categories of innovation, which are product innovation, process innovation, position innovation, and paradigm innovation (Francis & Bessant, 2005).

Product Innovation is embodied into novel physical outputs of an organization, or changes in things (products/services) that an organization offers.

Process Innovation is a change in the way an organization conducts its business, such as the way it manufactures its products.

Position Innovation is a change in the context to which a product or service is introduced, for example using fruit juice as a nutraceutical (or natural drug).

Paradigm Innovation is a change in the underlying mental models in which the firm operates, which usually changes innovation at an industry level, such as online booking of tickets (Southwest Airlines) or mass customization (bath and body works).

Within these four broad categories, innovation can be considered *incremental* or *radical*. An incremental innovation (like the introduction of diet soda) builds upon existing knowledge and resources, whereas a radical innovation (like the introduction of mobile telephone) will require completely new knowledge and/or resources. Likewise, an incremental innovation will involve modest technological changes and the existing products on the market will remain competitive, whereas a radical innovation will involve large technological advances, rendering the existing products non-competitive and often obsolete. Many other distinctions can be made about the type of innovation whereby different management techniques prove more of less successful.

Innovation Process

In focusing on product innovation, the *innovation value chain* (Hansen & Birkinshaw, 2007) present innovation as a sequential, three-phase process that is comprised of idea generation, idea conversion, and idea diffusion. Each of these three steps in the innovation value chain differs in the "key questions" they address and the "key performance indicators" (KPIs) they measure. The questions and measures help managers add value to every step of the innovation process.

Idea Generation. This involves the focused identification of an area in science, technology, or user need for a breakthrough. This can be achieved internally within a firm, in a business unit or across units or externally from sources outside of the firm. The key question that managers must ask themselves is if the people in the firm create good ideas on their own. Based on the KPI of number of high-quality ideas generated within a unit, managers can add value by improving the team dynamics within the firm or by finding additional sources of innovation externally.

Dynamics within the firm can be improved through the cross-pollination of diverse talents from diverse divisions, and by this method, the interactions between workers will add value to the process (Clark & Wheelright, 1992). There are four basic team structures that can be followed to achieve this cross-pollination:

Functional Teams can be developed where members work completely in their principal function and those members are coordinated by respective functional managers. This type of team would benefit product innovation that required high levels of expertise.

Light-Weight Teams can be developed where a dedicated project manager works with the functional managers to coordinate team members across functions. This type of team would benefit product innovation that required coordination and increased communication across functions.

Heavy-Weight Teams can be developed where a dedicated project manager has direct control over functional members, and these members work only with the project manager and other functional members. This type of team would benefit new developments that required focus and expertise.

Autonomous Teams can be developed where team members from different functional areas are committed and co-located with project manager. This type of team benefits from the isolation, allowing the most radical breaks from conventional ways of doing things.

Innovative manufacturing firms can also supplement the ideas sourced from internal employees with external sources, including suppliers and lead users. A manufacturer and its supplier can enter into a *strategic alliance*, i.e. arrangement between two companies who have decided to share resources on a specific project. Successful innovators also identify *lead users*, customers that are invested in identifying solutions and benefits months or years before the general marketplace. These are some of the different sources of innovation, or multiple innovation channels, available to a firm. It is important to understand that external and internal sources are often complements, and that firms with large internal product innovation teams are also the heaviest users of external collaboration networks. Innovation comes from different places and in different ways.

Idea Conversion refers to the notion that once ideas have been generated, they need to be screened and protected. Out of every 3,000 raw ideas there is approximately 1 commercial success. Selection should be made using standardized frameworks and guidelines that are unique to the firm. The standardization of the screening criteria is important in order to maintain consistency over evaluations and the firm will be able to make their choices objectively. The key question managers should ask is: Are we good at identifying and protecting good ideas? The KPIs include the percentage of all ideas selected that become fully developed (either internally or externally); the percentage of funded ideas that lead to revenues; and the number of months to first sales.

In order to quickly and effectively screen an idea, firms need to work on effective and prompt *prototyping*, to quickly fabricate a scale model of a product innovation. *Try-storming* is a more advanced type of prototyping that also simulates and tests the model in practice before committing to any one process or solution.

Once a prototype is found to work, the underlying innovation can be protected through the patenting process. A *patent* is a set of exclusive rights granted by a state (national government) to an inventor or their assignee for a limited period of time in exchange for a public disclosure of an invention. If patents are not obtainable or enforceable, innovation can be protected through secrecy, lead time and/or complementary resources (Arundel, 2001). Secrecy is the use of confidentiality or classified information to keep product innovation from being replicated by competitors. Lead time is the rapid turnaround of product innovation from initiation to execution of commercialization, in other words being the first to market. Complementary resources are resources that enhance the product innovation by extending or strengthening the whole package, including marketing, customer service, and other product innovations that can be included in a package or bundle.

Idea diffusion includes both *commercialization*, i.e. the production of the product and bringing it to the market, and *adoption and diffusion*, i.e. the product acceptance by the market. The key question that managers should ask themselves is if the company is good at getting products adopted by users. The KPI would be the percentage of penetration in desired markets, channels, or customer groups, and the number of months to full diffusion.

Managers can improve idea diffusion by managing the technology adoption life cycle (Moore, 1999). The *technology adoption life cycle* describes the adoption or acceptance of a new product or innovation, according to the demographic and psychological characteristics of defined adopter groups. The first 2.5% of adopters are labeled *innovators* and are characterized as venturesome; educated; having multiple sources of information; showing greater propensity to take risks; appreciating technology for its own sake; motivated by the idea of being a change agent in their reference group; and willing to tolerate initial problems that may accompany new products or services. The next 13.5% of adopters are labeled *early adopters* and are characterized as social leaders; popular and educated; visionaries in their market and are looking to adopt and use new technology to achieve a revolutionary breakthrough that will achieve dramatic competitive advantage in their industries; attracted by high-risk, high-reward projects and not very price sensitive because they envision great gains in competitive advantage from adopting a new technology. After the early adopters is a chasm representing a critical phase or opening from the last early adopters that allows for mainstream acceptance of the product. This chasm can be effectively crossed through increased education and word-of-mouth recommendations from early adopters to the next category. The next 34% of adopters are labeled *"early majority"* and are characterized as deliberate and have many informal social contacts; and rather than looking for revolutionary changes to gain productivity enhancements in their firms, they are motivated by evolutionary changes. The next 34% of adopters are labeled *"late majority"* and are characterized as skeptical and of lower socio-economic status;

very price sensitive and require completely preassembled, bulletproof solutions; motivated to buy technology just to stay even with the competition and often rely on a single, trusted adviser to help them make sense of technology. The last 16% of the adopters are labeled "*laggards*" and are characterized as traditional and want only to maintain the status quo. They tend not to believe that technology can enhance productivity and are likely to block new technology purchases.

Outcomes of Innovation

An important facet of understanding innovation is effectively and efficiently managing the outcomes of innovation. Besides the actual creation of a new product, service or process, the outcomes of innovation include job creation, economic growth and improvements in quality of life.

However, products often have unintended effects in addition to the ones intended by the manufactures (Tenner, 1997). Sometimes, those unintended effects can even be contradictory, creating bigger problems than the ones they were meant to solve in the first place. Examples include the indiscriminate use of antibiotics, yielding hardier strains of bacteria and viruses that do not respond to pharmaceutical treatment and the wide-scale use of air conditioning that has raised the outdoor temperature in some cities places by as much as 10 degrees, adding stress to already-taxed cooling systems. In addition to unintended consequences, products influence the values of a society by changing expectations and realities including efficiency and social progress. Products influence lifestyles making some aspects simpler and others more complex, and add issues of privacy, security, ethics and environmental impact.

Often firms must issue a *product recall*, a request to return to the maker a batch or an entire production run of a product, usually due to the discovery of safety issues (Berman, 1999). The recall is an effort to limit liability for corporate negligence (which can cause costly legal penalties) and to improve or avoid damage to publicity. A recall is costly to a company because it often entails replacing the recalled product or paying for damage caused by use, although possibly less costly than consequential costs caused by damage to brand name and reduced trust in the manufacturer. A country's consumer protection laws will often have specific requirements in regard to product recalls. Such regulations may include how much of the cost the maker will have to bear, situations in which a recall is compulsory (usually because the risk is big enough), or penalties for failure to recall. The firm may also initiate a recall voluntarily, perhaps subject to the same regulations as if the recall were compulsory. Product recalls can be prevented with the use of more extensive and robust testing, the fourth of the six broad steps of product innovation.

The new challenge of innovation is the outcome of environmental sustainability through *green product innovation*. These products are non-toxic, energy and water-efficient, and relatively harmless to the environment. *Life Cycle Assessment* (LCA) is a method that allows systematic analysis of a manufactured item into its components and their subsidiary industrial process, and allows measurement of impacts on nature from the beginning of the product to the final disposal (Goleman, 2009). In designing for sustainability, the entire life cycle of the product in is analyzed from birth of the innovation to re-birth in an infinite cycle. This approach highlights all the impacts that a product will have from a sustainability stand point and this insight helps to make more informed decisions very early in the products life cycle at the design face. Moreover, the implementation of LCA relies on the overall supply chain. The outcome of LCA innovation is a *sustainable (or green) supply chain,* where the management of a product from raw materials to manufacturer to consumer with explicit consideration of improvement to the social and environmental impacts, in a way that allows for reverse supply chain flows and network communication. Therefore, it is important to understand that the manufacturer of the product is not alone in managing the product innovation's overall impact on the environment.

The outcome (in this case sustainability) of a product cannot be determined on an individual firm basis but rather in the context of the ecosystem that the product is a part of in terms of its social, economic and environmental impacts. This ecosystem has distinct components which include the processes in place, the people and the products, a system of organizations, people, technology, activities, information and resources involved in moving a product or service from raw materials, to manufacturer, to supplier, to customer. In following with the LCA, sustainable supply chains must integrate issues and flows that extend beyond the traditional supply chain, including manufacturing by-products, by-products produced during product use, product life extension, product end-of-life, and recovery process at end-of-life.

Innovation can also elevate all of humanity, including the poor, to be seen as creative entrepreneurs as well as value-demanding consumers. The phrase "*bottom of the pyramid*" (BOP) is used in particular by people developing new models of doing business that deliberately target that demographic, often using new product innovation (Prahalad, 2005). The BOP is the largest, but poorest socio-economic group, which in global terms is the four billion people who live on less than $2 per day, typically in developing countries. In the case of the BOP, the outcome of product innovation can bring quality of life improvements if innovative firms work with civil society organizations and local governments to create new local business models. However, bringing materialism to the masses introduces fuel to the fire on unsustainable consumption. BOP product innovation needs to develop sustainable products so that these human needs can be met not only in the present, but also for future generations. The BOP approach to targeting the poorest people in developing countries appears counter intuitive to the fundamental business philosophy of capturing and sustaining value. However, there is an underlying fallacy that misrepresents the poorest people in the world. In many parts of the developing world, for example in India and Africa, the richest of the land and the poorest of the land often live in startling proximity to each other and have the desire to live in equality. Another important consideration is the role of infrastructure and basic amenities in supporting a sustainable approach to development among the people at the bottom of the pyramid. Innovative firms, like all corporations have a sole objective of maximizing returns; however, they must find incentives in investing the basic infrastructure that will allow them to create sustainable value to the bottom of the pyramid.

Implications for Management

The process of managing innovation and turning uncertainties into secure competitive advantage is a difficult process. Success is by no means guaranteed and history is ripe with examples of good ideas which failed to make it through the three broad stages of development, including Sony's Betamax, Apple's Lisa, Pepsi's Crystal Pepsi and Ford's Edsel.

What can managers do to encourage innovation? As this chapter highlights, managers must engage in the innovation process, understanding the doing nothing is rarely an option in dynamic industries. Innovation should be seen as a core process that helps the organization renew what it offers, the way in which these offerings are created and/or delivered, the context in which offerings are made, and/or the underlying frame in which the company operates.

Managers need to pick up and process signals about potential innovation internally (from strong teams) and externally (from alliances and lead users). Managers then need to strategically select from potential opportunities to those ideas which the firm will commit resources to completing. The challenge lies in selecting those innovations which offer the best chance of competitive advantage and consumer adoption. Moving quickly to prototyping allows for fast failure and the ability to try out ideas to find success quickly. Managers then need to grow the prototype to commercial product, paying attention to feedback from the market across different stages of adoption. Most importantly, managers need to reflect upon previous stages of development and review successes and failures in order to learn about managing the innovation process, and improving it for the future. All of this should be done with an eye towards social responsibility, ethical behavior and sustainability to meet the needs of today without compromising those of future generations.

At the macro-level, innovation requires supportive leadership, a learning culture, and a flat and flexible organizational structure. People and corporate culture should not only encourage but also manage, track, and measure innovation as a core element in a company's growth aspirations. An innovative culture is based on trust among employees. In such a culture, people understand that their ideas are valued, trust that it is safe to express those ideas, and oversee risk collectively, together with their managers. Such an environment can be more effective than monetary incentives in sustaining innovation.

Questions for Students

1. Describe in one or two sentences the four types of idea generation teams described in the chapter.
2. Identify the two key elements of the idea conversion stage of the innovation process.
3. How does the concept of idea diffusion apply to an assignment you had in a college class or work assignment?
4. What are the reasons for developing innovations for the Bottom of the Pyramid?

Exercise

Research the development of the iPod by Apple and mp3 players in general. Write-up a page in review of the development of the product from idea genera-tion to idea conversion to idea diffusion at Apple as you find it. Summarize the main strategic decision(s) faced by the managers in developing this product. Where could the development of the iPod have diverged significantly? On a second page, capture what you have written in words into a diagram, using the notation for process flow diagrams (rectangle for process/verb/action, arrows for direction of flow, diamond for decision resulting in at least two paths, and a circle for start and stop). Share your diagram with a classmate and note the differences and similarities. An example of a process flow diagram regarding online auctions can be found below:

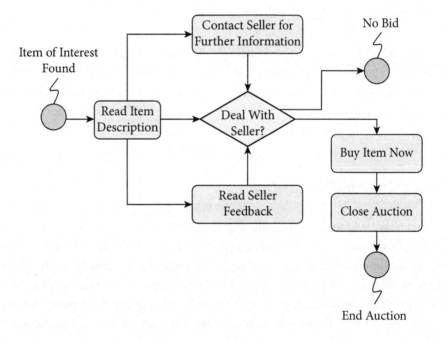

Source: adapted from Thomke, S. (2000). IDEO Product Development. HBS Premier Case Collection No. 600143–PDF–ENG.

Case: IDEO's Innovation Process

IDEO (http://www.ideo.com/) is a leading product design firm that grosses between $40 million and $60 million annually, and whose client list includes innovative firms such as Apple, BMW, Nike, Pepsi, and Canon. Headquartered in California's Silicon Valley, the company's motto is to "fail often to succeed sooner." IDEO is a flat organization, were all work is organized into product teams formed for the life of a project and then disbanded. As a result, there are no organization charts or titles to distract from the quality of work. Project leaders often emerge on the basis of personal excitement about a project. Though the company has established a free-flowing approach to the innovation process, IDEO uses the following five-phase system to provide structure to the development process:

Phase 0: Understand/Observe

In this phase, the project team attempts to understand the new client and its business. The team will research everything it can about previous product models, including cost structure and how the product was used. By the end of this phase, the project team would have constructed a feasibility record as well as recorded its insights about the users and market.

Phase 1: Visualize/Realize

In this phase, the team will create prototypes to visualize the direction a product solution is heading. This phase involves close coordination with the client to ensure timely feedback. By the end of this phase, the team will have three-dimensional models of the product and would have outlined the manufacturing strategy. Brainstorming goes hand in hand with rapid prototyping and vice versa, using the following principles: stay focused on the topic; encourage wild ideas; defer judgment to avoid interrupting the flow of ideas; build on the ideas of others; hold only one conversation at a time; go for quantity; and be visual.

Phase 2: Evaluate/Refine

In this phase, fully functional prototypes are built so that the team can identify and resolve technical problems and issues in the ways users interact with the product. By the end of this phase, the emphasis has shifted from human factors to engineering, and the phase will culminate in the delivery of a complete product design with technical specifications.

Phase 3: Implement (Detailed Engineering)

The team verifies the manufacturability and performance of the completed product in this phase. Though the emphasis is on engineering, engineers stay in close contact with design team members to ensure that the product is evolving in a way that meets both manufacturability and usage goals. At the end of this phase, the team will begin selecting vendors.

Phase 4: Implement (Manufacturing Liaison)

In this phase, the team coordinates the release of the product design to the manufacture. The team will supervise production of tooling, regulatory testing and approvals, and pilot runs of the manufacturing process. At the end of this phase, the team officially will turn the product over to the client.

Suggestions for Further Reading

McDonough, W., & Braungart, M. (2002). *Cradle to cradle: Remaking the way we make things.* New York: North Point Press.

Banerjee, P. (2008). Leveraging existing technology: The role of alliances in cross-application. *Strategic Management Review,* 2 (1), 1–22.

Dyer, J. H., Gregersen, H. B., & Christensen, C. M. (2009). The innovator's DNA. *Harvard Business Review*, 87 (12), 60–67.

References

Arundel, A. (2001) The relative effectiveness of patents and secrecy for appropriation. *Research Policy, 30,* 611–624.

Berman, B. (1999, March–April). Planning for the inevitable product recall. *Business Horizons,* pp. 69–78.

Clark, K., & Wheelwright, S. (1992). Organizing and leading 'Heavyweight' development teams. *California Management Review, 34* (3), 9–28.

Goleman, D. (2009). *Ecological Intelligence.* New York: Penguin Books.

Francis, D., & Besant, J. (2005). Targeting innovation and implications for capability development. *Technovation, 25* (3), 171–183.

Hansen, M., & Birkinshaw, J. (2007). Innovation value chain. *Harvard Business Review, 85* (6), 121–130.

Luecke, R., & Katz, R. (2003). *Managing creativity and innovation.* Cambridge, MA: Harvard Business Press.

Moore, G. (1999). *Crossing the chasm.* New York: Harper Perennial.

Prahalad, C. K. (2005). *The fortune at the bottom of the pyramid: Eradicating poverty through profits.* Philadelphia, PA: Wharton School.

Tenner, E. (1997). *Why things bite back: Technology and the revenge of unintended consequences.* New York: Vintage.

PART V

Learning and Knowledge Management

11. Organizational Learning

Ozgur Ekmekci
The George Washington University

Afzal Rahim
Center for Advanced Studies Management

Organizational learning is a significant construct, but it has not received the kind of attention from organization theorists that it deserves. There is greater need to improve our knowledge about organizational learning than ever before so that organizations can effectively respond to the fast-changing environment. Competition is increasing on a global scale, which calls for greater emphasis on developing effective processes for enhancing collective learning. The issue for the organizations is not whether they want to learn; they must learn as fast as they can.

Nature of Organizational Learning

Definition

Organizational learning involves *creation and/or acquisition of knowledge, transfer or distribution of knowledge, interpretation of information,* and *preservation of information* (for future access and use) (Rahim, 2002). This enables organizational members to collectively engage in the process of diagnosis of and intervention in problems. Argyris (1990) define learning as *detection* (cognitive) and *correction* (behavior) of error and discusses two types of organizational learning: single-loop and double-loop learning.

Types of Organizational Learning

Single-Loop Learning. This involves the diagnosis of and intervention in problems without changing the underlying policies, assumptions, and goals. In other words, single-loop learning results in cognitive and behavioral changes within an existing paradigm (i.e., the old paradigm or mindset).

That is, single-loop learning generates cognitive and behavioral changes within an existing organizational structure. In this type of learning, the social and cultural context in which decisions are made is largely ignored—instead, solely concentrating on treatment of the symptoms.

Double-Loop Learning. This occurs when the diagnosis and intervention require changes in the underlying policies, assumptions, and goals. In other words, double-loop learning involves cognitive and behavioral changes outside the existing paradigm (i.e., the new paradigm or mindset). Double-loop learning is very similar to second-order learning, or "learning how to learn." Bateson (1972) describes this type of learning as deutero-learning.

In this type of learning, not only are the symptoms treated, but the root cause of the symptoms—often grounded in a social and cultural context—are also investigated. Hence, it is important for organizational members to construct and exchange knowledge through double-loop learning, if their individual learning is to translate into organizational learning and then, in turn, into better organizational performance and sustainable change.

It should be noted that individual learning is a necessary but not adequate condition for organizational learning. There must be processes and structures for transferring what is learned by individuals to the collective. In other words, organizational learning occurs when members of the collective have successfully learned from the individuals. There must also be mechanisms for preserving and accessing knowledge acquired by the collective.

How Organizational Learning Occurs?

Organizational learning involves the transfer of knowledge and/or skills from the individuals to the collective, and the expansion of the collective's capacity to take effective action. The diffusion of learning occurs when the members of the collective or the organization are no longer dependent on the original holders of the knowledge for making decisions (Tompkin, 2005). Tompkin's model shows four stages of collective learning:

- Collaborative climate for managing conflict;
- Continuous improvement in organization's clarity of vision, principles, and purpose;
- Searching ways to improve the organization's competence by sharing and dispensing individual knowledge and skill; and
- Focusing on improvement in performance and satisfaction.

The factors which facilitate the process of learning are as follows.

Individual Defensive Reasoning

Argyris (1990) has persuasively argued and provided evidence that double-loop learning is inhibited by defensive reasoning of organizational members. This type of reasoning takes place when members fail to take responsibility for their decisions and attempt to protect themselves against the complaints of errors of judgment, incompetence, or procrastination by blaming others. This psychological reaction has something to do with the mental models humans develop early in life for dealing with embarrassing or threatening situations. Other scholars have described this type of defensive behavior as executive blindness. As a result of this, "Organizational members become committed to a pattern of behavior. They escalate their commitment to that pattern out of self-justification. In a desire to avoid embarrassment and threat, few if any challenges are made to the wisdom and viability of these behaviors. They persist even when rapid and fundamental shifts in the competitive environment render these patterns of behavior obsolete and destructive to the well-being of the organization" (Beer & Spector, 1993, p. 642).

Organizational Defensive Routines

Organizational defensive routines consist of procedures, policies, practices, and actions that prevent employees from having to experience embarrassment or threat. Also these routines prevent them from examining the nature and causes of that embarrassment or threat. Organizational defensive routines make it highly likely that individuals, groups, intergroups, and organizations will not detect and correct errors that are embarrassing and threatening. It is not possible to design an effective learning organization unless the problems of defensive reactions and routines are recognized and confronted.

Problem Solving

Individual defensive reasoning and organizational defensive routines impede members of an organization to engage in problem solving process effectively. Creative problem solving involves the processes of problem recognition, solving problems, and implementation (see Figure 1):

Figure 1
Problem-Solving Process

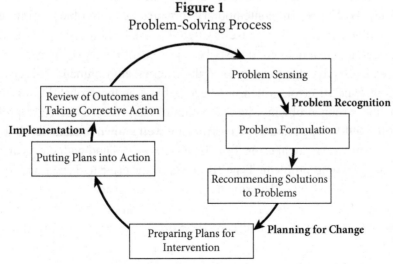

Source: Adapted with permission from Rahim (2002, p. 214)

1. **Problem Recognition involves:**
   - Problem sensing—This is associated with becoming aware of a discrepancy or error in one or more activities.
   - Problem formulation—This is associated with collecting and analyzing relevant information and stating a problem formally.
2. **Solving Problems involve:**
   - Recommending solutions to problems—This involves articulating alternative solutions to the stated problem.
   - Preparing plans for intervention—This involves preparing plans designed to implement recommended solutions to the problem.
3. **Implementation involves:**
   - Putting plans into action—This is associated with the implementation of the planned activities prepared in the previous step.
   - Review of outcomes—This involves evaluating the outcomes of the plan that was implemented and recommending corrective actions.

Because organizations neglected to recognize and deal with the problems of defensive reactions of employees and organizational defensive routines, organizations do not have the culture that encourages members to engage in real problem solving process. The first phase of problem solving is problem recognition, which involves confronting political and other risky problems. Even if some organizational members overcome their defensive reactions, organizational defensive routines will not allow them to formulate the real problems. Organizational members who create "dissent" become the bad "guys."

Type III Error. In contemporary organizations, problem formulation in the problem recognition phase is often distorted. As a result, old policies, procedures, and practices continue to be followed although they may have been rendered ineffective due to changes in the external environment. This typically results in Type III error, which has been defined as the probability of having solved the wrong problem when one should have solved the right problem (Mitroff, 1998). Type I and Type II errors are well known in statistics, but Type III error is not a statistical error. Type III error is associated with the probability of solving a wrong problem. Type III errors occur prior to Type I and Type II and it is also more basic. "Uncritical thinkers focus on and attempt to minimize Type I and Type II errors; critical thinkers focus on the Type III Error before they get caught up in Type I and Type II Errors. In other words, critical thinkers first attempt to insure that they are working on the right problem before they attempt to solve it in detail" (Mitroff, 1998,p. 18).

Organizational members may have to deal with another type of error. Sometimes good plans for intervention may not be put into action or a part of the plan may be put into action for a variety of reasons. This results in Type IV error: the probability of not implementing a solution properly. Mitroff's (1998) excellent book, *Smart Thinking for Crazy Times,* has provided detailed guidelines for avoiding Type III Error to solve the right problem. These are summarized as follows:

1. **Select the right stakeholders.** Managers often assume that stakeholders share their opinion or try to select stakeholders who share the same opinion. To avoid Type III error, Mitroff suggests that managers need stakeholders who challenge their views.
2. **Expand your options.** To avoid Type III error, managers should look at problems from more than one perspective: *scientific/technical, interpersonal/social, existential,* and *systemic.* An individual or group can determine whether a Type III error is committed "by comparing two very different formulations of a problem. A single formulation of a problem is a virtual prescription for disaster" (Mitroff, 1998, p. 61).
3. **Phrase problems correctly.** Phrasing a problem incorrectly may lead to Type III error. The effectiveness of the formulation of a problem depends to a great extent on the language one uses.
4. **Extend the boundaries of problems.** Managers should enlarge the boundary or scope of a problem so that it is inclusive enough. In other words, "never draw the boundaries of an important problem too narrowly; broaden the scope of every important problem up to and just beyond your comfort zone" (Mitroff, 1998, p. 29).
5. **Think systemically.** Managers should not focus on a part of the problem or ignore connection between parts. Failure to think and act systemically can lead Type III error

Effectiveness of Organizational Learning

Organizational learning needs to be well understood and managed, as it influences organizational outcomes. Organizational learning helps firms better develop their competence and resources that contribute to better performance and satisfaction and commitment of members. Spicer and Sadler-Smith (2006) suggest that organizational learning has a positive impact on financial, as well as non-financial performance. Organizations that formally promote learning seem to enjoy higher profitability and increased employee job satisfaction (Rowden & Conine, 2005). Studies suggest that organizational learning also leads to greater innovation, internal efficiency, project performance, and organizational competitiveness (Osterloh & Frey, 2000; Wang Cheung, & Fan, 2009).

Implications for Management

With the publication of *The Fifth Discipline* (Senge, 1990) the term *organizational learning* became a permanent part of business lexicon and has continued to draw significant interest from scholars of organizational studies ever since. Learning organizations essentially need appropriate leadership to foster a culture that promotes learning, design a flat and flexible organizational structure; and select top management that fully supports and models learning. Collaborative network—as opposed to rigid and hierarchical organizational structures—allow firms to more effectively adapt to their environment through efficient knowledge acquisition and dissemination (Peters, Johnston, Pressey, & Kendrick, 2010).

Leadership

Senge (1990) maintains that a different set of leadership roles will be needed with more emphasis on leaders as teachers, stewards, and designers. These leaders, "articulate a clear and challenging vision for their firm based on their insights into key industry trends that can be the catalyst for redefining the foundation of competition. ... they focus on developing the people around them, motivating them to want to learn and take greater responsibility. ... they lead in 'unlearning'—the conscious effort to challenge traditional assumptions about the company and its environment" (Slater, 1995, p. 33). General Electric's former CEO Jack Welch and Chrysler's former CEO Lee Iacoca fit this description of leadership.

To some extent this type of leadership fits Bass's (1985) description of transformational leadership that has three distinct factors: charisma, intellectual stimulation, and individualized consideration. Transformational leaders encourage their subordinates to engage in critical and innovative thinking that are needed for problem solving. These leaders, sometimes referred to as charismatic leaders, use their personal power to inspire employees to new ways of thinking and problem solving.

Conflict and tension will go up as more people challenge the old ways of thinking and doing things. As result, the problems are surfaced (problem recognition), which leads to recommendations for change in the process and structure (solving problems), and implementation of recommendations.

Organizational Culture

Conflict management to support organizational learning and long-term effectiveness would require cultures which support experimentation, risk taking, openness, diverse viewpoints, continuous questioning and inquiry, and sharing of information and knowledge. This implies that employees would be encouraged to take responsibility for their errors and not blame others for their mistakes or incompetence.

Such a culture would encourage substantive or task-related conflict and discourages affective or emotional conflict. For example, Honda Corporation encourages its employees to explicitly surface and handle conflict in a constructive way. Honda holds sessions in which employees can openly (but politely) question supervisors and challenge the status quo. "This is not an empty ritual but a vital force in keeping Honda on its toes. It sustains a restless, self-questioning atmosphere that one expects to see in new ventures—yet Honda is into its fourth generation of management. Its founders retired in 1970" (Pascale, 1990, p. 26).

Effective programs require an incentive system that encourages risk taking. An organization may have to reward failures; otherwise organizational members will learn to do what is safe and avoid risk-taking behaviors. B. F. Skinner's operant conditioning, which refers to voluntary learning of behavior through positive reinforcement, is particularly appropriate here. This was acknowledged by Schein (1993): "This is the kind of learning symbolized by the use of the carrot instead of the stick, the creation of incentives to do the right thing, and the immediate rewarding of correct behavior. In this model, errors and wrong behavior are not punished but are ignored so that the learner remains focused on improving and refining correct behavior" (p. 86). Managers need to know how to use reinforcements to elicit conflict management behaviors which are not only associated with effective performance and creativity, but also with risk taking for improving long-term performance.

Organization Design

This intervention attempts to improve the organizational effectiveness by changing the organization's structural design characteristics, which include differentiation and integration mechanisms, hierarchy, procedures, reward system, etc. This approach mainly attempts to manage conflict by altering the perceptions of the intensity of conflict of the organizational members at various levels.

Although Duncan and Weiss (1979) indicated more than two decades ago the need for designing organizations for encouraging organizational learning, scholars have not yet provided adequate attention to this issue. Many organizations have responded to competitive pressures by creating flatter, decentralized, and less complex designs than others. The shift is reflected in new organizational forms, such as the modular organization, virtual corporation, and the horizontal organization.

Many organizations have responded to competitive pressures by downsizing. Unfortunately, downsizing does little to alter the single-loop learning and consequently the basic way work gets done in a company. To do that takes a different model, the organic design. This design is flatter, decentralized, and less complex than others. Some of the biggest corporations, such as GE, Xerox, DuPont, and Motorola are moving in this direction. Unfortunately changes in organization design, without corresponding changes in culture, may not alter single-loop learning and consequently the basic ways of doing work.

Questions for Students

1. What is the difference between single-loop learning and double-loop learning?
2. Why is the double-loop learning more effective than single-loop learning, in terms of creating sustainable change in organizations?
3. What are some of the things that a manager can do to promote double-loop learning in an organization?

Case: Disney Institute

Disney Institute began as a vision, and the visionary was Walt Disney himself. Not only did Walt Disney redefine the world of entertainment, his legacy is found in a worldwide scope of motion pictures, Theme Parks, stage shows, books, magazines, television, merchandise, music, apparel, radio, resorts, a cruise line and more. Of course, none of this would have been possible had he not also rewritten the rules of business.

Walt Disney was, and will always remain, that rare breed: an artistic genius who, with the unflagging and essential support of his brother, Roy, created an effective organizational model and efficient work environment where employees were recognized for their achievements, encouraged to work as a team and, by striving for excellence, continually broke the confines of the status quo to surpass the expectations of the world.

Your Opportunity

Since Disney Institute opened in 1986, millions of attendees representing virtually every sector of business from every corner of the globe have had an opportunity to witness and experience these innovative business strategies.

Disney Institute remains the only professional development company where you will literally step into a "living laboratory" at Disney Theme Parks and Resorts for guided behind-the-scenes field experiences. Disney's brand of business excellence is also being taught at locations across the U.S. and, to date, in more than 45 countries around the world.

We have inspired leaders to change not only their business practices, but also to examine their business issues in an entirely new light. Like them, you will find your organization has more in common with Disney than you ever imagined.

Our Methods

Whether you tune into a Disney Institute WebCast, attend a workshop in your city, or immerse yourself in a multi-day program at a Disney Destination, the lessons we've developed are rooted in the time-tested visions and ideals of Walt Disney. As you "experience the business behind the magic," you'll discover our innovative training methods focused on three key program outcomes: Knowledge, Comprehension, and Application. These outcomes will clearly illustrate ways that you can adapt and apply these lessons into your organization.

As vital as the message are the messengers. Disney Institute facilitators include accomplished business leaders, entrepreneurs, educators, and executives who use dynamic and entertaining stories and demonstrations to explain effective business models and concepts. Depending on the program length and location, these sessions may be enhanced by facilitated discussions, team-building exercises, case studies, experiential activities, and behind-the-scenes guided tours at Disney Destinations. Disney Institute programs provide you with a business map that will help you chart a course for your organization, your division, and yourself.

Your return on this investment is across the board improvement. You'll realize this improvement in processes, your work environment, and the delivery of customer service. You'll sense it in yourself and your employees who are inspired to strive for excellence. Above all, you'll see it in increased productivity and a renewed sense of purpose and potential.

Source: Disney Institute. (2011). Our story. http://disneyinstitute.com/about_us/our_story.aspx. Retrieved on 8/19/2011.

Exercise: Types of Organizational Learning

A. Stated problem

An electronics manufacturing plant is suffering significant production delays.

B. Potential questions management may ask to solve the problem

- Which step in the production process constitutes a bottleneck?
- Which unit suffers most from production delays?
- IIow do production delays hurt our sales?
- What do our customers think about the production delays?
- How can we redesign the assembly line to reduce production time?
- What alternative technologies can be used to improve production times?
- What are the bases for setting the expected production cycle time, and are these bases still valid in this situation?
- If the production delays had been documented for a while, what may have prevented us from doing something about it?

- Do employees hesitate to offer suggestions for improving production times—despite knowing that something may be done? If so, what may be the reason for organizational silence?
- Is there an unwritten convention to avoid raising issues that might be noted with employees or processes, for fear of embarrassing others or not stepping on others' toes?
- Have production delays been accepted as a way of life in our? If so, since when and for what reasons?
- Is problem diagnosis and resolution often viewed as the exclusive responsibility of a few select individuals? Why might there not be shared responsibility?

C. Instructions for student activity

1. Each student in the class is asked to classify the above questions into two categories: (1) questions that promote single-loop learning; and (2) questions that promote double-loop learning.
2. The class is then divided into groups (of three members each) and each group is asked to discuss the reasons behind members' classification of these questions.
3. After members discuss their rankings within their groups, each group as a whole (re)classifies the questions.
4. A representative from each group explains to the class how their group benefited from this exercise.
5. The instructor then facilitates a class conversation on what students have learned from the exercise.

Suggestions for Further Reading

Argyris, C., & Schon, D. A. (1996). *Organizational learning II: Theory, method, and practice.* London: Addison-Wesley.

Crossan, M., Lane, H., & White, R. (1999). An organizational learning framework: From intuition to institution. *Academy of Management Review, 24,* 522–537.

Sadler, P. (2001). Leadership and organizational learning. In M. Dierkes, A. B. Antal, J. Child, & I. Nonaka (Eds.), *Handbook of organizational learning and knowledge* (415–428). New York: Oxford University Press.

References

Argyris, C. (1990). *Overcoming organizational defenses: Facilitating organizational learning.* Boston: Allyn and Bacon.

Bass, B. M. (1985). *Leadership and performance beyond expectations.* New York: Free Press.

Bateson, G. (1972). *Steps to an ecology of mind.* San Francisco: Chadler.

Beer, M., & Spector, B. (1993). Organizational diagnosis: Its role in organizational learning. *Journal of Counseling & Development, 71,* 642–650.

Osterloh, M. & Frey. B. S. (2000). Motivation, knowledge transfer, and organizational firms. *Organization Science, 11,* 538–550.

Pascale, R. T. (1990). *Managing on the edge: How the smartest companies use conflict to stay ahead.* New York: Simon and Schuler.

Peters, D., Johnston, W., Pressey, A. & Kendrick, T. (2010). Collaboration and collective learning: Networks as learning organisations. *Journal of Business & Industrial Marketing, 25,* 478–484.

Mitroff, I. I. (1998). *Smart thinking for crazy times: The art of solving the right problems.* San Francisco: Berrett-Koehler.

Rahim, A. (2002). Toward a theory of managing organizational conflict. *The International Journal of Conflict Management, 13,* 206–235.

Rowden, R. W. & Conine, C. T. (2005). The impact of workplace learning and job satisfaction in small US commercial banks. *Journal of Workplace Learning, 17,* 215–230.

Schein, E. H. (1993). How can organizations learn faster? The challenge of entering the green room. *Sloan Management Review, 35* (2), 85–92.

Senge, P.M. (1990). *The fifth discipline: The art and practice of the learning organization.* New York: Currency Doubleday.

Slater, S. F. (1995, November–December). Learning to change. *Business Horizons,* pp. 13–20.

Spicer, D. & Sadler-Smith, E. (2006). Organizational learning in smaller manufacturing firms. *International Small Business Journal, 24,* 133–158.

Taylor, G. S., Templeton, G. F., & Baker, L. T. (2010). Factors influencing the success of organizational learning implementation: A policy facet perspective. *International Journal of Management Reviews, 12,* 353 364.

Tompkins, T. C. (1995). Role of diffusion in collective learning. *International Journal of Organizational Analysis, 3,* 69–85.

12. Knowledge Management

Sajjad M. Jasimuddin
Kedge Business School, France

Knowledge management entails the exploration and exploitation of organizational knowledge. Knowledge is treated as one of the strategic resources for generating market value and economic rent for products and services of an organization. Producing a good or rendering a service typically requires the application of many different types of knowledge. Knowledge management allows organizational members to create, acquire, transfer, store, and use their knowledge individually and in group so as to improve organizational performance. The successful implementation of knowledge management is essential for improving the sustainable competitive advantage of an organization.

Nature of Knowledge Management

Definition

Knowledge management is an integrated approach that identifies, captures, stores, retrieves, and transfers knowledge so as to enhance strategic advantage of an organization over its competitors. There is a confusion over the meaning of knowledge management, which has somewhat restricted its theoretical development. Scholars have even found difficulty to distinguish it from other related concepts, such as knowledge engineering or information management. Difficulty in defining the concept actually arises from the broad domain of the field, which covers different research areas and levels of analysis. Several attempts are made to offer a comprehensive definition with an aim to integrate various dimensions that knowledge management involves. In the broadest sense, the term *knowledge management refers to the effective and efficient collection, distribution, utilization and retention of knowledge with an aim to ensure an organization's sustainable competitive advantage.*

Roots of Knowledge Management

Karl Wiig coined the 'Knowledge Management' concept for the first time in 1986 at a conference organized by the International Labour Organization (ILO) held in Switzerland. Since then, knowledge management has matured from fad to enduring management subject with its own dedicated consulting companies, journals and management gurus. However, information management is thought to be the forerunner of knowledge management.

The fact that knowledge management has received increased attention over the last two decades among academics and practitioners from across a broad range of subjects. Broadly speaking, academic disciplines such as organizational learning, strategic management, information systems, human resource management and economics, to name a few, help develop the understanding of knowledge management field.

In this regard, there are few scholars who claim that that knowledge management appears to represent an extension of information systems. Others argue that there is little to distinguish knowledge management from information management. They think it is little more than a repackaged form of information management. Several other scholars contend that that information management plays a role in providing fresh insights into the development of knowledge management discourse. It is true that knowledge management has borrowed terminologies and technologies from information management discipline. As a result, there is a debate among academics and researchers to resolve whether knowledge management and information management are the two distinct disciplines or are the same.

Similarly, there are scholars who believe that knowledge management and organizational learning can be used synonymously as they are closely related. There is strong logic behind linking knowledge management with organizational learning. In this regard, Rahim's (2002) definition of organizational learning supports this claim. According to him, organizational learning is associated with knowledge acquisition, knowledge distribution, information interpretation, and organizational memorization (i.e., preserving information for future access and use). However, there are scholars who treat the two fields as distinct subjects. Knowledge management is about the creation, distribution, and application of knowledge, whereas organizational learning is more concerned with the processes of collective leaning.

Knowledge Hierarchy

Philosophers like Plato defined knowledge as "justified true belief," which is widely cited in knowledge management literature. Knowledge is a catalyst for purposeful action of an individual as it increases his (her) capacity to take effective decisions. Although the terms data, information, and knowledge can be used with a similar meaning, knowledge differs from information and data. Davenport and Prusak (1998) provide a comprehensive discussion of the distinctions between data, information, and knowledge, suggesting that data are simply facts, which then become information by the addition of meaning, while knowledge originates in peoples' heads, drawing on information which is transformed and enriched by personal experience.

It is helpful to view data, information, and knowledge as separate constructs. However, they are also linked sequentially. For example, the list of stock prices is data; information is the meaningful data that is extracted for various stocks' price; and finally knowledge is the processed information, taking into account various information, such as stock price, company profile, industry information, portfolio risk, and availability of funds, that helps one to make decisions

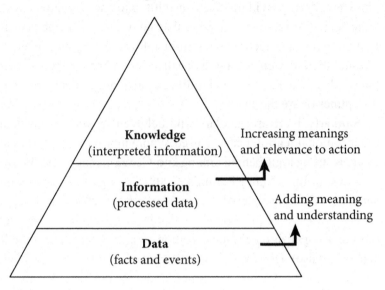

Figure 1
Knowledge Hierarchy

regarding stock investments. Hence, data are simply events or fact which are interpreted to form information. While information is data with meaning which is possessed by simple data, and knowledge is structured information which is the outcome the interpretation of information. The relationship between data, information, and knowledge as a hierarchy is shown in Figure 1. The three constructs can be viewed as a hierarchy of increasing meanings, depth and relevance to action.

Knowledge Management Process

Knowledge management deals with the creation, transfer, use, and storage of organizational knowledge. Knowledge management process involves various activities, such as the creation, interpretation, dissemination, application, preservation, and refinement of knowledge. It is not surprising that there are diverse views of what the components of knowledge management process are. The idea of knowledge management process is difficult to describe. In the broader sense, there are differences both in the understanding of the term 'knowledge management process' and its elements. Scholars have discussed knowledge management process probably in hundreds of ways in the relevant literature. Drawing on the extant literature, we categorize knowledge management processes into four components.

Knowledge Creation

Knowledge creation is widely regarded as a strategic issue of knowledge management. A growing body of literature indicates that knowledge creation is crucial because at the cutting edge of innovation knowledge generators provide the engine for change in process and products of an organization. The fact that knowledge creation embraces a continual dialogue between explicit (that is, codifiable and transmitted in a formal document) and tacit (that is, personal, context-specific, difficult to formalize and articulate) knowledge through the interaction of internal and external sources, which eventually boosts the creation of new ideas and knowledge.

Knowledge Transfer

Knowledge transfer is identified as a major focus area for knowledge management. Knowledge transfer refers to the process of exchanging knowledge among the members of an organization. The terms 'knowledge transfer', 'knowledge share', and 'knowledge exchange' are interchangeably used. Knowledge sharing is basically seen as the process by which an organization makes relevant knowledge available to other members. Most specifically, knowledge transfer is an act of transmission of knowledge among actors using a communication channel so that they can make decisions and take purposeful actions to do their job.

Knowledge transfer process can be discussed in terms of the information system (an operational level of analysis) or the interpretative system (a conceptual level of analysis). While the information system views knowledge transfer as a communication process with information-processing activities in which knowledge is exchanged by a medium, the interpretative system treats knowledge transfer as the concept of the learning organization.

Knowledge Storage and Retrieval

Knowledge storage and retrieval is one of the key elements of knowledge management. The preservation of knowledge (which is popularly referred to as "organizational memory") is a major building block in the implementation of knowledge management as it helps to reuse the existing knowledge and create new knowledge. The terms 'organizational memory' and 'knowledge storage' are used synonymously. Knowledge storage and retrieval can be defined as a system that preserves and stores perceptions and experiences beyond the moment when they occur, so that knowledge can be retrieved and used at a later time (Probst, Raub, & Romhardt, 2000).

Viewing knowledge as a crucial resource, organizations recognize the value of knowledge storage not only for present use but also for future use. If knowledge is not kept in a storage bin, that may be simply forgotten, represents a waste of organizational resources. At the time of need, we have to reinvent the wheel. If such transferred knowledge is stored and retained in a repository so that other members of the organization could get access to retrieve it for future use, it is more useful. But all knowledge of the organization should not be preserved and retained in a knowledge repository. If irrelevant and unused knowledge is stored then knowledge storage will be filled with garbage. So knowledge, which is perceived as current, relevant, and correct, should be stored into and should also be retrievable from knowledge repositories for use.

Knowledge Application. Knowledge application at individual and collective levels within an organization is considered to be a crucial task in modern organizations. The task of knowledge management does not end with the exploration of knowledge from inside and outside of an organization. Additionally, it should ensure that right knowledge is used in the right place at the right time. It is to be noted that the knowledge exploration function will be productive if it is used in an organization over and over again. In fact, knowledge that is in the head of a person or in a knowledge repository has limited value, while the value of knowledge can increase exponentially when it is used and reused, and quickly integrated into business practices and processes.

If transferred knowledge or stored knowledge are not utilised properly, it is a loss for the organization Knowledge that is created through interaction, transferred among the organizational members through an appropriate mechanism, and stored in a knowledge repository is likely to be more useful when it is applied. In this regard, huge investment is needed to spend by an organization at the time of creation, transfer, and storage of knowledge. Hence, it is important to make sure that right knowledge is used in the right place at the right time, immediately after its exploration from the right source.

Outcomes of Knowledge Management

In the knowledge based society, the success of an organization depends on how well knowledge is exploited. Since knowledge is the heart of a modern, knowledge-driven economy, knowledge management has become critical to organizational survival and growth. The benefits as derived from knowledge management initiatives are many. Knowledge management helps to improve the exploitation of the organizational knowledge and to protect it from imitation by competitors. Furthermore, KPMG (1999) describes knowledge management goals and provides a list of benefits derived from its application, which are mentioned below.

- supporting innovation, the generation of new ideas and the exploitation of the organization's thinking power;
- capturing insight and experience to make them available when, where and by whom required;
- making it easy to find and reuse sources of knowhow and expertise, whether they are recorded in a physical form or held in someone's mind;
- fostering collaboration and knowledge sharing; continual learning and improvement;
- improving the quality of decision making and other intelligent tasks;
- understanding the value and contribution of intellectual assets and increasing their worth, effectiveness and exploitation.

Knowledge management is assuming a greater role in all types of organizations (e.g., private firm, educational institution, public enterprise, military establishment, hospitals, government and non-government organization). Most specifically, leading multinational enterprises (MNEs) around the world are involved in knowledge management practice since 1990s. Most successful and innovation companies today are considered knowledge based organizations. Companies such as Accenture, Buckman Laboratories, Cable and Wireless, DaimlerChrystler, Dow Chemical, Earnest & Young, Ford, Hewlett Packard, IBM, Skandia, Siemens, Unilever, and Xerox, just to name a few, have implemented knowledge management initiatives. ShareNet, Siemens' Information and Communication Networks division is a global knowledge sharing Intranet that serves as an instrument to transfer and leverage existing knowledge so as to create new knowledge in a division based in one part of the world and make available for reuse by its employees elsewhere.

The Fortune 500 companies spent $12 billion by duplicating knowledge work. Thousand of companies across the world have incorporated managing knowledge as a part of their business function. As a result, many organisations have established a knowledge management department and created a position called a Chief Knowledge Officer (CKO), who will be responsible for managing and maintaining knowledge. Eighty percent of Fortune 500 companies currently have knowledge management staff, one fourth of which have knowledge administrator-equivalent. Such an officer may engage in developing a knowledge management strategy, and managing knowledge content for the company (Jasimuddin, Connell, & Klein, 2012).

The implementation of knowledge management initiative is not an easy task. Rather its implementation is generally a formidable challenge. There are a variety of reasons for its failure. It is essentially needed to identify the problems faced. Its implementation can be very expensive, time consuming and resource intensive. Sometimes top management is not ready to assemble resources. The resistance of employees to any change in an organisation is a common phenomenon. This might be the case that could limit the impact of knowledge management in practice.

Implications for Management

Knowledge management has turned into a crucial agenda for organizations around the world. The main focus of knowledge management practice has been on how an organization discovers and deploys its knowledge. Both academics and practitioners recognize that knowledge management is an important functional area for an organization. Senior management support is crucial to launch a knowledge management initiative in which leaders have to share a vision on knowledge management, and provide such a program with ongoing support. Most specifically, top management should take the following measures for the successfully implementation of knowledge management.

1. Assembling of people, time and money to put knowledge management into practice;
2. Building of a knowledge sharing culture in the organization;
3. Creating a knowledge management infrastructure;
4. Establishing a full-fledged knowledge management department which will be headed by the Chief Knowledge Officer (CKO). Hence the CKO needs to be created so that he (she) dedicatedly manage organizational knowledge.
5. Knowledge management has a bright future. It will expand as a scholarly discipline. Knowledge management is far from being a narrow management initiative, or 'fad'. Knowledge management is now a well-established subject. Although knowledge management is developed first by the professional services firms, it has quickly been practiced by manufacturing, financial services, government and non government, military, and intelligence organizations. In this regard, academics and researchers are making an effort to foster knowledge management in management education with an aim to sustain its popularity. A notable thrust in recent curriculum development within higher education sector focuses on designing modules and degree schemes on this subject to offer knowledge management education.

Questions for Students

1. Does knowledge differ from data and information?
2. How does a thorough understanding of knowledge management processes can help a manager to implement knowledge management initiative?
3. Do you think senior management has role to ensure the successful implementation of knowledge management? Justify your argument.
4. Why does a company need to establish its knowledge management department headed by a Chief Knowledge Officer?

Exercise

Graphically represent the following table of articles counts for the following management techniques for each year from 1992 to 2007.

Year	Knowledge Management No. of journal articles	Year	Knowledge Management No. of journal articles
1992	8	2000	121
1993	2	2001	151
1994	8	2002	249
1995	9	2003	274
1996	16	2004	388
1997	22	2005	358
1998	37	2006	470
1999	69	2007	480

1. Form a group of six members and explain the reasons behind understanding management fads.
2. After each group member explained the rationale to the group, the group as a whole will provide their argument whether KM is another management fashion.
3. A representative from each group explains what they learnt from this exercise.
4. The instructor encourages the class to make further comments on what they learnt from the exercise.

Case: Knowledge Management Practice in WHO

The World Health Organization (WHO) realizes the importance of knowledge and knowledge management. With an aim to treat its workforce as knowledge worker, the WHO has launched an independent unit, *Department of Knowledge Management and Sharing.*

WHO defines the term 'knowledge management' to describe how the secretariat uses technology to enable people to create, capture, store, retrieve, use and share knowledge. The vision of WHO knowledge management is to improve the understanding and application of knowledge management in the pursuit of WHO's mandate in order to ensure a world with better and more equitable health outcomes. The mission of its knowledge management strategy is to make efforts to bridge the know–do gap in global health by fostering a culture that encourages the creation, transfer, and application of knowledge to improve health. Broadly speaking, the objectives of its knowledge management strategy are (i) to contribute to strengthening country health systems through better knowledge management; (ii) to promote the principles of knowledge management as a fundamental aspect of public health research and practice; and (iii) to enable the WHO to become a better learning and knowledge sharing organization. In order to implement knowledge management initiative successfully, the WHO is engaged in various activities including:

1. **Dissemination of health related information.** The WHO publishes, markets and disseminates in priority languages, relevant and high-quality information products to reach a widespread, targeted readership in both print and electronic formats. Its establishing publishing policies and guidelines ensures efficiency and quality of the publications. WHO is promoting access to high-quality, relevant, targeted information products and services.
2. **Building capability in knowledge management methods in public health practice.** The WHO assists public health communities to develop the capacity to translate knowledge into policy and action in their local context.
3. **Sharing and reapplying experiential knowledge.** Knowledge management methods and tools offer new opportunities for WHO and public health. The WHO provides guidance and facilitates the adoption of knowledge management methods so that experience is reapplied and built upon in practice.
4. **Fostering a conducive knowledge sharing culture.** The WHO creates an environment for the effective use of knowledge that is vital to achieving its mission. WHO is strengthening organizational capacity, advocating adoption of knowledge management in the field of public health, and improving capacity for implementing knowledge management at country level. Such a culture helps to encourage the routine capturing, sharing and application of knowledge to better deliver expected results.
5. **Developing and delivering knowledge management training programmes:** The WHO arranges training programmes surrounding knowledge management to build WHO and country capacity with emphasis on innovation, knowledge sharing and translation, and managing the reapplication and scaling-up of successful interventions.

WHO is claimed itself as a knowledge-based organization. The sharing, dissemination, and application of knowledge and information about health conditions and the maintenance of health has been its central activity since its inception. In collaboration with regional offices and external partners, *Department of Knowledge Management and Sharing* is engaged in a range of activities which are aimed at achieving its strategic goals. The WHO knowledge management strategy focuses on national policy makers, WHO programmes, and health professionals. It also targets other audiences including the academic and research community, nongovernmental organizations (NGOs), the private sector, donors, the media, development institutions and the general public.

Suggestions for Further Reading

Alavi, M., & Leidner, D. (2001). Knowledge management and knowledge management systems: Conceptual foundations and research issues. *MIS Quarterly*, *25* (1), 107–136.

Hansen, M. T., Nohria, N., & Tierney T. (1999). What's your strategy for managing knowledge? *Harvard Business Review*, *77* (2), 106–116.

Jasimuddin, S. M. (2012) *Knowledge management: An interdisciplinary perspective*. Singapore: World Scientific.

References

Davenpport, T. H., & Grover, V. (2001). Special Issue: Knowledge management. *Journal of Management Information Systems*, *18* (1), 3–4.

Davenport, T. H., & Prusak, L. (1998). *Working knowledge: How organizations manage what they know*. Boston: Harvard Business School Press.

Jasimuddin, S. M., Connell, N., & Klein, J. H. (2012). Knowledge transfer frameworks: An extension incorporating knowledge repositories and knowledge administration. *Information Systems Journal*, *22* (3) 195–209.

Jasimuddin, S. M., & Zhang Z. (2011). Storing transferred knowledge and transferring stored knowledge, *Information Systems Management*, *28* (1), 84–94.

Jasimuddin, S. M., Klein, J. H., & Connell, C. (2005). The paradox of using tacit and explicit knowledge: Strategies to face dilemmas. *Management Decision*, *43* (1), 102–112.

Jasimuddin, S. M. (2006). Disciplinary roots of knowledge management: A theoretical review. *International Journal of Organizational Analysis. 14*, 171–180.

Jasimuddin, S. M. (2008). A holistic view of appropriate knowledge management strategy. *Journal of Knowledge Management, 12* (2), 57–66.

Jasimuddin, S. M., Connell, N. A. D., & Klein, J. H. (2006). What motivates organisational knowledge transfer? Some lessons from a UK-based multinational. *Journal of Information and Knowledge Management, 5* (2), 165-171.

KPMG (1999). *The power of knowledge: A business guide to knowledge management,* London: The KPMG Management Consulting.

Nonaka, I., & Takeuchi, H. (1995). *The knowledge creating company.* Oxford, UK: Oxford University Press.

Probst, G., Raub, S., & Romhardt, K. (2000). *Managing knowledge-building blocks for success.* Chichester, West Sussex: Wiley.

Rahim. M. A. (2002). Towards a theory of managing organizational conflict. *International Journal of Conflict Management, 13*, 206–235

Wiig, K. M. (1997). Knowledge management: Where did it come from and where will it go? *Expert Systems with Applications, 13/14*, 1–14.

PART VI

Organization Design, Project Management, and Multinational Enterprises

13. Organization Design

David Biggs
University of Gloucestershire, UK

Afzal Rahim
Center for Advanced Studies Management

Don G. Schley
Colorado Technical University

Organizational design is arguably one of the most important tasks undertaken by CEOs or senior management. While organizations often evolve on an *ad hoc* basis, at crucial times they must be reorganized in a manner more conducive to their effective operation. In addition, different types of organizations demand different styles of behavior from their employees, and different organizational types also elicit the kinds of behaviors from employees necessary to make the organization work. Thus, understanding organizational types and the behaviors such types both demand and elicit becomes a critical survival issue for persons building their careers in the modern, corporate world.

Nature of Organization Design

Definition

Organization design refers to the arrangement and the process of arranging various resources (human, informational, technological, financial, and environmental) to overcome physical and psychological limitations of individuals so that organizational objectives can be accomplished. This definition makes it clear that design is as much a process (designing) as a structure (the resultant design). Organization design is a process by which top managers make decisions that result in the creation of a specific organization structure. Organization design should be distinguished at the macro-level from job design at the micro-level. Job design includes job rotation, job enlargement, and job enrichment.

Job Design. This refers to deciding what activities will constitute individual jobs. Job design method can follow two approaches. The classical approach involves structuring the task activities to make full use of the division of labor and specialization. Job design was reduced to highly simplified work with standardized operations, and these jobs could be done by relatively untrained persons. The main purpose of this approach to job design was to create economic advantages; nevertheless, this process ignored the individuals performing the routine repetitive jobs to such an extent that efficiencies created were largely negated by a demotivated workforce. This job engineering is still a popular job design strategy. The four approaches job design are as follows:

- Job simplification—this involves simplifying tasks down to their most basic form,
- Job rotation—this involves rotating workers among different jobs that require similar skills,
- Job enlargement—this involves increasing job range, i.e. the number of tasks performed by the workers, and
- Job enrichment—this approach involves changing the job to make it more challenging and satisfying.

Job enrichment. This is a practical solution to deal with the boredom, de-motivation and alienation involved particularly in job simplification. It involves increasing *job range*, i.e. the number of tasks that a jobholder

Figure 1
A Model for Job Design

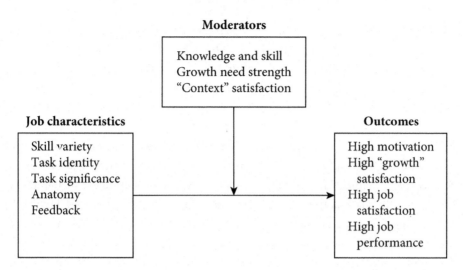

Moderators

Knowledge and skill
Growth need strength
"Context" satisfaction

Job characteristics

Skill variety
Task identity
Task significance
Anatomy
Feedback

Outcomes

High motivation
High "growth"
  satisfaction
High job
  satisfaction
High job
  performance

Source: Adapted from Hackman, J. R., & Oldman, G. R. (1980). *Work redesign*. Reading, MA: Addison-Wesley, p. 90.

performs, and *job depth*, i.e. the amount of discretion that an employee has to decide on job activities and job outcomes. An approach to job enrichment that enhances range and depth was developed by Hackman and Oldham (1975) and a simplified model is shown in Figure 1. Their approach attempts to make jobs more meaningful by increasing or adding certain core job characteristics, such as skill variety, task identity, task significance, autonomy, and feedback.

These five core job characteristics are positively related to "job satisfaction, growth satisfaction, and internal work motivation as well as to other outcomes such as outcomes such as organizational commitment, coworker satisfaction, burnout, and role perception" (Parker, 2014, p. 664). The five core dimensions can be described as follows:

1. **Skill variety.** This refers to the degree to which a job requires a variety of activities that involve the use of a number of different skills and talents of employees.
2. **Task identity.** This refers to the degree to which the job requires an employee to perform a complete piece of work, that is, doing a job from beginning to end with a visible outcome.
3. **Task significance.** This refers to the degree to which the job has an impact on the lives or work of other people, within or outside the organization.

4. **Autonomy.** This refers to the degree to which the job provides freedom, independence, and discretion to the employee in scheduling his or her work and in determining the procedures to be used in carrying it out.
5. **Feedback.** This refers to the amount of information that results from the performance of a job by an employee about how well she or he is performing.

The core characteristics influence three critical psychological states. The jobs that are high on skill variety, task identity, and task significance influence experienced meaningfulness of the work. Psychological states, such as experienced responsibility for outcomes of the work, and knowledge of the actual results of the work activities, are influenced by job autonomy and feedback, respectively. Although evidence is lacking, the theory suggests that higher levels of psychological states lead to positive personal and work outcomes, such as high work motivation, high growth satisfaction, high job satisfaction, and high job performance. Hackman and Oldham (1975) devised the following equation for computing an overall index, the Motivation Potential Score (MPS):

$$\text{MPS} = [(\text{Skill Variety} + \text{Task Identity} + \text{Task Significance}) \div 3] \times \text{Autonomy} \times \text{Feedback}$$

The MPS was hypothesized to be positively related to personal and work outcomes. But because individual employees differ, the researchers suggested that every employee does not respond to the MPS identically. Three factors moderate the relationship between the core job characteristics and outcomes. These are:

1. **Knowledge and skill** of the employees to perform job well.
2. **Growth need strength** (i.e., need for learning, self-direction, and personal growth of the employees).
3. **"Context" satisfactions** (i.e., the level of satisfaction, particularly with job security, compensation, coworkers, and supervision).

The employees who report higher on one or more of the above mediators should respond more positively to jobs that score high on MPS.

The researchers designed an instrument called the Job Diagnostic Survey (JDS) for measuring each of the variables in the job characteristics model (Hackman & Oldham, 1975). On the basis of the employees' responses to the JDS, it is possible to compute the MPS for employees. This instrument is used to predict the extent to which the characteristics of a job motivate employees to perform such a job. A number of studies have found moderate to strong support for this theory (Hackman & Oldham, 2010).

The job descriptive model appears to be a useful conceptual framework for studying the effects of job design on work behavior and performance of individual employees. Longitudinal field experiments are needed to assess the effects of job design interventions on different types of conflict discussed in this chapter. Other approaches to improving job characteristics are:

Flextime or Flexi-time. It is a work schedule arrangement that allows variation in the starting and departure time of employees without changing the total number of hours worked within a week. Essentials of this arrangement are:

- A core period (say 10:00 a.m.–3:00 p.m.) in a day when all the employees must be working.
- The rest of the day (say 7:00 a.m.–10:00 a.m. and 3:00 p.m.–7:00 p.m.) is flextime during which employees have the discretion over when they can come and leave work.
- Employees have to work to reach the total hours daily, weekly or even monthly which depends on the nature of work and employer approval.

3–Day or 4–Day work week. The four-day workweek is an arrangement in which a worker works 8 or 10 hours per day. The three-day workweek is another arrangement in which an employee works 12 hours a day (1.e., 36 hours per week).

It appears that these work arrangements enhance morale and productivity and reduce turnover and absenteeism (Olmsted & Smith, 1994).

Differentiation and Organization Structure

Organization at the macro-level includes the processes of differentiation and integration which are the broadened terms of division of labor or specialization and coordination. Organizations generally are differentiated into subunits with specialized goals, policies, and tasks so that they can effectively respond to the needs of internal and external environments (Lawrence & Lorsch, (1967; see also Lawrence, 2001). Organizations establish mechanisms of integration so that specialized activities for different subunits are channeled toward the attainment of their objectives. Organizations are structured in several different ways to meet the needs of the external environment. These are as follows:

Functional Structure. In the functional (U–Form) form of departmentation, employees with similar skills are grouped together. Figure 2 shows that a small manufacturing company is organized according to functions, such as marketing, production, human resources, and finance. The benefits of this structure are supporting specialization, reducing duplication, high quality technical decisions, and task assignment based on training and experience.

Figure 2
Functional Organization Structure

In a small corporation this type of structure may work out. But as the organization expands and develops many new products, the CEO may find it difficult to keep up with all the different functions of the corporation, and this form of structure loses its advantages.

Product Structure. The product or divisional structure (M–Form) is associated with creating divisions which are responsible for developing, producing, and distributing single products or an assortment of similar products (see Figure 3). Units attached to this type of design are usually quite autonomous in their own right. General Motors Corporation's design remains divisional, and the auto-manufacturing divisions include Chevrolet, Buick, Cadillac, and GMC Trucks. Support divisions originally included AC Delco (electronic parts) and Fisher Body (auto-body design and manufacturing). Ford Motor Company mirrored GM with its Ford, Lincoln, and Mercury divisions. Other organizations such as Hilton, Hewlett Packard, and Walt Disney maintain this type of design. The rationale behind the divisional structure is that this design encourages creativity

Figure 3
Product or Divisional Organization Structure

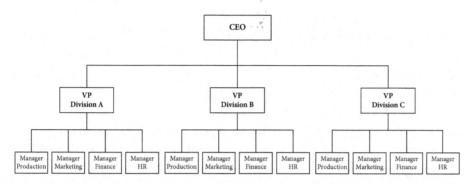

and innovation in the separate units, while promoting internal competition between the divisions yet allowing central management to retain overall control. These divisions are product focused and divisional leaders are responsible for improving the quality of their products and customer satisfaction.

Conglomerate Structure. The conglomerate (H–Form) structure occurs where a holding company or parent company owns and manages several

Figure 4
Matrix Organization Structure

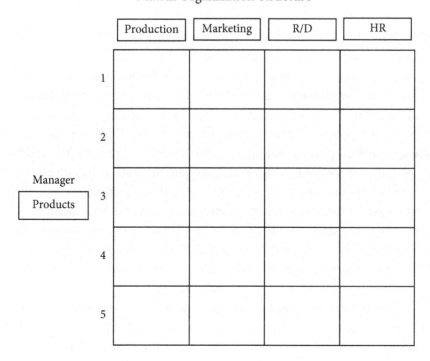

unrelated businesses. These other businesses are typically "wholly owned subsidiaries" and may function with a high degree of independence from one another. Dubai World is an example of such a holding company. Its portfolio includes DP World, Drydocks World, Dubai Maritime City, Economic Zones World, Istithmar World and Nakheel. Each of these companies constitutes a large multinational organization in its own right.

Matrix or Project Structure. The matrix design utilizes functional and product bases of departmentation. Figure 4 demonstrates the design of this kind of organization. This figure shows that personnel assigned in each cell belong to not only to the functional departments, but can also find themselves working for a particular product or project department. For example production, marketing, R/D, and finance personnel can be assigned to work on one or more projects or products (A, B, C, and D).

In this type of structure, employees report to managers in the functional and product departments. This dual authority system is one of the distinguishing characteristics of matrix organizations. These kinds of matrices are detailed in the chapter on project management. Advantages of this type of structure include cross-fertilization of ideas, timely response to the needs of environmental conditions, and efficient use of resources by reducing duplication.

Other Forms of Structure. Variations on these types can also be found, including the following.

Customer Departmentation. Here the grouping of functions is done according to the needs of customers. The design is similar to the functional form, but departments are created on the basis of the needs of customers. For example, Sears products are grouped for Big and Tall, Women, Men, and Children sections. A paper distribution company may be organized according to the markets it serves, e.g. public sector, private sector, and retail sector.

Geographic Departmentation. In addition to the grouping of activities, discussed above, some firms, such as large pharmaceutical manufacturers or some of the multinational companies, may group their functions geographically into Asian, North American, South American, and European divisions.

Emerging Organizational Structures. Three emerging organizational designs must also be considered: *team-based, virtual,* and *learning organizations.*

Team-based organizations. This form of organization structure derives from the field of project management and relies on teams to achieve its objectives. The advantage of team based-organizations is that they are innovative, their members trust each other (based on professional competency and performance), and the teams are self-directed and self-motivated. Such organizations empower their employees to excel in operational performance, in planning, and in leadership. Team-based organizations depend on highly competent individuals who have mastered not only their own technical area of expertise, but who are familiar with other technical areas as well. These teams and their members work "cross-functionally", so stand as polar opposites to tradition functional (U–form) organizations, where work and advancement are based on individuals staying within strictly defined technical specialties. In addition, because these teams work in a cross-functional manner, they can carry out work both more effectively and in a far more timely fashion than would have been possible in a functional organization.

Virtual organizations. These structures are a product of modern technology, particularly the Internet. They comprise formally organized companies with geographically dispersed members, and are typified by firms such as the University of Phoenix, Google, and Amazon.com. A virtual organization is defined by that fact that it lacks a central physical or geographic locus. Instead, it exists "virtually"—i.e., usually via the Internet or some other electronic means. The virtual organization can take various forms. It may be an alliance of independent legal entities consisting of limited companies, sole traders and partnerships, or it may be a single corporation with principles operating out of various locales. Typically there is an organizing base but work is distributed out to the alliance of partner firms, or to the individuals making up the organization. A major piece of the project work at the redevelopment of the Anschutz Medical Complex in Aurora, Colorado, was carried out by such a virtual team.

Learning organizations. MIT's Peter Senge (2006), one of the developers of the idea of the learning organization (out of pioneering work by Chris Argyris), has defined it as dynamic system in a state of constant learning and adaptation. In this sense, learning organizations are diametrical opposites of the classical mechanistic hierarchies—epitomized by the functional (U-Form) organizations—which are stable and rigid, and which do not adapt well to changing environments (arguably one of the primary reasons for the failure of the American auto companies in 2008 and 2009 was the fact that in the dynamic and fast-changing world of the international auto markets, they were structured as early twentieth-century hierarchies, and were thus unable to respond effectively to environmental changes!). Another distinction between classical hierarchies (mechanistic organizations) and organic, learning organizations is the way knowledge is treated. In classical hierarchies, knowledge is guarded within the individual functional silos to enhance functional performance over and against other functional areas. In organic organizations, and especially learning organizations, knowledge is rapidly distributed laterally throughout the organization to facilitate organizational learning, adaptability and effectiveness.

Chain-of-Command and Span of Control

Another crucial feature in organization design has to do with the relationship between chain-of-command and span of control. Chain-of-command is the most basic element of this relationship. It establishes who the boss is and who the subordinates are. In rigid, formal structures, such as the military, the chain-of-command establishes the "reporting structure" based on rank. In this structure, it is the rank that holds authority, and one respects the rank before the person holding it. Nevertheless, organizational roles in the business world may not necessarily be as stable as they are in the military. In fact, the strength of the chain-of-command structure varies dramatically outside of the military, and not every organization adheres to the military principles of chain-of-command, which are meant to guarantee the first principle of organizational design— "unity of command."

Span of control refers to the number of employees who report directly report a supervisor. The span of control determines the structure of an organization. Wide spans of control mean flatter, more efficient organizations, and narrow spans of control create taller, steeper hierarchies, that are less efficient than flatter ones.

Integration

Integration is the process of coordinating the activities of various subsystems so that they can work together to attain their common goals and not engage in dysfunctional conflict. The previous section discussed differentiation which is necessary to respond effectively to the need of the external environment. Yet differentiation creates the challenge of integrating the activities of the diverse departments, units, and divisions so that so that their energies are channeled toward the accomplishment of their common organizational objectives. The higher the differentiation, the greater is the difficulty of effective integration. "In complex organizations having differentiated subsystems with different goals, norms, and orientations, it appeared that intergroup conflict would be an inevitable part of organizational life" (Lawrence & Lorsch, 1997, p. 42). There are several mechanisms for attaining integration:

1. Hierarchy of authority—This is the classical coordinating mechanism which establishes who reports to whom and it is expected that this system will coordinate various organizational roles.
2. Liaison roles—In a fast-changing environment, members from each sub-unit are given the primary responsibilities for coordinating the activities of the subunits.
3. Task forces—When an organization increases its size and complexity, a task force composed of members from various units can be set up to deal with specific intergroup problems.
4. Integrating role—A full-time managerial position can be created to improve communication between departments and divisions.

Interdependence

An organization is a complex social entity consisting of many interrelated parts. Accordingly, the emergence of new organizational models can make organizational design very complicated. The complexity of organizational design derives from the *interdependence* of human activities, which is the primary reason for integration. In an organization, interdependence can be defined as the dependence of units on each to accomplish their tasks. Interdependence therefore influences organization design and three types of interdependence are generally identified in the literature: *pooled, sequential* and *reciprocal.* There are other types of interdependence, such as immersive, purposive, compound, and role which are beyond the scope of this book (cf. Mackenzie, 2001).

Sequential Interdependence. This occurs when the output of one department (Department A) becomes the input of another department (Department B), and the output of this department becomes the output of another department (Department C), and so on as in the case of an automobile assembly plant. A similar situation can be found in manufacturing companies, for instance, where marketing analysis precedes design, design precedes engineering, and engineering precedes production. By way of example, in creating say a mouse mat, the raw material of rubber may be initially processed by one firm; this material then is delivered to another firm, which adds material, and cuts the mouse mat to size. These firms together demonstrate sequential interdependence.

Reciprocal Interdependence. Reciprocal interdependence is similar to sequential interdependence, but the output of say Department C (as in the above example) comes back to Department A and then the output of this department becomes the input of Department D. The assembly of a jet aircraft involves reciprocal interdependence. The management of this interdependence is the most complex.

Pooled Interdependence. This occurs where a relatively fluid and loose dependency is in place. Here each part of the business performs its own function with minimal interactions with other units. However, the combined success of all functions leads to the success of the entire organization. This type of interdependence exists in academia where a student can take appropriate courses from various departments so that he or she can graduate without much coordination of activities among the various departments.

The Organizational Environment

In stable environments, complex undertakings were broken down into simple tasks that could be done repetitively by semi-skilled, semi-literate workers with a minimum of training. In addition, product design periods were long, and product life cycles were even longer. Thus, organizations worked in a relatively stable environment, where both products and markets were relatively stable. A major factor influencing the emergence of new organizational types has been the dramatic changes in the business environment, when the entire world moved from the earlier system of long and stable production sequences and markets, to a rapidly changing world, in which not only markets, but also products had to change with extreme rapidity. Technological advances have been the primary cause for this shift, but other changes have included rapid globalization, and with it, the constant introduction into the marketplace of new tastes, demands, and cultural influences.

Mechanistic Design. In facing this new economic environment, one has to deal with one further division among organizational structures: the *mechanistic* and the *organic*. Mechanistic patterns of organizing date back to the eighteenth century and the beginnings of the industrial revolution, when the machine came to be seen as the ideal organizational model. Mechanistic organizations were structured as pyramidal hierarchies, where roles, responsibilities and procedures were clearly defined, and where power and authority inhered in position, not person. These organizations centralized decision-making at the top to preserve unity of command, and to impart a machine-like efficiency. Human beings in such structures were generally regarded as disposable or interchangeable, on the model of "interchangeable parts", introduced by the American inventor, Eli Whitney at the end of the eighteenth century. In addition, these "mechanistic hierarchies" were and remain divided horizontally between vertically structured "functions"—or specific work areas (e.g., legal, finance, marketing, design, engineering, production, etc.), usually headed by a "Vice President" at the executive level. Each functional area in a mechanistic organization operates as a distinct separate entity with direction given from the top. Such organizations continue to be hierarchical, stable, and predictable, and are best suited to the predictable and stable environments.

Organic Design. Organic organizational designs differ from mechanistic designs in that they are biological in conception, as proposed by Marx in *Das Kapital* and a century later by Bertalanffy (Schley, 2009). Organic organizations arose from multiple objectives. One of these was scalability—that is, the organization had to be able to grow in a cellular fashion, one cell at a time. A second objective was for the organization to be as open and responsive as possible to the environment. Thus, decision-making had to be decentralized, with authority given to the most appropriate person rather than to a distant figure at the top of a hierarchy. Alfred Sloan structured the early General Motors Corporation in this manner, and he viewed the essential problem of such organizations as the distribution of functions between the cells and the center (Schley, 2009). Decentralization requires that organic organizations have a high degree of integration—a feature often achieved through training and education. These organizations do not rely on a strict, scalar chain-of-command, with authority derived from rank or position, so individual roles may change, depending on the situation, and leadership may vary depending on expertise. Precisely because people operate within an accepted overarching framework inculcated through training and education, cellular organizations are adaptable and flexible in the face of changing environmental circumstances and opportunities.

Such organizations tend to be flat as opposed to steeply pyramidal and hierarchical. Organizations adopting this model include franchise organizations, particularly McDonalds, as well as transportation and distribution companies, such as Schneider National, Inc., and Swift Transportation, two of the largest American trucking firms. Each of these companies places special emphasis on training and education. Schneider National, in Green

Bay, Wisconsin, is renowned for its national, cold-weather driving facility, Swift for the high-quality driver training and safety programs offered at its Phoenix, Arizona, headquarters, and McDonald's for Hamburger University in suburban Chicago.

Variations on the organic structure include *circular*, *cellular*, and *socio-technical* systems (the latter pioneered by Eric Trist in British mines after World War II). Circular structures have been heavily influenced by Peter Senge (2006) and have been important in entrepreneurial and customer service organizations. Socio-technical systems have been proven to work well in industrial settings, but they cut away functional lines, and one of their standard features is that workers are trained in multiple functional areas. The distinguishing feature between mechanistic and organic designs is that the former are best suited for stable environments, while dynamic and turbulent environments require organic organizational designs.

Outcomes of Organizational Design

Appropriate organization designs are needed to enhance performance and other outcomes in organizations. Mechanistic organization designs are suitable for stable environments. As shown in the case study later in this chapter, the mechanistic design is grounded in stability and structure. It is relatively easy for an individual to see where he or she can next be promoted to due to the organization's hierarchical nature. Tall organizations have more of a hierarchy to climb than flat organizations, but are far less responsive to environmental changes. Span of control is important to consider in these types of design: the larger the span of control, the more challenging the management, and the greater the reliance on skilled, well-trained, educated personnel. Certain military spans of control, such as the structure of three (mostly in the U.S.), is highly dysfunctional from a business perspective, as it creates tall, steep hierarchies that do not adapt well to environmental changes.

In organic organizations, this hierarchical nature may be largely absent. Indeed, individuals who like a hierarchical working environment are not well-suited to this type of organization, which requires a serious degree of personal autonomy for workers, and where the chain-of-command is weak. The value of organic designs is that they can adapt quickly to a changing environment. Thus, individuals who crave spontaneity, change, responsibility, and the freedom to meet new demands are better suited to the organic organization.

Implications for Management

Organizational design is a crucial aspect of management. Organizations are complex social systems run by human beings. However, the socio-technical systems perspective promote the use of technology in organizations as a way of maintaining control and motivating staff. Typically, it is the underlying structures, both divisional and political, that are important. This format can be seen as either mechanistic or organic. Nevertheless, for organizations to survive in the 21st century this dichotomy may be rather simplistic. Recognizing the differences in approaches in organization design is crucial as some rely on simplification to arrive at a solution, whereas others absorb the complexity of the organization leading to a particular design.

Differentiation of staff in terms of whether there are supervisors or managers is important. Depending on the design adopted, it is essential that the personnel understand their roles and are integrated into the organization itself (Jones, 2012). For instance, in a management consultancy with an organic organization design on one project, person X may manage person Y. However, on a different project person Y may manage person X because that person has a more suitable skill set for that particular project. In a firm with a more mechanistic design, it is unlikely that individuals would swap places in terms of management and supervision. However, with this type of organization comes the stability of knowing who manages particular individuals.

Specialization and coordination are also vital for managers to ascertain in organizational design. A wide span of control may overstretch a manager if the personnel are poorly trained and educated and require excessive supervision. On the other hand, highly trained, highly skilled workers prefer to be free to do their jobs, so they will generally respond positively to a broad span of control. Indeed, a broad span of control over highly skilled, highly trained workers frees the manager to *manage*, not merely *supervise*.

How does the structure of the organization relate to specialization and how are the various work specializations coordinated? In a mechanistic design, specializations will be demarcated in a straightforward fashion, whereas in an organic design there may be considerable overlap or cross-functionality.

The last implication for management concerns organizational strategy and culture. Organizational culture relates to the values shared within the organization. These may be in part set by specific strategy. This strategy differs from organization to organization. However, it can be set along a particular course through mission statements and senior leadership (Jones, 2012). This is a key implication for management to understand where the organization is going and then set out the values of the organization that will take it towards its strategic direction.

Finally, some organizational structures are wholly unsuited for the kind of work involved. For instance, two very influential Americans, both of whom built significant organizations, Fred Smith of FedEx and George Bush, who built the Department of Homeland Security, were educated at Yale University in the 1970s, where mechanistic organizational hierarchies were being taught. Consequently, FedEx, one of the world's great distribution organizations, which ideally should be structured in a cellular fashion around a hub-and-spoke system (as are other first-rate distribution organizations such as Swift and Schneider National), was designed as a strict hierarchy with certain matrix elements in its IT division. How much more profitable would this world-class company be were it structured in a more logical fashion?

Similarly, the best intelligence and counter-intelligence organizations, such as the OSS and FBI in World War II, have been structured in a cellular fashion, to match the adaptability and changeability of their adversaries. Yet George Bush structured the Department of Homeland Security as a strict hierarchy and filled it out with military persons of a strict hierarchical mindset. This edifice thus seems wholly unsuited for its assigned task: dealing with and countering terrorist organizations deliberately constructed along cellular lines for adaptability and scalability.

Thus, the lesson of management history for organizational design and structures is that the modernist project—the development of the one organizational structure which would be attuned to every circumstance and function—failed. Instead, we live in a world where multiple organization designs exist, each proven effective in its own circumstances and in its own environment. Accordingly, those charged with designing and structuring organizations need to make their structural choices based on a multiplicity of considerations, rather than relying on a single hierarchical model, as too many leaders have done in the past, and continue to do today.

Questions for Students

1. What is an organization?
2. What is organizational design?
3. What is the rationale behind organizational design?
4. How do mechanistic and organic organizations differ?
5. How would you feel working in a matrix design organizational structure?

6. What problems may be faced in a virtual organization design?
7. What are the broad three approaches that can be taken in organization design?

Exercise: Organization Design

This simple exercise can be used to explore the inherent features of organization design.

Requirements

For this task, you will need access to a few sheets of paper to write down your thoughts.

Steps

1. Write down some ideas of what would be your perfect organization
2. Think about the industry it is involved with how would it look
3. Think about how many staff would be needed in this organization—don't forget about support functions such as Administration, Human Resources, Information Computer Technology, etc
4. Mark on another piece of paper how those people report—is it hierarchical or flat or is it more organic and less well defined?
5. Do you have a boss, and do they have a boss? Is there a chain of command? And if you don't have a boss do you report to share holders?
6. Mark on the organization paper how you report into your boss (if relevant)
7. Try and work out the best structure of the organization, is it mechanistic or organic
8. Think about how the organization may expand in the future

Further work

This exercise is an imaginative fun trip. However, it is useful as it may uncover your own career aspirations and what you want out of a job. In my own experience, I have found a HR director working for an organic organization absolutely detesting that of a hierarchical mechanistic firm. For further work, think about a career path you may take that allows you to fulfill your work aspirations. Make a plan that will take you along your career path in terms of the next year, the next 3 years and then the next 5 years. Share this plan with others to see their feedback.

Case: Organization Design in a Railway Firm

A railway company operated a network of 3 services across a small European country situated in Mainland Europe. These 3 services consisted of fast town to town services (Intercity), city and regional services. The services were considered to be rather poor through customer service reports. The regional service was considered to be really poor and even "cattle class" by customers. Part of the poor service was attributable to the attitudes of staff. Roles and responsibilities of individual job holders were not clearly defined. And a clear succession planning system, used to promote good workers, was not evident. This led to a certain amount of hostility especially between divisions such as estates management who operated the train stations and the train operations which included train drivers, mobile ticket inspectors, etc. The management was also seen as confusing as they were typically based in the estates division or in specialist departments such as engineering and maintenance. Promotion was seen as going into dead man's shoes and due to the high levels of role ambiguity staff motivation was low.

As a result, the organization hired a management consultancy with specialist skills in operating a railway and in human resources/work psychology. The purpose of the project was to produce clearly defined job roles using job design. The other aim of the project was to put forward an organization design that incorporated the newly defined job roles.

Organizational analysis was done taking a rational model type approach. This initially involved securing the commitment of key senior managers. By securing this senior management commitment to the project, the justification of conducting the organizational analysis was understood. As in many rational based designs the Analysis and Design of the solution was produced by the consultancy. The final report put forward solutions to remedy the existing issues within the client firm. The design was for a more mechanistic structure where individuals knew their reporting structures. It also enabled succession planning to be more transparent than in the previous organization that was more organic in nature.

The project was seen as a success by railway company who were then involved with the implementation and subsequent evaluation of the new organization design. Since this date the attitudes of the staff and the service of the railway has improved as noted through customer satisfaction surveys.

Suggestions for Further Reading

Beckman, S. L. (2009). Introduction to a symposium on organizational design. *California Management Review. 51* (4), 6–10.

Huber, G. P. (2011). Organizations: Theory, design, future. In S. Zedeck (Ed.), *APA handbook of industrial and organizational psychology*, Vol. 1: *Building and developing the organization* (pp. 117–160). Washington, DC: American Psychological Association.

Cropanzano, R. S., & Rupp, D. E. (2002). Organization structure and fairness perceptions: The moderating effects of organizational level. *Organizational Behavior and Human Decision Processes, 89,* 881–905.

References

Hackman, J. R., & Oldham, G. R. (1975) Development of the Job Diagnostic Survey. *Journal of Applied Psychology*, 60, 159–170

Jones, G. (2012). *Organizational theory, design, and change.* Upper Saddle River, NJ: Pearson Education.

Lawrence, P. R. (2001). The contingency approach to organization design. In R. T. Golembiewski (Eds.), *Handbook of organizational behavior* (2nd ed., pp. 7–17). New York: Marcel Dekker.

Lawrence, P. R., & Lorsch, J. W. (1967). *Organization and environment.* Homewood, IL: Irwin-Dorsey.

Mackenzie, K. D. (2001). The organization of organizations. *International Journal of Organizational Analysis, 9,* 116–148.

Oldham, G. R., & Hackman, J. R. (2010). Not what it was and not what it will be: The future of job design research. *Journal of Organizational Behavior*, *31,* 463–479.

Olmsted, B., & Smith, S. (1994). *Creating a flexible workplace* (2nd ed.). New York: AMACOM.

Parker, S. K. (2014). Beyond motivation: Job and work design for development, health, ambidexterity, and more. *Annual Review of Psychology. 65*, 661–691.

Schley, D. G. (2009) Origins and development of the cellular organization. In M. A. (Ed.), *Current topics in management* (Vol. 14, pp. 119–147). New Brunswick, NJ: Transaction Publishers.

Senge, P. M. (2006) *The fifth discipline: The art and practice of the learning organization.* New York: Random House.

14. Project Management

Don G. Schley
Colorado Technical University

Brook Henderson
Colorado Technical University

Project management has become the "new management" approach of the technological world. In the rapidly changing modern technological marketplace, almost all employees, both technical and non-technical, will find themselves drawn into project work. Thus, employees need to know project management basics in order to survive and to be effective within their organizations. Two generations ago, they only needed to know the basics of classical hierarchical management—their technical proficiency, and the rules for operating under a scalar chain of command, as one finds in the military. Today's employees therefore need to understand the dynamics of working in a matrix organization and the pitfalls of dual reporting. They need to know that while answering to a functional manager, they may also have to work for a project manager. The project context, in fact, will be much more common to them than the classical or functional context, where one simply had to come to work and do the same job every day. Understanding project management basics, then, constitutes a critical survival skill in today's job market.

Nature of Project Management

Definition

Aimed at delivering quality outcomes in shortened periods of time while maintaining strict cost controls and achieving high quality and customer satisfaction, "project management," or PM, is an emerging management discipline. This discipline involves the management of temporary (or time-constrained, meaning there are definitive start and end dates) undertakings to deliver a product or service on time, at budget, and according to specific and pre-defined quality and performance requirements.

Project Management vs. Traditional Management

A basic distinction has to be made here between the temporary work of project management and the ongoing operations of classical or traditional management. To begin, there is history. Functional or classical management was born with the industrial revolution in England in 1750, and it was gradually refined from there until it reached its zenith 1960s. This type of management was a product of the industrial revolution, so its focus was on ongoing operations and delivery of products with very long life cycles, produced by having semi-skilled, semi-literate workers do simple, repetitive tasks to create some complex finished products. For instance, the Oldsmobile OHV 350 cubic inch V–8 was produced in various configurations from the 1940s until sometime in the 1990s—a 40-year-plus production run! Ford's Bronco ran 10 years in its original configuration, and 20 years in the "full-size Bronco" configuration (1977–1996). Classical management was thus perfected for industrial management, but it did not readily adapt to the fast-changing world of modern product development, where technological products may be obsolete within 18 months or less of entering the market. Consequently, project management, with its adaptability to changing demands of customers and markets has emerged as the preferred management discipline of the technology sector.

Project management differs from traditional management in other ways, too. For instance, projects utilize a higher caliber of personnel from the traditional, semi-skilled, semi-literate workers of the industrial era, where workers were trained in and limited to working in a single area or craft (welder, riveter, pipefitter, driller, press operator, mechanic, etc.). Instead, today's project workers are often proficient in one or more complex skill sets. They are also highly trained and collaborate as members of "cross-functional teams." This approach allows project teams to achieve previously unattainable efficiencies in performance., and to find quality, holistic solutions to project problems that would not be possible in the more fragmented, or "siloed" traditional environment. Highly efficient, cross-functional project teams, comprised of multi-disciplinary experts, are a primary reason all kinds of organizations are coming to prefer project management to the classical management approach. The results are seen in the efficiency and reliability of many of the most advanced new car models, such as Honda and Toyota, which have been employing project management methodologies for over a decade. All of these advances are achieved within the threefold constraint—time, cost, quality. Resources, and even customer satisfaction constitute further constraints (or limitations) under which PMs may work. Modern projects managed in this way stand in contrast to the "command economy" projects of the pre-modern world, when potentates of various sorts initiated projects and drove them through regardless of resource, cost or other constraints.

Additionally, distinctive project management methodologies were pioneered from the 1940s through the 1960s, mostly among U.S. Department of Defense contractors. These methods included scheduling techniques and a special emphasis on risk assessment using brainstorming and controlled surveys of expert opinion (Delphi method). Further techniques emerged in the succeeding years, especially with the Japanese auto industry's emphasis on TQM, or Total Quality Management (Morris, 2013). Thus did project management emerge as a separate management discipline with its own methods and with its own unique demand for quality technical human resources.

Typology of Project Management

True to project management's eclectic nature, its typology can follow several lines—by industry (aerospace and defense, commercial aviation, manufacturing, energy, IT, etc.), by organizational structure, or internally, according to the five processes and ten knowledge areas prescribed by the Project Management Institute (PMI; 2013) in its definitive manual, *The Guide to the Project Management Body of Knowledge* (PMBOK). Since a typology of project management by industry would be very complicated, this text will lay out project management in two other ways: according to the PMI's processes and knowledge areas, and according to organizational structure.

The Five Project Management Processes

The PMI identifies five project management processes, which, while overlapping, are managed horizontally across the project, from start to finish. They are initiating, planning, executing, monitoring and controlling, and closing. The PMI has overlooked, however, the critical pre-initiation phase (Morris, 2013).

Pre-Initiation. Really large projects—mega-projects—begin with an idea. Because they consume vast amounts of money and public resources, mega-projects should go through multiple stages of evaluation before initiation. These are identified in the USBOR's definitive *Earth Manual* (2005) as *reconnaissance, feasibility,* and *specification*. A *reconnaissance* (or *pre-feasibility*) *study* involves examining the project through available public documents. If, after a thorough professional review, the project appears to be feasible, the project sponsor (the party or organization developing the project) may spend a large sum of money (often in the neighborhood of $5 million or more) to commission a practical, on-ground, engineering-based *feasibility study*. This additional cost is justified because, if well done, the feasibility study will steer the sponsor clear of wasting further funds on a non-feasible venture, while identifying advantages of a beneficial project. The engineering work carried out during the feasibility study—seismic testing, soil testing, surveying, and the like—should also result in the production of real project specifications: that is, how the project must be technically built if it is to succeed, and the first had cost and performance figures. *Reconnaissance, feasibility,* and *specification* are the necessary preliminary steps to major project initiation. Failed projects, such as the Denver International Airport and Boston's Big Dig, never went through these steps.

Initiation. Every project has a beginning point—an action, cause or event—that sets it in motion, or gets it started. Without initiation, there would be no project. Once the project has been deemed feasible through a formal, technical evaluation process, the project gets its first formal description (the preliminary project scope statement) which is incorporated into an initiating document called the project "charter." This document, signed by a senior executive (the project "sponsor", defines the project, designates the project manager, and authorizes him or her to begin building a team, drawing funds, and planning the project. In many cases in the business world, the project charter is replaced by a contract or Statement of Work (S.O.W.) with the firm that is being authorized to carry out the project. In construction, this firm (or person) would be the general contractor, whether the project is a new home, a shopping mall, a factory, or a highway.

Planning. Once initiated, a project enters the planning phase. Detailed planning lies at the heart of successful project management. During the massive COSMIX project in Colorado Springs, the Project Manager and the Project Engineer negotiated with the sponsor, Colorado Department of Transportation (CDOT) for six extra months of detailed planning time. Although the contractor thus began executing the project 6 months later than anticipated, the extra detailed planning time allowed the crews to complete the project 1 year and four days earlier than the contract required. The detailed planning time actually allowed the project manager to cut eighteen months off the overall project schedule, saving millions of dollars in the process. The US Army, a long-time sponsor of quality projects, has a saying about the importance of project planning: "Proper Prior Planning Prevents Poor Performance." This saying is known as "the six Ps." Another commonly used saying among PMs is "failing to plan means planning to fail." Both proverbs make the same point.

Execution. Once planned, the project work must be carried out according to plan. This process is called "execution." Generally, execution begins with a "kick-off meeting" between the sponsor, the project manager, the project team, and all the important persons and parties who have a vested interest, or "stake" in the project. These parties are called "stakeholders." The kick-off meeting is designed to make sure that everyone is on board with the project and is committed to project success. After this meeting, the project manager and project team set to work directing and carrying out the work of the project.

Monitoring and Controlling. Every project must be monitored for adherence to standards of schedule, budget and quality performance. Project personnel must be on hand to ensure that the project cost and schedule targets are being met, and shortcuts that would impair the project's quality are not being taken. Monitoring and controlling, including managing and controlling project change, are among the most difficult aspects of project management.

Closing. Every project must be brought to completion, and this process begins during the latter part of the execution phase. Work must be inspected and signed off on, contractors and subcontractors must be paid, formal approval and acceptance must be received from the sponsor or customer, and all final documents must be signed. Proper closing is necessary to ensure that all issues are resolved prior to closing, and that after closing, there are no unexpected problems. On a successful major project, such as COSMIX, the closing may be marked by an official closing ceremony, attended by all the major stakeholders, and even public officials such as the Mayor, the Governor of the State, County Commissioners, and other important stakeholders, contributors and participants.

The Project Management Knowledge Areas

The PMI, through its *PMBOK*, specifies ten "knowledge areas" that a project manager must master in order to carry out projects successfully. These knowledge areas, with their respective special tools are:

Integration: defining, unifying, and coordinating the project processes. The project charter is the basic document of project integration.

Scope: defining and specifying the requirements, activities, tasks and work packages (a work package is the smallest unit of work that can be defined, staffed, and costed) necessary to complete the project successfully.

Time: using the activities, tasks and work packages defined under "scope" to build a detailed schedule to complete the project requirements on time.

Cost: making estimates based on the work items from the scope statement, and using the estimated durations of each activity, task, or work package.

Quality: specifying the level of quality required to satisfy the customer and meet contractual obligations, determining whether the organizational process are in place to achieve this level of quality, and monitoring the project to ensure that is level of quality is met for each of the project deliverables.

Human Resource Management: ensuring that the organization has the proper personnel to complete the project work on time, within budget, and to the prescribed level of quality.

Communications: building a communications plan to ensure that all stakeholders are consulted & informed properly and in a timely fashion, and making sure the means are in place to carry out timely and effective communications.

Risk: assessing both positive and negative risks—opportunities and threats—and planning effective steps to manage these, and updating the project cost estimates accordingly.

Procurement: determining what must be purchased for the project, the methods necessary to make these purchases in a timely fashion for project completion, and revising the cost estimates based on this information.

Stakeholder Management: identifying the persons, groups or entities that affect the project, or who are affected by it; analyzing their expectations of and potential impacts on the project, and managing these, and the communication modes and strategies required for project success. Stakeholder management was formerly a subset of communications.

Synopsis: Processes and Knowledge Areas

Mastering the discipline of project management thus requires three different and complex tracks of thinking: (a) acquiring some grasp of project management theory, (b) learning the five process groups and the ten knowledge areas, and how they work (the execution–delivery approach), and (c) spending time in the field managing projects (historically, project management has relied on an apprenticeship system to develop project management talent).

Project Management and Organizational Structures

Despite the demands of the technological era, nearly all companies still employ organizational structures based on the classical hierarchy and its methods, so most project managers find themselves working in some form of hierarchy. When a project manager (PM) is working in a strictly classical organization, arranged according to vertically aligned functional areas or silos (such as design, engineering, production, finance, contracting, marketing and the like), that PM is laboring within a hierarchical "functional" organization. When lateral lines of communication are formalized across the functional "silos," the PM is working in some kind of a "matrix." If the PM is in charge of his or her own processes, with control over his or her own budget, resources, team, etc., that PM is working in a "projectized" organization. Finally, the PM may work within a composite organization that shares the features of both a functional organization (in which the PM is merely a scheduler, expediter or "lead" working under a functional manager) and a strong matrix, in which the PM has the authority from the Project Management Office to draw resources from across functional lines. A further breakdown follows.

Functional Organization

Functional organizations are separated into vertically aligned work areas, or "silos," each controlled by a "functional manager." The functional manager

(FM) holds the legitimate authority (that is, the legal authority to make decisions, including budgeting, hiring and firing) required to manage and control his or her specific area of work and expertise. In a functional organization, projects are carried out within single functional areas, with the project manager (PM) reporting directly to the functional manager, and having little to no authority or control over resources or the budget. Here the PM serves only part-time, with any PM staff holding part-time status as well.

Weak Matrix

A "weak matrix" is a functional organization which has made some formal provision for cross-functional project work—in other words, for the project manager can draw resources from one or more functional areas, thus working "cross-functionally." Here the PM has nominal or limited authority and resource availability, no control over budget, and is still part-time, with a part-time project staff. The difference between a "weak matris" and a functional organization is that the PM will enjoy limited support (see chapter on power bases) from a project sponsor—an executive higher up in the organization—who authorizes the PM to form the project team and draw funds for the project.

Balanced Matrix

The balanced matrix expands the PM's authority and resource availability from the weak matrix and allows some shared budgetary control. In addition, the PM will hold that position full-time, though the PM staff will still serve part-time. Still, the PM's authority in a balanced matrix is held only by reference to a sponsor higher up in the organization—hopefully high enough up to command respect from the functional managers and sufficient to provide the resources and funds necessary to ensure project success.

Strong Matrix

This structure is the first where the PM has legitimate authority to manage and control his or her own projects. The strong matrix achieves this result by incorporating a "Project Management Office" headed by a "Manager of

Project Managers" as a separate functional area. Thus, the PMs answer to their own functional manager who holds formal, legitimate power alongside the other functional managers in the organization. The strong matrix imparts to the PM a moderate to high level of power and resource availability, total control over the budget, and a full-time position and staff. Here the PM holds the legitimate authority to draw the resources necessary to ensure project success, so that the project does not depend solely on referential power for success.

Composite Organization

Composite organizations include a Project Management Office or Manager of Project Managers, but also have projects carried out on a functional basis. Thus, such organizations follow the lines of a strong matrix, but still allow for projects to be carried out within individual functional areas, where a "project coordinator", expediter, or scheduler works under the direct supervision of a functional manager. High-tech companies such as Oracle and FedEx exhibit very strong functional characteristics as well as pronounced commitments to cross-functional project management. Many such organizations are built *ad hoc*, with executives implementing various structural elements to cope with the immediate demands of company performance, and without consideration to the most efficient structural form.

Projectized Organization

The projectized organization is a creature of the construction industry. There, the "site superintendent" is usually the *de facto* project manager. In these organizations, the *de facto* project manager holds almost total authority over the project, resources and budget, while holding a full-time position and managing a full-time staff. Construction project management has its own professional organizations outside the PMI, such as the Construction Specifications Institute (CSI), the American Institute of Architects (AIA), and produces its own reference works as well. These latter include the US Bureau of Reclamation's (USBOR) *Earth Manual* (2005), and a host of other works.

Influence of Structural Types on Project Management Practice

The functional, matrixed and composite organizations are found largely in the defense and technology industries, while the projectized organization remains the standard of the construction industry. One reason for this dichotomy is the fact that construction lives and dies by individual projects, whereas in these other industries, projects co-exist alongside ongoing repetitive operations. An anomaly of construction project management is that the *de facto* PM remains the site superintendent, in whose hands all authority rests, while the site superintendent may have several assistants who are termed "project managers" and whose real duties are those of a scheduler or expediter, not of a true project manager.

The much higher level of success in construction projects versus defense and technology projects derives directly from the much greater power over budget, schedule and resources wielded by construction project managers ("site superintendents") in comparison with their counterparts in these other industries where project authority is merely referential (for project failure rates see, Anbari, 2005). Where major construction projects fail, a common feature appears to be the lack of an empowered PM on site. Another is a lack of proper planning. Although Kerzner (2013) advocates a systems approach to project management, actual organizational approaches are in reality traditional, piecemeal and *ad hoc*, outside of the large-scale construction projects that have been the historical *forte* of project management. Dysfunctional carryovers from functional management still occur in project management, from the classical management methodology of conflict resolution (cf. Rahim, 2011) to the preference for functional structures and weak matrices, which disempower the PM.

Other Project Management Issues

Skills that are basic to Project Management. Project managers have much in common with traditional functional managers, but they also must have or develop other skills if they are to be successful. First among these is the ability to make sound, on-the-spot decisions about the work that actually must be done for a project to succeed. Second is the ability to develop accurate cost estimates based on real-world experience and knowledge of the project area. Software programs exist in both construction and IT, for example, that allow a fairly accurate development of cost estimates. Third is the ability to build a realistic schedule and hold one's work teams to that schedule. Fourth is the ability to identify, assess and manage risks.

Soft Skills and Project Management. Besides mastering these technical management skills, the greatest challenge project managers face is the demand for "soft", hands-on people skills. Historically, construction project managers were engineers and masters of the hard or technical skills, who then had to use people skills to get work done on-site. With the rise of the technological and defense industries, work became much more technical, and technicians were required to maintain such a high level of proficiency in their own skill sets that project management duties increasingly fell to "generalists" with superior "soft" skills.

The problem here is that "soft skills" managers often come aboard who are not conversant in the technical issues, and who thus cannot make sound judgments regarding technical issues in their projects. This reality has created a split in professional opinion as to whether a project manager should be a technician with good soft skills, or a good soft skills manager who was conversant with technology. This dichotomy still exists, and first-rate project managers of both stripes can be found.

Negotiating is another necessary project management skill, but the ultimate soft skill in the project environment is probably conflict management. This is a critical and emerging discipline which is at odds with the older classical method of conflict resolution (Rahim, 2011). Practicing project managers need experience and training in conflict management, because good conflict management can increase organizational and project performance, while poor conflict management, or simply "conflict resolution", can result in negative project performance. The introduction of *stakeholder management* in the 5th edition of the *PMBOK* as a separate knowledge area illustrates the increasingly high value placed on soft skills.

Cross-Cultural Issues. American management culture is much more attuned to time concerns than other cultures; thus, American project managers may find themselves frustrated when working in other countries and cultures where time does not have the same value. Africa and the Middle East afford good examples. In addition, project work overseas may require the payment of bakshish (or a gratuity; in American law understood as a bribe) to advance the project's progress through public approval processes—a reality strictly forbidden by the Foreign Corrupt Practices Act (the FCPA; cf. Marinelli, 2007). American project managers will certainly confront practices outside the US with a certain degree of moral shock.

In addition, international project management requires a fluency in both language and culture, skills woefully lacking throughout modern American culture. Foreign currency exchange rates today fluctuate widely, making it possible that a properly and accurately costed overseas project may in fact run over budget owing to changes in the currency rates. Other pitfalls also exist, including the necessity, even in some Western European cultures, of respecting class lines American project managers often operate with a high degree of social familiarity with their workers, and this situation is not universally accepted across cultural lines. Accordingly, international project management requires education and training in language and culture, personal sensitivity on the part of the project manager to other cultures and their practices, as well as technical project management expertise. Thus, the threefold constraint of time, cost and performance has to be met in the overseas context within various cultural constraints as well. Historically, high-quality international project companies, such as Bechtel Corporation, have maintained world-class cultural training programs for their employees.

Outcomes of Project Management

Properly implemented, project management results in better enterprise planning, more precisely defined projects, more accurate and manageable cost estimates, better and more forthright risk assessment, and superior control over work and schedule outcomes. These outcomes can be seen in the great and successful infrastructure projects of the 20th century United States: the Hoover Dam, the Golden Gate Bridge, the Empire State building, and other undertakings. Quality project management is also employed in the successful, on-time, to-budget and specification delivery of every other kind of enterprise, from the building of a computer hardware assembly facility in Moorpark, California, to the construction of Toyota's giant light truck facility in San Antonio, Texas, to the construction of large commercial warehouses, to the building of residential houses. When a homeowner contracts with a builder for a custom home, every aspect of the work must be tightly managed to a pre-approved amount in a fixed construction loan. Moreover, each feature of the residence must also comply with the local building codes, and the schedule must be perfectly aligned with the purchaser's need to vacate the present residence and move into the new residence without the need to spend a week or two and a thousand dollars more in a hotel awaiting final construction to be completed. Every successful fast-food chain, such as Sonic, McDonald's and a host of others, depends on world-class quality project management to get new stores up and operating on time and within budget. So does every capable custom homebuilder.

The modern auto industry, led by Toyota and Honda, turned long ago to project management methodologies in order to keep up with increasing pressures to turn out new models of vehicles more quickly and frequently. Microsoft has been working with the US automotive industry for more than a decade and has established the Microsoft Automotive and Industrial Equipment Solution Group to facilitate cross-functional processes from new model design to communications among teams. Nissan and PSA Peugot-Citroen have also benefited from the introduction of these methodologies (Gale, 2011). The methodology of "management-by-projects" has long been an integrated part of the Toyota Production System (Towill, 2010) Thus, project management continues to develop alongside and even within the traditional industries it supports.

Where project management processes are less stringently applied, entire chains may fail, or entire corporate expansions, such as Rite Aid in Colorado. With failed mega-projects, such as Denver International Airport (DIA), the negative outcomes can be staggering—450% cost overruns (estimated at $1.2 bn, delivered at $5.4 bn!), failed systems throughout, and years of delays while debt piles up. Such disastrous projects rob deserving, well-planned projects of desperately needed funds, and deny the host community the prosperity that a well-managed project would have brought.

Where project management was good, but where organizational and cultural difficulties led to large-scale delays, such as the English–French Channel Tunnel project, the outcome may be a technologically successful result with extreme long–term financial burdens on the investors. The optimal development of modern infrastructure—transportation, electronic communications, water storage and conveyance, power generation, etc.—depends on successful project management. Boondoggle projects, with their huge cost overruns and systemic failures, burn up funds that could have gone to better planned, better specified, better costed and better managed projects that would have yielded far higher economic value to the community footing the bill. In all cases, effective project management leads to better quality, lower costs, more rapidly delivered outcomes, and greater capital reserves for investment in further undertakings, and thus increased levels of prosperity.

In the Information Technology (IT) sector, where software project management remains its own subdiscipline (Caulfield, Veal, & Maj, 2011), PM works well where applied. One serious impediment here seems to be the difficulty of communication among technologists, who seem to a large degree to despise the "soft" skills of communication, conflict management and negotiation—the bread-and-butter of good project management.

In every project management sector, project risk management depends on a project manager's first-rate skills in communication and in conflict management (Rahim, 2011). In the defense sector, the disjunction between the vertical silos of the organizations and the lateral communications and work of cross-functional teams remains an ever-present reality (cf. Viaene & Van den Bunder, 2011). In change management, project management offers a disciplined approach to initiating, planning, executing, and monitoring and controlling change processes. Here what is needed is executive attention and follow-through (cf. Senaratne & Sexton, 2008). Thus, project management remains a discipline in flux.

Implications for Management

Project management is distinct from classical management in that project management processes are managed horizontally across organizations, while classical management is pushed down through an organization's vertical chain of command. Project management also relies on a much less rigid, far better trained, and more flexible workforce than classical management. Project workers tend to be goal-oriented, rather than task oriented, as they are generally moving from one project to another. Accordingly, those who work well in a classical management environment may not do well in a project context, and good project personnel may find classical environments too boring or restrictive.

Newer applications of project management include using project management methodologies in change management programs, and in conjunction with Six Sigma programs (Anbari, 2005). To improve project outcomes, four basic steps can be taken. First, every project requires a strong sponsor in the executive suite. Second, if the project manager is going to get the buy-in of the critical functional managers, the project must have a clear tie to the organization's strategic plan. Third, every successful project begins with a detailed project plan. Fourth, that plan must be followed. In most cases of failed projects, all or some of these elements are missing. The lack of clear-cut, detailed planning is pandemic; but even worse is the fact that once a project has been planned, the chances are that no one will follow that plan. Seeing that each of these four elements is secured within the corporate culture can improve financial performance 40%–50% per element!

Questions for Students

1. How does project management differ from classical management?
2. What personal characteristics may be required of project personnel that might not be important in classical operational personnel?
3. How and why did project management emerge as a separate management discipline/
4. Describe some of the unique management tools utilized in project management.

Exercise for Students

Using the following project scenario, and following the process sequence laid out in the *PMBOK* (PMI, 2013, p. 61), the instructor helps students form 3–4 person teams. Each team will then develop a basic project plan to complete this project, including a scope statement with defined deliverables and tasks, a schedule, a cost estimate, a communications plan, and a risk assessment plan. Students are encouraged to obtain real-world estimates for this project.

Case: The Rehab-to-Rent Project

The meltdown in the housing market in 2008 and 2009 led to millions of homeowners across the U.S. losing their homes and being forced into the rental market. The US thus faces an era of declining home ownership and increased rental demand which will continue until at least 2019. Some estimates are that as many as a million former homeowners will be entering the rental market each year until 2020. Accordingly, the US housing market remains depressed, and houses generally do not command the prices they would have six years ago. In this context, houses are relatively inexpensive to acquire (by historical standards) but are difficult to sell at a substantial profit. Therefore, buying distressed properties and rehabilitating (or "rehabbing") them for rent is a good business strategy. It also requires project management skills.

The project exercise for this class then is as follows. With a maximum budget of $100,000 to acquire and rehabilitate a property to rent, each student team of 3–4 persons needs to locate a real local property that is distressed (undervalued in the market and that has not been able to sell), inspect it, decide what work needs to be done to rent it out (determine the project scope), assess the project costs (establish a budget), and plan and schedule the work. The instructor shall assist the students in locating properties, in determining what work needs to be done, at what cost, and over what period of time. Project deliverables will be as follows:

1. Project charter, identifying the property, giving a preliminary project scope statement, a rough order of magnitude estimate (50% over to 25% under real costs), a projected timeline, and an authorization from the instructor to proceed. The instructor should be prepared to provide a real-world critique of each project charter;

2. Finalized project scope statement, coupled with real costs attached and a final, realistic cost estimate;

3. Project schedule (all at least 30 days to close the purchase on the property; project timeline begins the day the property is scheduled to close; fix-up should take no more than 30 days and should be done in such a way that the property can be shown to potential renters after two weeks).

4. Project communications plan: should include primary, secondary and tertiary modes of communication chosen, and a RACI chart.

5. Project risk plan: should include a prioritized risk register with the highest impact risks (in dollar amounts) first, the lowest last, not to exceed 10 identifiable risks.

6. Executive summary: written at the conclusion of planning, but the first document presented, outlines the project with its costs and potential financial benefits, including an estimated Return on Investment (ROI).

   - Overall, the plan should employ the methodologies and techniques that are taught in this course. The *PMBOK* (PMI, 2013) should serve as a basic reference, plus any other relevant materials or templates that can be legally accessed. Outside materials are acceptable as long as they are pertinent to this exercise. All sources need to be cited. Students will conclude the exercise with a formal presentation of the project plan by each team to the rest of the class (briefing not to exceed 20 minutes).

Suggestions for Further Reading

Fuller, P. A., Dainty, A. R. J., &Thorpe, T. (2011). Improving project learning: A new approach to lessons learnt. *International Journal of Managing Projects in Business, 4* (1), 118–136.

Kerzner, H. (2009) *Project management case studies.* Hoboken, NJ: Wiley.

Morris, P.W. G. & Hough, G. (1988) *The anatomy of major projects.* Hoboken, NJ: Wiley.

Prawdzik, B. (2011). Problems facing our energy infrastructure. *Yale Economic Review, 7* (1), 41–43.

References

Anbari, F. T. (2005). Innovation, project management, and Six Sigma method. *Current Topics in Management, 10,* 106–116.

Bertalanffy, L. (1950). An outline of general system theory. *British Journal for the Philosophy of Science, 1,* 134–165.

Bertalanffy, L. (1969). *General systems theory.* New York: George Braziller.

Bredillet, C. (2008). Exploring research in project management: Nine schools of project management research (Part 6). *The Project Management Journal.* 39 (3), 2–5.

Bureau of Reclamation, US Department of the Interior. (2005). *Earth manual: A guide to the use of soils as foundations and as construction materials for hydraulic structures.* Honolulu: University Press of the Pacific.

Caulfield, C., Veal, D., & Maj, S. (2011). Teaching software engineering project management: A novel approach for software engineering programs. *Modern Applied Science, 5* (5), 87–104.

Gale, S. (2011, January). Driving innovation. *PM Network,* pp. 10–11.

Kerzner, H. (2013). *Project management: A systems approach to planning, scheduling and controlling* (11th ed.). Hoboken, NJ: Wiley.

Marinelli, M. (2007, September). Is U.S. business hampered by foreign corrupt practices ban? *World Trade,* p. 8.

Morris, P. W. G. (2013). *Reconstructing project management.* Chichester, West Sussex: Wiley.

Project Management Institute (2013). *A guide to the project management body of knowledge* (PMBOK) (5th ed.). New Town, PA: Project Management Institute.

Rahim, M. A. (2011). *Managing conflict in organizations* (4th ed.). New Brunswick, NJ: Transaction.

Senaratne, S., & Sexton, M. (2008). Managing construction project change: a knowledge management perspective. *Construction Management and Economics, 26* (12), 1303.

Towill, D. R. (2010). Industrial engineering the Toyota production system. *Journal of Management History, 16,* 327–345.

Turner, J. R. (2006) Towards a theory of project management: The nature of the project. *International Journal of Project Management, 24* (1), 1–3.

Turner, J. R. (2006) Towards a theory of project management: The nature of the project governance and project management. *International Journal of Project Management, 24* (2), 93–95.

Turner, J. R. (2006). Towards a theory of project management: the functions of project management. *International Journal of Project Management, 24* (3), 187–189.

Turner, J. R. (2006) Towards a theory of project management: the nature of the functions of project management. *International Journal of Project Management, 24* (4), 277–279.

Turner, J. R. (2009) *The handbook of project-based management* (3rd ed.). London: McGraw-Hill.

Viaene, S., & Van den Bunder, A. (2011).The secrets to managing business analytics projects. *MIT Sloan Management Review, 53* (1), 65–69.

15. Managing Multinational Enterprises

In Hyeock Lee
Loyola University Chicago

As the global economy continues to expand, the demand for managerial knowledge in international business is higher than ever and expected to increase. The United Nations (UN) has identified over 60,000 multinational enterprises (MNEs) worldwide. The United States has 5,331 foreign-affiliated firms operating, and there are almost 25,000 U.S. firms in overseas markets which generate 10 million jobs and $4.2 trillion of revenues abroad. Virtually every management decision made today is influenced by international events. As a result, only managers who understand the diversity of international business/management can be valuable participants in this era of global business.

Nature of MNEs

Definition

MNEs are defined as companies conducting business transactions across national borders—between their home country and host countries (Rugman & Collinson, 2009). It should be noted that three key components in the definition of MNEs represent important aspects of international business/management. First, main objective of MNEs is to maximize *profits*. MNEs attempt to provide low-cost and/or high-quality goods and services in the world market, so as to attract potential customers willing to pay their asking prices in exchange for the benefits of their goods and services. Second, such business transactions between companies and customers must take place *across national borders*. If a firm's production and consumption of goods and services occur within a single country, it is not an MNE; it is simply a domestic business conducted by purely domestic enterprises. Third, as a result of transactions taking place across national borders, the company's entire business operations should be distributed across at least two different countries—a *home country* and *host countries*—for it to be an MNE. A home country is where MNEs are headquartered, and host countries are where MNEs locate their foreign subsidiaries for either manufacturing or service activities that can serve foreign local customers. Therefore, the MNE headquarters coordinates the value chain activities of its foreign subsidiaries, which are distributed across one or multiple host countries, in the most efficient manner.

MNEs conduct business transactions across national borders through two primary types of activities: trade and foreign direct investment (FDI). Trade is defined as the flow of goods and services from one country to the other. When goods and services are produced in a home country and consumed in host countries, this process of international activities is called export. Import is the opposite flow of goods and services—they are transported from foreign host countries to the home country where they are consumed. FDI, on the other hand, is a flow of *funds*, not final goods or services, from one country to another. As a result, outbound FDI implies a flow of investment funds from a home country to host countries where the physical production of goods and services takes place, whereas inbound FDI is the opposite. It should be noted that among over 60,000 MNEs, the 500 firms on the *Fortune Global 500* list account for about 50 percent of world's trade, both exports and imports, and over 80 percent of the world's FDI.

Characteristics of MNEs

MNEs strive to maximize their profits by going beyond their domestic borders to further enhance their profitability from foreign operations and consumers. By operating in foreign countries, of which they are unfamiliar (e.g., business practices, regulations, laws, geography, language and culture), MNEs take on major characteristics that set them apart from purely domestic enterprises: (1) liability of foreignness; (2) firm-specific advantages; and (3) country-specific advantages.

Liability of Foreignness. MNEs incur additional costs when entering into new foreign markets because foreign markets usually carry more risk than their domestic countries due to differences between the home and host countries, which Ghemawat (2001) describes as "four distances."

Cultural Distance. This is due to differences in language, cultural traditions and perceptions, and religious values in the host countries that may create barriers for MNEs' marketing operations aimed to target foreign customers, resulting in additional downstream expenses.

Institutional Distance. When MNEs enter into transitional economies during a country's transition from one political or economic structure to another, such as from communism to capitalism, institutional differences in political, regulational, and/or administrative regimes arise, called *institutional distance*, which add to MNEs' adjustment costs for cultivating new foreign markets.

Geographic Distance. By distributing their value chain activities across different geographic regions and countries, MNEs take on additional transportation costs to physically deliver their intermediaries and their final products/services from one location to the other, called *geographic distance*.

Economic Distance. When MNEs based in developed countries enter into developing countries to expand their markets, they often must devise different business models for these countries, because their new foreign customers may have different purchase patterns and behaviors due to their limited income and spending power which Ghemawat (2001) calls *economic distance*.

The diverse types of distances between different countries generally produce additional costs for MNE operations in unfamiliar foreign markets, which Zaheer (1995) calls as the *liability of foreignness*.

Firm-specific Advantages. To counteract the liability of foreignness, MNEs must possess something uniquely internalized within their boundaries—such as core resources and capabilities. Otherwise, MNEs cannot outperform domestic competitors in host countries, and, as a result, they may not survive in this increasingly competitive world market. These core resources and capabilities are called *firm-specific advantages* (FSAs) in the international business, and they are hard-to-replicate, tangible and intangible assets over which successful MNEs should maintain control (Rugman, 2005). FSAs may come from upstream value chain activities of MNEs such as R&D investment, innovation, and manufacturing technologies, and, they may also originate from downstream activities of the vertical value chains such as marketing expenses, brand names, and distribution channels among others. In short, FSAs are fundamental sources of superior competitive advantage and translate into higher performance for MNEs operating in seemingly risky, unfamiliar foreign markets.

Country-specific Advantages. In addition to the firm-specific factors, successful MNEs also exploit country-specific factors to their advantage for building superior capabilities in the global market by conducting trans-border businesses across countries. This means that, when MNEs lack a certain FSAs for their successful foreign operations, they attempt to compensate by securing unique access to certain location-specific assets available only in certain parts of the world, called *country-specific advantages* (CSAs). Dunning (1998) categorized them into four groups based on different objectives of MNEs' foreign investment.

Natural Resources. The first group includes natural resources such as oil and gas, timber, copper, diamonds, a cheap labor force. In this case, MNEs carry out FDI in foreign countries that have the physical, financial or human resources that they need. Therefore, one precondition for this natural resource-seeking foreign operation is that the host country government allows foreign investors to access these resources.

Market Size. This is the second type of CSAs in which countries with a large market would prompt MNEs to situate their subsidiaries in these foreign countries. Therefore, this type of CSAs would be the presence of customers willing and able to purchase final products and services provided by MNEs.

Strategic Assets. This include knowledge- or reputation-based resources such as scientific knowledge in the upstream end, marketing knowledge in the downstream end, and administrative knowledge or reputational resources possessed by other counterparts in certain host countries. By being an insider in foreign knowledge business clusters, or by purchasing companies that possess these resources, MNEs can gain access to the advanced resources in the foreign countries.

Efficiency. The last group of CSAs is efficiency that MNEs use to capitalize on environmental changes leading to reduced manufacturing costs or increased productivity of production processes. Interestingly, this efficiency can be achieved by combining the other three groups of CSAs. For example, by accessing cheap labor forces and new technological knowledge in foreign countries, MNEs can pursue cost reduction and productivity improvement simultaneously, leading to increased efficiency of their operations.

Internationalization Process by MNEs

Since foreign markets are perceived as new, unfamiliar, and risky to MNEs, they conduct business transactions across national borders through a step-wise internationalization process by increasing resource commitment slowly as time goes by (Johanson & Vahlne, 1977, 1990). As a result, at the initial stage of internationalization, MNEs would like to have foreign companies use their patents, trademarks or technology in exchange for a fee or royalty through *licensing or franchising contracts*. As MNEs accumulate experience about the foreign markets, they usually start to work with a local agent/distributor and/or to set up an office for their sales representatives or sales subsidiaries located in the host country markets for conducting direct *exporting activities* to enter the foreign markets. As MNEs accumulate more experience in the foreign markets, they may decide to set up *semi-manufacturing activities* such as local packaging and/or assembly operations by committing more resources in the host countries. Finally, MNEs are tempted to set up wholly-owned subsidiaries by conducting 100% *foreign direct investment* (FDI) only when they perceive no more risks from doing business in the foreign country markets.

During the course of diverse international activities conducted by MNEs, they are subject to the emergence of global and regional trade and investment liberalization mechanisms such as GATT, WTO, EU, and NAFTA. General Agreement on Tariffs and Trade (GATT) was established in 1947 in order to liberalize trade and to negotiate trade concessions among member countries. The GATT was succeeded to World Trade Organization (WTO) in January 1, 1995, an international organization that deals with specific rules of trade among member countries. As a result, the WTO not only enforces the provisions of the GATT, but also acts as a dispute-settlement mechanism among their member countries. The European Union (or EU27) is composed of the countries in the EU15 (Austria, Belgium, Denmark, Finland, Germany, Greece, France, Ireland, Italy, Luxembourg, the Netherlands, Portugal, Spain, Sweden, and the UK) and twelve new, mainly Central European, countries that joined in 2004 and 2007. The North American Free Trade Agreement (NAFTA) was established in January 1, 1994 to remove barriers to trade and investment among the US, Canada, and Mexico.

MNEs and Strategic Management Issues

In spite of the liability of foreignness that increases costs of operating in unfamiliar foreign countries, MNEs attempt to maximize profits from their overseas businesses by achieving the best configuration of FSAs internalized within their boundaries and CSAs accessible from their current foreign locations (Rugman, 2005). Similar to purely domestic enterprises in domestic markets, MNEs also face strategic challenges that may jeopardize their profitability when doing business in foreign markets, and, as a result, MNEs cope with the challenges by formulating and implementing the following five major strategies based on their FSAs and CSAs: (1) multinational, (2) organizing, (3) innovation/R&D, (4) collaboration, and (5) location.

Multinational Strategy

When conducting a strategic process, MNEs must navigate through four stages, (1) identification of business goal(s), (2) evaluation of external and internal environments, (3) implementation of strategic plans, and (4) control of the strategic process.

Goal. The first stage of identifying a business goal is to set a long-term mission and objective to pursue in the world market.

Evaluation of Environments. The second stage of evaluating external and internal environments is to formulate detailed strategies to achieve the long-term mission and objective identified at the first stage by matching business opportunities in external industry environment and MNEs' core internal resources and capabilities. As a result, external environmental analysis focuses on evaluating the attractiveness and/or competitiveness of the markets/industries where the MNE would like to operate by assessing five major external forces including the threat of substitutes, threat of new entrants, the level of firm rivalry, and bargaining powers of suppliers and buyers (Porter, 1991) surrounding MNEs. Internal environmental analysis, on the other hand, focuses on evaluating both the strengths and weaknesses of the MNE's core resources and capabilities that it possesses in order to decide what resources and capabilities to use to serve the business opportunities in the market (Barney, 1997).

Implementation. The third stage of a strategic process is to implement strategies in the world market as planned at the second stage, and, for this purpose, MNEs must possess an organizational structure to be explained in the following sub-section.

Control. The last stage of controlling the strategic process is to compare the MNE's business goal set at the first stage and the actual results and performance it has realized in the market so that it can take corrective actions to improve its performance in its next business cycle.

Organizing Strategy

After successfully formulating strategies by matching external opportunities and internal resources and capabilities, the next task for MNEs is to successfully implement the planned strategies in the real market. With headquarters in a home country and multiple subsidiaries in host countries, MNEs must devise an appropriate organizational structure to implement its strategies efficiently and effectively in the world market, and the final choice of a certain organization structure depends on which strategic orientation MNEs possess over the relationship between their headquarters and subsidiaries in the world market, i.e., *ethnocentric*, *polycentric*, and *geocentric* orientations.

When MNEs possess an *ethnocentric* strategic orientation, product managers in the MNE's headquarters usually dominate the entire overseas business process, and aim to achieve efficiency advantages by providing standardized products and services to foreign markets with no modifications. As a result, MNEs usually would like to organize their global structure based on products that it provides to its customers (Rugman & Collinson, 2009), and this product-based organizational structure commonly results in the implementation of cost leadership strategies based on an economically integrated perspective over the homogeneous world market.

On the other hand, when MNEs possess a *polycentric* strategic orientation, area managers in the MNE's foreign subsidiaries typically maintain important decision-making powers over the overseas business process, and seek differentiation advantages by providing heterogeneous products and services targeted for its local customers in each of its foreign markets. As a result, MNEs organize their global structure based on geographical areas/markets that they are currently serving (Rugman & Collinson, 2009), and those MNEs with an area-based organizational structure usually adopt differentiation strategies based on a nationally responsive perspective to satisfy the specific needs of local foreign customers in the heterogeneous world market.

The last way of organizing an MNE is to combine both the economic integration and national responsiveness perspectives so as to pursue both cost leadership and differentiation strategies simultaneously in the world market (Rugman & Collinson, 2009). This hybrid type of organizational structure is usually chosen when MNEs possess a *geocentric* strategic orientation where both product managers in the headquarters and area managers in the foreign subsidiaries maintain a balanced degree of power in communication, decision-making, and coordination processes over the whole overseas operations. A matrix structure and/or a transnational network structure are the best examples of the balanced organizational structure with product and area focuses (Bartlett & Beamish, 2011).

Innovation/R&D Strategy

As competition in the world market continues to grow, the acquisition and/ or accumulation of innovation capabilities become indispensible for MNEs to survive. MNEs must continuously provide new or improved products and services to their customers to outperform their local competitors, and one way to achieve this is through R&D investments, which, if successful, create new knowledge and/or innovative products and services. Two key questions relate to an MNE's innovation/R&D strategy. The first is whether the MNE should aim to achieve a standardized innovation process for all its overseas subsidiaries, or whether it should customize its innovation process to each local foreign market it serves. The second question is where an MNE should locate its innovation-related R&D activities—within the home country or across its host countries. These two questions are closely related because, if an MNE wants to pursue the standardized innovation strategy, then it needs to locate its major innovation/R&D activities in its home country. In this case, the new knowledge created by innovation/R&D activities flows from the central R&D headquarters to the foreign subsidiaries. Kuemmerle (1997) calls this a *home-base exploiting* innovation/R&D strategy, because it exploits current domestically developed R&D capabilities in home country for use in the MNE's foreign operations. On the other hand, if the MNE decides to customize its innovation process to each of its foreign markets, then it needs to locate its major innovation/R&D activities in each of its host country markets by establishing foreign R&D subsidiaries. In this case, the direction of knowledge flows from the foreign R&D subsidiaries to the MNE's headquarters in the home country, which Kuemmerle (1997) calls a *home-base augmenting* innovation/R&D strategy.

Collaboration Strategy

When an MNE implements its overseas business plans in foreign countries, it usually identifies local counterparts to work within the host countries. The MNE must decide what complementary resources to use from its external local host-country partners—such as technology providers, licensees, local distributors, joint venture partners. This means that by accessing complementary resources provided by local external actors, MNEs can reduce the level of risk that comes from the four (previously described) distances between their home country and host countries. The most popular way of collaboration in host countries is to establish international joint ventures (IJVs) with local partner firms (Hennart, 1988; Kogut, 1988). An IJV is a new entity created by an MNE and its local partner firms under an ownership contract. An IJV is complementary and mutually beneficial to both partner firms, since the foreign partner (an MNE) contributes new technology/knowledge, marketing skills, and/or globally established distribution channels to IJVs based on its FSAs, whereas the domestic partner (a local firm) provides local market knowledge, land and buildings, local legal expertise, and labour force, etc. to the IJVs.

Location Strategy

When MNEs decide to expand abroad beyond their domestic markets, they have to make a decision of where to locate their foreign operations. Some may argue that our world is 'flat' because a large proportion of international business takes place through off-shoring activities across the world, which has led to globalization (Friedman, 2000). According to this view, companies usually go through four stages of development before they become global MNEs: first, they must be successful in their domestic markets to achieve economies of scale enough for pushing them abroad (i.e., *domestic stage*); second, successful domestic companies typically choose a single strategic foreign country where they can export domestic surplus of their products or services to enhance their performance (i.e., *international stage*); third, as the exports into the single foreign market become more successful, the international companies further expand their geographic scope by cultivating multiple foreign markets (i.e., *multinational stage*); and, lastly, the multinational companies may achieve the status of global MNEs by reaching every corner of this global market with their upstream and/or downstream value chain activities distributed across the world (i.e., *global stage*).

However, the empirical data from the world's largest MNEs on the list of *Fortune Global 500* actually show that this world is spiky, not flat. Diverse barriers exist among different countries/regions, and, as a result, MNEs should pay more costs when they attempt to cross the boundaries of other countries or regions (Rugman, 2005). For example, Rugman and Verbeke (2004) introduced four types of MNEs based on the sales revenue realized across a triad—North America, European Union (EU), and Asia-Pacific. Among them, they defined home-region oriented MNEs as companies that achieve at least 50% of their sales revenue in their home region whereas global MNEs were defined as firms that realize at least 20% of their sales revenue from each of the three regions of the triad. Based on this categorization, Rugman and Verbeke show that, among 380 MNEs with available sales segment data on the *Fortune Global 500* list, only nine were global MNEs, and that 320 out of 380 MNEs were highly home-region oriented MNEs accounting for 80% of intra-regional transactions. As a result, the nature of international business is regional, not global, and focused on the home region of the triad. International expansion does not necessarily mean global expansion because most MNEs implement regional location strategies by pursuing market opportunities within their home region. Since local competitors are usually more adept at satisfying the local demands of their regional markets, MNEs should prefer their home region over remote regions when they go abroad seeking foreign operations.

Internationalization of Small and Young MNEs

As small- and medium-sized enterprises (SMEs) generate new jobs, innovations, and economic wealth in most countries, the rapid internationalization of small and young MNEs has attracted both academic and practical interests in the new field of international entrepreneurship over the past decade. Many small and young ventures have been observed as pioneering new market opportunities and scarce resources from foreign countries despite their double liabilities of smallness and newness in the competitive market. Such a new breed of firms has been referred to as international new ventures (INVs) or born global ventures in the international entrepreneurship, which are "business organizations that, *from inception*, seek to derive significant competitive advantages from the use of resources and the sale of outputs in multiple countries (Oviatt & McDougall, 1994, p.49)."

The rapid internationalization of small and young MNEs such as international new ventures is counter-intuitive to the traditional internationalization process of large-sized and already-existing MNEs. Since foreign markets are perceived as risky and uncertain, even to large and incumbent MNEs, resulting in the liability of foreignness, the majority of MNEs commonly need a substantial amount of time to learn about their new foreign markets before cultivating new markets and/or scarce resources rapidly and aggressively from unfamiliar new foreign countries. As such, domestic firms are inclined to develop their home country market before becoming multinational, and when they decide to expand into foreign countries as MNEs, they would like to target nearby foreign countries first followed by remote foreign countries next in a step-wise incremental process as time goes on (Johanson & Vahlne, 1977, 1990). International new ventures are recognized to defy the step-wise internationalization process by combining (1) entrepreneurs' prior foreign experience, (2) their innovative, proactive, and risk-taking behaviors, and (3) new ventures' network relationship with external resource providers to create future goods and services (McDougall & Oviatt, 2000; Oviatt & McDougall, 2005).

Implications for Management

Recognition of foreign markets as additional workplace brings about both opportunities and challenges to the general management of MNEs, and managers working therein. First of all, transactions across national borders may enhance overall firm performance compared to when companies are confined to their domestic markets. Internationalization strategies usually lead to the positive net benefits from expanded foreign markets, because MNEs can provide standardized low-cost goods and services to their customers by achieving the economies of scale. In addition, when MNEs are successful in understanding the specific needs and preferences of local customers in each of the foreign markets, they may attempt to further enhance their performance by providing highly differentiated products and services to the local customers in segmented foreign markets.

Prospective managers of MNEs, however, need to recognize that an internationalization process may be costly in some cases, and, as a result, the enhanced firm performance of MNEs from internationalization strategies may be possible only when they possess hard-to-replicate firm-level resources and capabilities (i.e., FSAs) and/or unique access to country-level factors in either their home or host countries (i.e., CSAs), both of which should outweigh the additional costs from internationalization, the so-called liability of foreignness. Since the possession of FSAs and/or CSAs may be costly as well, it is both important and challenging to the managers of MNEs for them to identify the best configuration between the two over the course of their international business.

It is especially worth mentioning that, since MNEs' business operations are distributed across *home* and *host* countries, there may be on-going conflicts and tensions between *headquarters* and *subsidiaries* of MNEs in the world market. Therefore, it should be noted that, when MNEs possess ethnocentric strategic orientations, the product managers in the headquarters of MNEs' home country typically dominate the entire overseas business process, aiming to achieve the standardization advantages in the formulation and implementation of multinational, organizing, and innovation/R&D strategies. On the other hand, when MNEs lean toward polycentric strategic orientations, the area/market managers in the subsidiaries of MNEs' host countries commonly seek differentiation advantages by considering the heterogeneity of their local customers in each of its foreign markets over the course of multinational, organizing, and innovation/R&D strategies.

Lastly, managers of MNEs should fully understand the benefits of cultivating their near-by countries in their home region rather than striving to become global MNEs across the entire world market. Partly due to the cultural, institutional, geographic, and economic distances between the home and host countries of MNEs, the nature of international business is actually regional, not global. As such, for example, Japanese MNEs usually operate their foreign businesses in their near-by Asian countries rather than in North America or European Union, and Mexican MNEs would like to pursue foreign market opportunities within the NAFTA in order to get the full benefits from the removal of trade and investment barriers among the US, Canada, and Mexico in the region.

Questions for Students

1. How do you define multinational enterprises (MNEs)? What are the main characteristics of MNEs that are different from purely domestic enterprises?
2. The liability of foreignness refers to additional costs for MNE operations in unfamiliar and risky foreign markets. Explain "four distances" that may affect the liability of foreignness for MNEs' foreign business.
3. When MNEs lack certain firm-specific advantages (FSAs), they may attempt to compensate by securing unique access to certain country-specific advantages (CSAs) that are available only in certain parts of this world. Suggest some examples of CSAs.
4. Explain the three types of strategic orientations that MNEs possess over the relationship between their headquarters and subsidiaries in the world market (i.e., *ethnocentric*, *polycentric*, and *geocentric* orientations), and link them to the choice of organizational structure by MNEs.
5. Compare home-base exploiting and home-base augmenting innovation/R&D strategies.
6. What are international joint ventures (IJVs)? How are they complementary and mutually beneficial to both domestic and foreign partner firms?
7. Is the nature of MNEs' foreign operation global or regional? Explain it in relation to MNEs' location strategies.
8. How do you define international new ventures (INVs)? What are the main characteristics of INVs that are different from traditional MNEs?

Case: McDonald's as an MNE

McDonald's has evolved from a small American company started by two brothers, Dick and Mac McDonald, in San Bernardino, CA in 1940 to a hugely successful international restaurant chain with 35,000 restaurants in over 100 countries across six continents as of 2013. Across the globe McDonald's restaurants represent an American franchise success story, not just in its home country, but across its host countries. McDonald's is clearly an MNE, as it is headquartered in the US with subsidiaries in multiple foreign countries. According to list of *Fortune Global 500* in 2014, McDonald's ranked 433rd with sales revenue of $28.1 billion and profits of $5.6 billion.

McDonald's implemented internalization strategies that differ from most manufacturing companies in order to enter new foreign markets: it could not simply import materials from other countries, combine those inputs to produce final products, and then export those goods to other countries via international trade. When McDonald's launched its internationalization efforts from 1967, going into foreign markets with potential consumers was the best route. McDonald's has used the franchising strategy for internationalization, since it can increase the size of the company and its sales revenue rapidly without requiring too much money on FDI. About 80% of the McDonald's worldwide are franchises, meaning that McDonald's sells the right to use its name, patents, and processes, etc., and to uphold its standards and replicate its products, to local partners who in turn pay franchising fees and open new stores in foreign markets.

With respect to FSAs, McDonald's strong competitive advantages originate mainly from its expertise in marketing-related downstream activities to serve their local customers. Based on the fierce competition in the American fast food industry, McDonald's has held its lead in the international fast food market due in part to the dedicated local managers who are passionate about delivering the most efficient and economical restaurant experience to their local customers to outperform their competitors. This atmosphere of internal competition by local managers provides strong customer care service. In fact, McDonald's had the best service standard in the quick service restaurant (QSR) sector. In the fierce competition of the U.S. fast food industry, McDonald's has had to increase its speed of service, unlike grilled chicken items in Kentucky Fried Chicken (KFC) usually require a comparatively long wait for customers. The other example of FSAs possessed by McDonald's is that it is continually creating new menus (in McDonald's speak, *new combos*) to reach more customers. Since identifying customer demand has become more complex and customer tastes have become more varied, McDonald's has developed strong capabilities in market research, and delivered diverse and heterogeneous combination menus to satisfy wide-ranging customer needs. For example, McDonald's developed a $1 dollar item menu in recent years in addition to many diverse combinations of meals, from Kid's Meals of various types and ever changing kids "treasures" (plastic action heroes and popular film characters) to hamburger/fries/soda combos and "healthy" diet menu choices to satisfy various customers' diverse needs. Therefore, McDonald's has worked hard to maintain and develop its FSAs to keep its advantageous position in the acutely competitive fast food market in the US and internationally.

McDonald's also enjoys several very significant home CSAs. First and foremost, the US large population provides a large market for McDonald's to spread its "hamburger, French fries and soda" fast food culture. In addition, McDonald's restaurants are increasingly located in large department stores such as Wal-Mart, in most large shopping malls, and in subway stations and airports where passenger flow is tremendous, giving McDonald's easy access to large potential markets. In addition, McDonald's has developed good relationships with the vast American agricultural industry to secure cheap, adequate "big six" resources including chicken, beef, lamb, turkey, pork, and eggs. McDonald's also has franchised its brand names to some toy manufacturers in China to satisfy the demand of small plastic toys included in McDonald's Kids Meal menus. Even though the geographical distance between the McDonald's in the US and its toy manufacturers in China is huge, McDonald's enjoys host CSAs that originate from China's cheap labor force and raw materials.

To cater to the specific needs of local foreign customers, McDonald's maintains an organizational structure that is similar to a global area structure. As a result, area managers have the authority to create promotion strategies, add new flavors and ingredients hamburgers to match local customer tastes, and to modify its menus to suit regional markets. For example, McDonald's does not sell beef hamburgers in India, since the national religion, Hinduism, forbids the eating of beef. McDonald's has developed other types of sandwiches made of chicken and/or fish for the Indian market (called national responsiveness). On the other hand, McDonald's decision making process is quite centralized. Although foreign subsidiaries are authorized to make certain changes in the menu and marketing approaches, they must follow McDonald's rules and regulations set up and imposed from its headquarters in the US. This is why, in spite of several different recipes designed for different areas, most of McDonald's food products are standardized. This standardization supports economic integration leading to efficiency advantages that McDonald's has traditionally enjoyed in the US and global fast food industry.

Based on McDonald's sales segment data across the triad in 2013, it is now a global MNE. McDonald's brings in 31.5% of its sales revenue from the US market, 40.2% from the EU, 23.0% from the Asia-Pacific, Middle East, and African regions, and the rest 5.3% from other countries. Therefore, with at least 20% of total sales revenue in each of the three triad regions, McDonald's is truly a global MNE. The company continues to push its envelope of growth as can be seen in a 2013 analysis of the company. McDonald's increased its sales revenues in each of the three triad regions. McDonald's realized a 4.4% increase of sales revenue in the EU, a 0.4% increase in the US, and a 1.4% increase in the Asia-Pacific, Middle East, and Africa in 2013.

Exercise: Global versus Regional Strategy by Fortune Global 500 MNEs

Rugman and Verbeke (2004) characterized the following four types of MNEs based on the sales segment realized across the triad of North America, EU, and the Asia-Pacific region.

1. Home-region oriented MNEs: Firms that realize at least 50% of sales revenue in their home region.
2. Bi-regional MNEs: Firms that realize at least 20% of sales revenue in each of two regions, but less than 50% in any one region of the triad.
3. Host-region oriented MNEs: Firms that obtain more than 50% of sales revenue in a triad market other than their home region.
4. Global MNEs: Firms that realize at least 20% of their sales revenue from each of the three regions of the triad.
5. From the *Fortune Global 500* list published in 2014, choose three MNEs with one company from each of the three regions of the triad, and evaluate whether they are pursuing global or regional location strategies in the world market.

Suggestions for Further Reading

Dunning, J. H. (1998) Location and the multinational enterprises: A neglected factor? *Journal of International Business Studies, 29*, 45-66.

Ghemawat, P. (2001). Distance still matters: The hard reality of global expansion. *Harvard Business Review, 79* (8), 137–147.

Rugman, A. M. (2005). *The regional multinationals: MNEs and 'global' strategic management.* Cambridge, UK: Cambridge University Press.

References

Barney, J. B. (1997). *Gaining and sustaining competitive advantage*. Reading, MA: Addison-Wesley.

Bartlett, C. A., & Beamish, P. W. (2011). *Transnational Management: Text, cases, and readings in cross-border management* (6th ed.). New York: McGraw-Hill.

Dunning, J. H. (1998) Location and the multinational enterprises: A neglected factor? *Journal of International Business Studies, 29*, 45-66.

Friedman, T. L. (2000). *The Lexus and the olive tree*. New York: Farrar, Straus and Giroux.

Ghemawat, P. (2001). Distance still matters: The hard reality of global expansion. *Harvard Business Review, 79* (8),137–147.

Hennart, J. (1988). A transaction costs theory of equity joint ventures. *Strategic Management Journal, 9,* 361–374.

Johanson, J., & Vahlne, J.-E. (1977). The internationalization process of the firm: A model of knowledge development and increasing foreign market commitments. *Journal of International Business Studies, 8*, 23-32.

Johanson, J., & Vahlne, J.-E. (1990). The mechanism of internationalization. *International Marketing Review, 7* (4), 11-24.

Kogut, B. (1988). Joint ventures: Theoretical and empirical perspectives. *Strategic Management Journal, 9,* 319–332.

Kuemmerle, W. (1997). Building effective R&D capabilities abroad. *Harvard Business Review, 75* (2), 61–70.

McDougall, P. P., & Oviatt, B. M. (2000). International entrepreneurship: the intersection of two research paths. *Academy of Management Journal, 43*, 902-906.

Oviatt, B. M., & McDougall, P. P. (1994). Toward a theory of international new ventures. *Journal of International Business Studies, 25*, 45-64.

Oviatt, B. M., & McDougall, P. P. (2005). Defining international entrepreneurship and modeling the speed of internationalization. *Entrepreneurship Theory and Practice, 29*, 537-557.

Porter, M. E. (1991). Towards a dynamic theory of strategy. *Strategic Management Journal, 12* (S2), 95–117.

Rugman, A. M. (2005). *The regional multinationals: MNEs and 'global' strategic management*. Cambridge, UK: Cambridge University Press.

Rugman, A. M., & Collinson, S. (2009). *International business* (5th ed.). Essex, UK: Pearson Education.

Rugman, A. M., & Verbeke, A. (2004). A perspective on regional and global strategies of multinational enterprises. *Journal of International Business Studies, 35*, 3-18.

Zaheer, S. (1995). Overcoming the liability of foreignness. *Academy of Management Journal, 38*, 341-363.

PART VII

Entrepreneurship and Family Business

16. Entrepreneurship

Frederick D. Greene
Manhattan College

Carolyn E. Predmore
Manhattan College

Veena P. Prabhu
California State University, Los Angeles

Jeff Bezos, with a degree in computer science and electrical engineering, worked at several firms at Wall Street, becoming the youngest Vice President at D. E. Shaw in 1990. With such a successful career in Finance, one would rarely think of abandoning it altogether. That's exactly what Jeff did, when in 1994 Bezos resigned and took the risk of starting his own company. The Internet always fascinated him given the endless opportunities it could be used for—his idea was simple—an online book store. He moved to Seattle, and along with a few employees began building software and opened Amazon.com as an online site on July 16, 1995. In spite of hardly any advertising, Amazon.com was a huge success as it sold books not only in the United States but also across 45 foreign countries within 30 days of its inception. The rest is history. What did Jeff Bezos do? He followed his dream, converted his idea into a start-up company that is serving the masses. He is an *entrepreneur* and the process by which he made his idea a reality is referred to as *entrepreneurship*.

By studying entrepreneurship one can learn how to start a business, grow a business, and harvest a business and in the process serve the needs of the people and contribute to the progress of the society at large. Entrepreneurs have opportunities in both good and bad economic times. Entrepreneurs can start a business that employs the family members and is passed down through generations. Entrepreneurship, thus is important to our society, gross national product, and cultural mindset. Entrepreneurship gives us the new, the different, and the cutting edge ideas by which we can continue to compete in a global environment. Considering how important entrepreneurship is, we need to understand what it is.

Nature of Entrepreneurship

Definition

There have been many attempts to define entrepreneurship. Many times the terms of entrepreneurship and entrepreneur are often interchanged or substituted for each other in conversation, but they slightly differ as an entrepreneur is an individual practicing entrepreneurship. One view of entrepreneurship refers to a field of study concerning the creation of a new business, the individual risk involved, and the economic impact on society (Mohr & Sarin, 2009). Another view of entrepreneurship is that anyone who wants to work for himself or herself is considered to be an entrepreneur (Shane, 2008). A more recent view is that entrepreneurship may have several dimensions and may vary across countries for e.g. Americans pursue entrepreneurship as they are focused on high growth— expanding their business and increasing profit exponentially while Filipinos dive into the field to change their life style and lead a more balanced work family life (Prabhu, McGuire, Drost, & Kwong, 2012). The view we take has more of a practical orientation rather than an academic orientation. For purposes of this chapter, we use the following definition:

Entrepreneurship involves the establishment of an enterprise built around an innovative idea by an individual—an entrepreneur—who has certain characteristics that enable him or her to face the challenges and risk involved. They take the initiative and risk to start a business. They also bring an additional level of creativity and have the ability to think out of the box and recognize the opportunities present in a given situation.

Characteristics of Entrepreneurs

Creativity. Entrepreneurship entails the creation of a new business venture with a unique focus, structure or differential advantage. The start up can be a for-profit or a not-for-profit organization, but it must be more than merely an idea. It must be put into operation. An entrepreneur has the motivation to start a new business due to the need to succeed through either psychological motivation or by economic pressure (Carsrud & Brännback, 2011). The business concept is new or the product is new or even the process by which the product is manufactured may be novel thereby aiding in increasing efficiency and effectiveness.

Personality Traits. Entrepreneurship is not one personality trait that one can ask questions about on a survey. It is a combination of personality traits, including an ability to see themselves as being in control of their lives. These traits include: risk-taking, intrinsic motivation (Prabhu, Sutton & Saucer, 2008), flexibility, openness to experience (which is strongly correlated to creativity) social awareness, and a need to succeed. Entrepreneurs work on taking calculated risk and focus on the "what can be done" rather "what cannot be done", which allows the entrepreneur to think of the various possibilities for the challenges at hand, rather than brood about what is likely to go wrong. They are focussed, and able to change the status quo, accept change, cause dynamic change and embrace change. Entrepreneurs can be any race, gender, ethnicity or age. Anyone at any time may realize that they have seen the heart of a problem and have an idea of how to solve that problem, feel passionately about it and work towards changing solving that problem or changing that idea or dream into reality. These traits encourage a person to explore, question and then take risks to try something new, open a new business and put financial security in jeopardy.

Risk-Taking. Creating a new business brings a variety of risks. There is risk of bringing a product/service/idea to market before it is ready; risk of not understanding the target market well enough to have the right type of product/service/idea, risk of losing the investment of money that is needed to start the business, and the risk of being seen as a fool by friends and family. The entrepreneur brings a passion for the new business idea that helps lower the perception of risk (van Gelderen, Thurik, & Patel, 2011). Successful entrepreneurs take calculated risk by assessing their level of expertise and the level of ambiguity in a particular decision context and then tailoring their decision-making process to reduce risk (Murmann & Sardana, 2013).

Motivation. Entrepreneurs are self-motivated, want self-fulfillment, want to be hands-on, will get psychic satisfaction from the job, have an eye for coming changes, shifts in consumer attitudes and opinions and industry needs (Shane, 2008). They are interested in people and in being sociable, but are also willing to be alone in order to create the product/service/idea that they bring to market. They are able to postpone gratification in order to succeed.

Flexibility and Social Awareness. An entrepreneur is able to be flexible, able to cope with change, has the ability to see how a new methodology, new product or new service will be able to enter a market profitably. He/she must understand what talents need to be added to support his/her own shortcomings in order to form the networks needed to support the company. Entrepreneurs are also very involved with people. They are able to understand and absorb what others are telling them on business topics and would likely score highly on an emotional quotient scale. Entrepreneurs are able to gather talented people around them to move the firm forward (Vissa, 2011).

Need to Succeed. Entrepreneurs have a drive to succeed. Failures are perceived as learning experiences, especially for habitual or serial entrepreneurs. One can often learn more about the business model and consumers from a failure than from a success. Since many entrepreneurs start their companies based on their previous business experience, the entrepreneur can alter a business model until the firm succeeds (Shane, 2008).

Types of Entrepreneurs

Just as there are an infinite number of types of businesses, which can be created, there are also different types of entrepreneurs with diverse goals and business behaviors.

Habitual or Serial Entrepreneurs

Some habitual or serial entrepreneurs start and own multiple businesses at one time and others like the challenge of creating and starting a new business in a time series. When the firm becomes more of a managerially based business with routine challenges, the entrepreneur sells that company and starts a new one, becoming a serial entrepreneur (Westhead, Ucbasaran, & Wright, 2005).

Growth Entrepreneurs

Growth entrepreneurs create economic opportunities for their communities and neighbors by creating new businesses and jobs leading to an increase in local wealth and standards of living (Carsrud & Brännback, 2011). The establishment of a new business creates the environment for the growth of competition and the initiation of a new industry, which can support other new firms and small businesses.

Harvest Entrepreneurs

While harvest entrepreneurs carry the traits of being risk averse, self-motivated, and innovative, they are also driven to create as much value within the company as possible. They want to sell the company for the most profit. They may also be known as portfolio entrepreneurs when they own some part of at least two entrepreneurial firms (Westhead, Ucbasaran, & Wright, 2005)

Occasional Entrepreneurs

Occasional entrepreneurs create their businesses on a part-time basis and finance them with only their own money.They usually make a smaller profit since the new enterprise is run in their spare time. Creating a business with self-funding while continuing to work at another job is a typical starting scenario for entrepreneurs. Many entrepreneurs do not seek outside funding until their companies grow, either through a desire to retain managerial control or financial control (Shane, 2008).

Late Career Entrepreneurs

There are at least two different situations that can lead to late career entrepreneurships. They may have remained in their first career much longer than intended in order to provide financial security for themselves and their families. They have often built up extra funds in order to start the business of their dreams. The second situation is when the person has been let go from a company through early retirement packages or reductions in force and has to create a new career out of necessity. It is often difficult for the average over 50-year young person to find a corporate job, which leaves entrepreneurship as the best alternative (Shane, 2008).

Social Entrepreneurs

Social entrepreneurs feel passionately about solving a pressing social problem by addressing the root cause of the problem and in the process making it also a profitable venture. Mohammend Yunus, a noble laureate and one of the most famous social entrepreneurs developed the concept of microfinance and started Grameen bank. As opposed to the conventional bank which lend money only to people who have some money (collateral), Grameen bank lend money to those who truly have nothing but are working towards becoming self-reliant through thie small business. Started in 1977, Grameen bank served 7 million clients by 2006. Thus social entrepreneurs are those business people who not only see an opportunity for addressing a problem of the society but also at the same time see a possibility for growing a business. Sometimes the comment is that social entrepreneurs do well by doing good (Gorgievski, Ascalon, & Stephan, 2011; Murphy & Coombes, 2008)). Social entrepreneurs have a concern for the public good and want to fix a problem.

There are different models of social entrepreneurship. One model was created by TOMS Shoes. When a customer buys one pair of shoes, another pair of shoes is donated to a child in an underdeveloped country. The cost of the donated pair of shoes is included in the price of the shoes sold. Another model is where the business tries to improve the lives of their workers and their neighbors through good business practices as Tom's of Maine has done for years.

An example of a third model is when some entrepreneurial philanthropists want to have a direct say in how their charitable dollars are going to be used by a nonprofit organization. Bill Gates created the Bill and Melinda Gates Foundation (1994) in order to deliver new technologies and new ideas in health and education to underdeveloped countries. While there are many charitable organizations with a focus on education and/or health, starting a new business concern allows for greater control over the entire business operation. He and Warren Buffet have challenged the Fortune 400 billionaires to donate 600 billion dollars to charitable causes.

Hybrid Entrepreneurs

It's a known fact that many start-up ventures fail due to the high risk involved and uncertainty, leaving the entrepreneur discouraged and demotivated. Risk in an integral part of any new venture and hence cannot be overlooked. However it would greatly help if one could take calculated risks and is prepared to have a backup source of finance if the new venture failed. To that end a new trend is evolving referred to as "hybrid entrepreneurs" who on one hand continue to hold on to their secure "day job" while also venturing out and taking the risk of starting a new company (Raffiee & Feng, 2014). It has been found that individual characteristics such as risk averse need for security and long-term orientation (saving for the future) may be typical of hybrid entrepreneurs. Furthermore, risk-averse entrepreneurs would prefer to purchase an existing business rather than build a new venture from scratch given that the latter may be more risky (Block, Thurik, van der Zwan, & Walter, 2013)

Intrapreneurs or Corporate Entrepreneurs

There have been companies, which have set out to encourage entrepreneurship within the company. The environment would have to encourage time for thinking, for brainstorming and then considering what might be able to be put into production or application. 3M is one company with a very long history of encouraging innovative thinking starting with the beginning of the company in 1902. 3M has found that by hiring smart and inquisitive people and then giving them the time to innovate, corporate entrepreneurship can be encouraged.

Steve Jobs has said that his job is not to innovate, but to veto the ideas and products that would not fit the vision or strategy of the company while encouraging innovation. Sometimes an idea has to simmer until the consumer is ready for it, like the iPad. By allowing others to create new applications, the iPad also increased its own success. So in addition to needing to succeed, encouraging the invention of new uses by consumers can increase the public support for corporate entrepreneurships.

Entrepreneurship or Small Business?

Entrepreneurship is the creation of a new venture with a unique focus, structure or differential advantage. The venture is not necessarily the first mover in the market, but is the first with a significant market share and has viability. Entrepreneurship is different from small business management as the small business owner may be continuing a family business or has bought a successful business. A small business may be inherited within a family business succession plan and grow into an entrepreneurship as a new owner/manager brings new ideas, new business models and/or innovation into the creation of new products/services. Entrepreneurships may also grow into medium and large sized companies through the continual innovation and evolution in products/services and business practices. Continual growth is not a necessity as long as innovation and change remain at the heart of the business. An entrepreneurship may remain small to remain agile and lean enough to find change, react to change and be ahead of the curve in applications.

While small businesses carry a risk of business failure due to changes in the consuming market or changes in the environment, entrepreneurs take on additional risks. Entrepreneurs have additional financial risk involved in the creation of the company and the monetary outlay for office/manufacturing space, equipment and hiring new people. The company is new to the market-place and there is usually little or no financial cushion available to absorb the losses from a slow start up or a slowing economy. An additional risk is that the entrepreneur may not have good knowledge of the consuming market due to a lack of business experience in this industry category.

Entrepreneurship Myths

Genius

One myth would be that you need to be a genius in order to start a business that will be very successful. Many people think that you need to be like Bill Gates or Mark Zuckerberg in order to create that incredibly innovative and interesting new business that captures the attention of the consumers. Not true! You just need to see a new solution to a problem and create a new business as Blake Mycoskie did in creating TOMS shoes. He created a shoe to sell that could be made inexpensively enough that each customer is buying two pairs of shoes; one for themselves and one for a needy child.

Hi-Tech

Another myth is that an entrepreneurship needs to be hi-tech. Not true! TOMS Shoes are not hi-tech in the least. They are inexpensive shoes that let a customer act on a charitable thought—donate a pair of shoes. There are other simple ideas that can be seen on television. There is a reality show about two sisters who have created an entrepreneurship around cupcakes. They have high quality, custom-decorated cupcakes with a wide variety of flavors so that they have a cupcake for nearly every possible desire.

Wealth

Wealth—everyone becomes an entrepreneur in order to make lots of money. Not true! The great majority of entrepreneurs decide to take on the risk of starting a new business because they cannot ignore the passion that they have for their product/ service/idea. The need to succeed is really the need to see the passion passed on to others. The need to succeed is also a part of the passion that social entrepreneurs have to improve society and/or the environment. The need to succeed is also a need to have the company do well enough for the entrepreneur's family to be proud.

Failure

There is another myth that is promoted by many textbooks, newspaper articles and journal entries that 70% to 80% of new companies fail. Not true! Over a span of 4 years, 55% of new companies are still in business (Shane, 2008). It is also true that people who have received higher levels of education are more likely to become entrepreneurs (Shane, 2008). Budding entrepreneurs believe that being offered some training and help early would support their entrepreneurship success in the first two years (Roomi & Harrison, 2008). That means that getting help (from the Small Business Administration as well as other sources) is a good idea.

It is possible that you have a great idea but somewhere in the business plan, there is a flaw in your feasibility study. While a business failure is a failure of your idea, the experience of failure may help you learn what set of circumstances and business planning will be needed for a successful new business

Effectiveness of Entrepreneurship

One outcome of entrepreneurship is expansion of the economy. It is easy to expect large businesses to increase their hiring in order to expand job creation. Entrepreneurs create new businesses and new job opportunities. The rapid growth in social media websites like Facebook, Groupon, and Living Social that add in geographic identifiers to retailing suggestions show how the passion of one entrepreneur can excite the imagination of others to create a new industry.

Serial entrepreneurs create new businesses as they have the passion for each type and then sell as they form a passion around a new idea/product. The thrill is in the start-up of the company so the serial entrepreneur sees the seed of a new industry or new idea and nudges it into a growth cycle. The company attracts interest due to its innovative view of the product/service and attracts more people into the business. As this business grows, competitors come into the market, which creates an industry or reinvigorates an older industry. The economy in the geographic region benefits from new businesses congregating in a competitive industry with the influx of people to work in the industries. The new people bring with them the possibility of other ways of seeing the needs of a consumer or innovative manufacturing ideas further encouraging entrepreneurship growth. Entrepreneurs encourage other entrepreneurs to step out of comfort zones and into more new businesses. The emergence of Silicon Valley in California and Silicon Alley in New York are examples of this. Serial entrepreneurs tend to create within industries that are similar in nature and in location. Once successful, they continue to support and reinforce the creative spirit in the area.

Social entrepreneurs flourish when technology or business culture may have focused more on business success than the downstream effects on people and culture. With an understanding that it is realistic to have as business goals improving living conditions as well as creating a profitable business, social entrepreneurs give society the examples of what can be created when many questions are asked about why a situation has to be the way it is. Why can it not be better? What is holding society back from making an improvement? How can the improvement be done on a less costly basis? Changes in technology help stimulate possibilities for an active and imaginative person to use in a novel manner leading to a new product/service or new distribution system or a new method of donations.

Entrepreneurship frees members of society to think of how to do the process of living and working in a new way by giving people license to innovate. While Google is a multinational search engine, there are Chinese entrepreneurs who created a Chinese based search engine that works better within the Chinese culture. The creation and success of each new entrepreneurship opens the possibility of the next one to an entrepreneur.

Implications for Organizations

Expansion into new markets through creative innovation and corporate entrepreneurship helps support job growth and economic expansion. Even in a recession or slow economy, people will spend once their interest is excited. Corporate entrepreneurship is a great way to ensure that the company can continue to grow and survive in both good and bad economic conditions. Support for corporate entrepreneurship comes from top management encouraging creativity among company employees and a willingness to listen to new ideas.

With regard to innovation, there are three types of innovation: continuous innovation, dynamic innovation and discontinuous innovation. Nelson and Consoli (2010) support Schumpeter's ideas that consumer behavior is an active participant in this process. As people living in a consumption society, an individual can figure out a better way to solve a consumer problem. Just solve one problem, answer a need and give an easily defined benefit to using the product/service or idea and there is a seed of a new business and possibly a new industry. It is innovation that drives business and the economy forward. It is the individual entrepreneur who is willing to take a financial risk and perhaps a social risk to bring a new product/service to the market. It is entrepreneurs who create the future—either individually or within an organization. It is the constant creation of newness that keeps business alive.

What will encourage entrepreneurs in the 21st century? Difficult economic times create the need to succeed. New technologies and downward economic pressures create the environment for smart people with the ability to define problems and think creatively to become entrepreneurs. Computing in the cloud (Internet based computer programs) may support multitudes of possible innovations just as a need for alternative fuel supports innovation in transportation. Implications for management are that companies need to explicitly value thinking and innovation, by giving employees the time and freedom to develop creative ideas and products.

Questions for Students

1. Who is an entrepreneur?
2. Name the different types of entrepreneurs?
3. Which personality trait do you think is most important to becoming an entrepreneur?
4. Is social entrepreneurship realistic?
5. Is entrepreneurship only for the genius and wealthy? Why?
6. What does it take to be an entrepreneur?

Case: Exotics and Hybrid Motors

Exotics and Hybrid Motors is a privately owned car repair shop in Nassau County, Long Island. The co-owners, Robert and Peter Positani (father and son), prefer to work on high-end European cars. The Positanis can repair any type of car and motorcycle supported by their experience in the car repair business and commitment to education. They take advanced course work offered by a variety of car manufacturers and automobile service associations. The shop has been in business for 32 years when it was begun by the three Positani brothers (Pietro, Robert, & Paolo). They were born in Italy, but are all now U. S. citizens. The Positanis have great mechanical skills as well as intense attention to detail, which may have been inherited or learned from their grandfather and father who were cabinetmakers.

History

In 1976 Robert was thinking about going into business for himself or with family members. He found a location on Long Island, NY and told Pietro about it. In March of 1977, the two brothers opened Exotic and Hybrid Motors with a focus on European cars. At that time, European car manufacturers created most of the automotive innovations. Those car innovations trickled into the U. S. car market affording the Positanis the opportunity to service and repair both foreign and domestic cars. After a year the youngest brother, Paolo, joined his brothers in the shop.

For 10 years, the brothers worked together with varying degrees of rivalry and cooperation. It was sibling rivalry in their business. Their level of attention to detail brought a great deal of customer satisfaction since repairs were done right, well and quickly. Exotics and Hybrid Motors' reputation grew and there was often a one, two or three day wait before one could get his/her car in for repair.

The Positanis started to consider enlarging the shop in order to accommodate more cars in repair on the floor at one time, thereby reducing the wait time for getting a car in for repair. They also wanted to start to hire more of the second generation of the family as repair people and more space was needed in order to have more workers. They first wanted to enlarge the shop that they had, but there was no land available near their location for an additional building or for adding onto the existing premises.

The next possibility would be to relocate the company to an entirely different location, build a new shop and hope that the customers would follow. Each of the brothers had an idea of where they wanted to go and each investigated possible new company sites. Conflict over strategic planning, division of profits, vision of what the shop should become became a daily focus of divisive arguments among the brothers.

The first to leave was Paolo. He had an opportunity to partner with someone outside the family in a new location, one nearer where their customers lived. Pietro and Robert continued in business for another year when their disagreements over how to expand the business became excessive. The brothers decided to end their partnership, as they could not decide where to go or what the company should become or how to deal with a second generation in the shop and distribution of profits.

One of the Positani brothers (Robert) kept the same location and was able to keep the same name of the shop—Exotics and Hybrid Motors. While the breakup of the brothers in business was hard on the family and on the customers who were used to seeing their favorite brother at the shop, the remaining Positani brother has been able to gather enough customers to remain in business at the same location.

It is now 17 years later and Robert's oldest son (Peter) has joined him at Exotics and Hybrid Motors. Car repair is their life. The question is whether they can expand the customer base to be able to keep Robert, Peter and two other mechanics gainfully employed year round. It is not easy to find a skilled mechanic and once found, the Positanis do not want to hire for seasonal demand. While repair work has picked up significantly once the snow melted in the spring, Robert is concerned about what to do about next winter. He is worried that next winter will also see a seasonal decline, which has not been a typical pattern for the shop's customers. This is especially troubling since the county economy seems to have slowed as noted by the slower housing sales in the area.

Peter, the son, loves cars and motorcycles. While he had an opportunity to go to college, he did not enjoy the atmosphere or anything else about college. He came to the repair shop ten years ago and expects to own the shop when his father retires. While the future for car repair remains difficult due to better cars and longer warrantees, there are people who collect old and antique cars who look for craftsmen to do the work. That is where Exotic and Hybrid Motors sees their niche. Both Robert and Peter continue to take classes on the innovations in cars to be able to repair both old and new imports. Peter's future seems like a challenge in the present car ownership environment.

The 4 P's of Marketing

The product that Exotics and Hybrid Motors sells is service and the replacement parts that are used in the car repairs. Their differential advantages are that they create a personal relationship with the car owners, the Positanis' expansive knowledge of European and U. S. cars and a very short waiting time for getting a car into the shop. Their prices for repair are generally 75% of the price at car dealerships. Exotics and Hybrid Motors are able to repair any make or model of car at competitive prices.

The Exotics and Hybrid Motors shop is in an industrial automotive section of Mineola, New York. It cannot be seen from a well-traveled consumer road. The building appears to be at least 50 to 70 years old and is not inviting on the outside. The inside is well maintained and very clean. There are a few chairs for waiting but no amenities.

Exotic and Hybrid Motors has premiums to give to customers: imprinted pens, memo paper cubes, refrigerator magnets and similar items. There is no budget for promotion.

Exercise

Following is a list of four entrepreneurs: (a) Larry Page; (b) Bill Gates; (c) Steve Jobs and (d) Mark Zuckerberg

Choose any three and research about the following:

1. What is this entrepreneur famous for?
2. Describe briefly about their journey as an entrepreneur.
3. What are some of the factors that helped in building their first start up?

Suggestions for Further Reading

Downes, L., & Nunes, P. (2014). *Big bang disruption: Strategy in the age of devastating innovation.* Penguin Group, New York.

Gorgievski, M. J., Ascalon, E., & Stephan, U. (2011). Small business owners' success criteria, a values approach to personal difference. *Journal of Small Business Management, 49,* 207–232.

Khalifa, A. S. (2008). The "strategy frame" and the four Es of strategy drivers. *Management Decisions, 46,* 894–917.

References

Block, J., Thurik, R., van der Zwan, P., & Walter, S. (2013). Business takeover or new venture? Individual and environmental determinants from a cross-country study. *Entrepreneurship Theory and Practice, 37,* 1099–1121.

Carsrud, A., & Brännback, M. (2011). Entrepreneurial motivations: What do we still need to know? *Journal of Small Business Management, 49,* 9–26.

Gorgievski, M. J., Ascalon, M., & Stephan, U. (2011). Small business owners' success criteria, a values approach to personal differences. *Journal of Small Business Management, 49,* 207–232.

Mohr, J. J., & Sarin, S. (2009). Drucker's insights on market orientation and innovation: Implications for emerging areas in high-technology marketing. *Journal of the Academy of Marketing Science, 37* (1), 85–96.

Murmann, J. P. & Sardana, D. (2013). Successful entrepreneurs minimize risk *Australian Journal of Management, 38* (1) 191–215

Murphy, P. J., & Coombes, S. M. (2008). A model of social entrepreneurial discovery, *Journal of Business Ethics, 87,* 325–336.

Nelson, R. R., & Consoli, D. (2010). An evolutionary of household consumption behavior. *Journal of Evolutionary Economics, 20,* 665–687

Prabhu, V. P. McGuire, S., Drost, E. & Kwong, K. (2012). Entrepreneurial intent and proactive personality: Is entrepreneurial self efficacy a mediator or moderator? *International Journal of Entrepreneurial Behaviour & Research, 18* (5), 559–586.

Prabhu, V. P., Sutton, C. D., & Sauser, W. (2008). Creativity and certain personality traits: Understanding the mediating effect of intrinsic motivation. *Creativity Research Journal, 20,* 53–66.

Raffiee, J. & Feng, J. (2014). Should I quit my day job?: A hybrid path to entrepreneurship. *Academy of Management Journal,* 57 (4), 936–963.

Roomi, M. A., & Harrison, P. (2008) Training needs for women-owned SMEs in England. *Education & Training, 50* (8–9), 687–696.

Shane, S. A. (2008). *The illusions of entrepreneurship.* New Haven, CT: Yale University Press.

Van Gelderen, M., Thurik, R., & Patel, P. (2011). Entrepreneurial problems and outcome status in nascent entrepreneurship. *Journal of Small Business Management, 49,* 71–91.

Vissa, B. (2011). A matching theory of entrepreneurs' tie formation intentions and initiation of economic exchange. *Academy of Management Journal, 54,* 137–158.

Westhead, P., Ucbasaran, D., & Wright, M. (2005). Decisions, actions, and performance: Do novice, serial, and portfolio entrepreneurs differ? *Journal of Small Business Management, 43,* 393–417.

17. Family Business

Tracey Eira Messer
Case Western Reserve University

Family businesses play an important role in the global economy. World-wide, they account for 80–98 percent of all businesses and are a leading source of start-up capital. In the United States, family-owned or -controlled firms account for approximately 90 percent of all incorporated businesses, including one-third of all Fortune 500 companies. The words "family business" often conjures an image of a neighborhood grocery or other small enterprise, and many family-owned businesses fit this description. Family businesses can also be found among the largest corporations in the United States. Their names may be familiar to you—Wal-Mart, Levi Straus, L.L. Bean, Hallmark, Nordstrom, Smucker's, and The Wall Street Journal are all family-owned or -controlled businesses. Why should a manager care about family business? Managers need to understand family-owned businesses because they are likely to work with members of a family business as customers, suppliers, employees or employers. Family-controlled enterprises operate similarly to their non-family counter-parts, but with a few differences. Understanding these differences will help managers achieve their goals.

Nature of Family Business

Definition

Three criteria are generally present in family firms: *ownership control, strategic direction,* and the *intention to continue family ownership* of the enterprise. Ownership control refers to the rights and responsibilities held by family members as part of voting ownership and governance of the firm. Strategic direction reflects the influence which family members set for the venture through their involvement. The intention to sustain family influence and control into future generations deepens the owner's relationship with his employees, customers, and community. These elements combine to define a family business as a synthesis of the following elements (Poza, 2010, p. 6):

- Ownership control (of at least 15 percent) by two or more members of a family or group of families.
- Strategic direction by family members on the management of the firm. Direction may be expressed through active management or by serving as a board member or advisor.
- Concern for family relationships.
- Intention to continue the business across multiple generations.

In addition, stakeholders (i.e., family, owners, management) often hold multiple and overlapping roles. This overlap is unique to family business.

Family businesses come in many forms: sole proprietorships, partnerships, limited liability companies, and holding companies in addition to publicly-traded and family-controlled businesses. Different terms, such as, family enterprise, family venture, family-controlled, or family-owned are used to refer to family business. These terms are used interchangeably in this chapter.

Systems View of Business

In non-family business, two roles predominate: owners and management. In these firms, individuals are rarely both majority owners and managers (employees) at the same time. There are three primary roles in family enterprises: family, owners, and management. Overlaps between roles are common. *Systems theory* is a tool for understanding overlapping roles (Bertalanffy, 1972) and here it is applied here to family business (Taguiri & Davis, 1996).

Example of the Systems Model. The McIlhenny family, manufacturers of TABASCO Pepper Sauce, was founded in 1868. Today, revenues exceed $250 million and the seventh family member is at the company's helm. Ownership of the company has grown from founder Edmund McIlhenny through his two sons to approximately 145 shareholders (stock was inherited or given by a living family member). The family limits the number of family members in senior management at one time as part of an effort to keep management open to new ideas.

In the Systems Theory model (Figure 1), McIlhenny family members occupy the circle marked 1, owners who are not members of the family (if any) are in the circle marked 3, and the employees of the McIlhenny Company are represented in the circle marked 5. Each circle represents clear and independent roles. When the circles overlap, there is also an overlap of roles. Family members, who are also owners (shareholders), are represented in overlap 2. Shareholders, who are also employees, but not members of the family, occupy area 4. Family members who work in the business, who are not owners, are shown in overlap 6. Finally, overlap 7 identifies family members who are owners and employees, like the family member serving as CEO.

The Systems Theory Model of Family Business

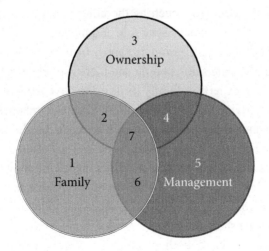

Note. Adapted from Taguiri and Davis (1996, p. 201).

Differences between Family and Non-Family Businesses

Family and non-family businesses are not necessarily different from one-another in there structure or operation (Stewart & Hitt, 2012). Differences, if they exist, can usually be seen in firm ownership, membership of the Board of Directors, and in the company's goals.

Ownership. In publicly traded businesses, ownership occurs when an individual purchases stock in the company through a market, such as the New York Stock Exchange. Share price is determined by the marketplace. Most family firms are privately owned and in these firms, the purchase or sale of company shares are handled privately. In addition, the company by-laws may limit who is eligible to own shares. For example, the by-laws might state that only family members working in the business or only family members related by blood (i.e. not an in-law) can own shares. Without an open market, financial professionals are often required to determine the value of the shares.

Board of Directors. There are two kinds of directors. *Inside director* is the term used for individuals who have significant relationships with the company (i.e., officer or owner) and are board members. *Outside directors* are board members who do not have significant relationships with the company other than serving on the board.

In large public companies, the board is composed primarily of outside directors who are elected by the stockholders. Inside directors tend to be senior level officers of the company, such as the chief executive officer. The board has a strategy-setting and supervisory role and management is delegated to the professional staff of the organization. In family firms, the directors and majority shareholders are often the same people and there are few, if any, outside directors. To gain outside expertise, family firms often have a board of advisors who provide objective advice based on their knowledge and business experience.

Goals. Management-controlled firms are profit-focused. The firm's primary goal is to generate economic benefits or profit to shareholders. Typically, senior management sets strategic direction which is then communicated to, and carried out by, the firm's employees. Employees are paid a salary. If employees own shares in the company, they will also receive dividend income and benefit from increases in the share price.

Family businesses have both economic and non-economic goals. Non-economic goals can include the survival and independence of the firm, social prestige for being associated with the company, jobs for family, philanthropy, and job security (Zellweger, Nason, Nordqvist, & Brush, 2011). Like management-controlled firms, they also seek to be profitable.

Another view of the difference between management-controlled firms and family-controlled firms suggests that the former seeks to maximize wealth and the latter seeks to maximize value, with wealth being only one aspect of the enterprise's value (Stockmans, Lybaert, & Voordeckers, 2010).

Resource Based View. Another way to look at differences between family and non-family firms is the Resource Based View (RBV), a management tool used to determine the strategic resources and capabilities that are available to a company. The central idea of the RBV is that the resources of an organization drives its success and those resources should be valuable, rare, not imitable, and non-substitutable (Wernerfelt, 1984). For example, the unique resources of Apple Computer, a public, management-controlled consumer electronics company, include:

- Exceptional brand loyalty, which creates a market when new products are released;
- products feature a user-friendly and unique visual vocabulary;
- channel control through Apple retail stores and on-line media, product and application stores;
- multiple patents plus commitment to strong R&D; and
- reputation for innovation and status as a "best place to work" make it a desirable employer and keeps employee turnover low.

In family businesses, the interaction between the family and the business is one source of the unique resource. Five Guys Burgers and Fries, one of America's fastest growing restaurants, led by Jerry and Janie Murrell and their four sons is an example. Each member of the Murrell family understands multiple aspects of their business and is responsible for a specific management role from training to franchising to baking hamburger buns. This cross-functional knowledge enables a family member to pitch in to when extra help is needed (Weise, 2011). The family's rapid success illustrates five resources that form the RBV and the advantages promoted by each (Poza, 2010).

- Overlapping responsibilities of owners and managers which support quick response time and speed to market.
- Concentrated ownership structure which promotes higher productivity and long-term commitment to investments in personnel and innovation.

- Focus on customers and market niches which result in higher return on investment.
- The family's desire to protect its name and reputation often promotes high product and service quality. This, in turn, may lead to higher return on investment produced by high-quality leaders.
- Family unity, ownership commitment, and interaction between the family business system (family, ownership, management) support lower administrative costs, knowledge transfer from generation to generation, and the ability to act quickly in changing markets.

Features of Family-Owned Enterprises

Family-owned and -controlled firms introduce a unique dynamic, the family, to the executive suite. Family presence can have both a positive and negative impact on business and it is useful for managers to be aware of these dynamics as well as the benefits, from patient capital (i.e., stakeholder capital invested for the long term) to quick response time, which are common to family firms

Family Impact. *Familiness* is a term representing the unique package of resources and capabilities arising out of family involvement in their business. The resources are assets that are available and may include knowledge and/or skills in addition to social, financial, and physical capital. Capability refers to the ways in which owners and managers are able to leverage those resources. In business families, the business represents a significant part of the family's context and, in turn, the family represents a big part of the business's context. Depending on how the resources and assets are used, familiness can drive, constrain or have a neutral effect on firm performance (Frank, Lueger, Nose, & Suchy, 2010).

Family Power and Influence. While the misuse of power and influence is not unique to family firms, two types of behavior are unique to family firms. In both instances, family members in ownership and/or management positions take actions to benefit family members at the expense of the company. The first, *nepotism*, occurs when family members are hired based on their blood ties and not as a result of managerial skill or merit. The second behavior, *altruism*, is defined as having concern for the welfare of others. It can have a positive impact on a company or can become a problem when an owner-manager allows family members to break rules that non-family employees are expected to follow. An owner-manager's failure to reprimand children-employees for laziness or other improper behavior is one example. Corporate reporting structures which minimize the time that employees spend reporting to immediate relatives can also help avoid this kind of altruism, as well as provide the family employee with objective performance evaluations and critical advice.

Outcomes of Family Business

Successful family firms create jobs, wealth, and help to fund new ventures. These firms are able to take advantage of the business' traditional focus on performance and the family-centered values of long-term loyalty and nurturance. Together, these elements promote the many of the behaviors discussed as part of the resource based view (RBV), including quick decision making and speed to market. Family firms play an important role in the new venture creation process in two ways: by mobilizing both financial and non-financial resources for new start-up ventures and by spinning new businesses off of existing family enterprises. Family provides a larger percentage of finding to start-ups than venture capital firms, especially critical in the early venture stages before a venture has gained credibility from other potential funders (Matthews, Hechavarria & Schenkel, 2010).

Implications for Management

What behaviors are most crucial to the success of family ventures? Three areas are critical to family business success: *trust, communication* and *planning*. While these areas are not unique to family enterprises, they are especially import to them. Understanding each of these elements can help managers work more effectively with family businesses no matter whether the manager's relationship is that of employee, customer, supplier or owner.

Trust. Trust is a psychological state that occurs when one is willing to uphold their commitments and relies on others to do the same. The five dimensions that underlie trust are integrity, competence, consistency, loyalty and openness. With these dimensions in mind it is easy to understand why trust is important to business success and how it facilitates cooperation, reduces harmful conflict, and supports group effectiveness (Rousseau, Sitkin, Burt, & Camerer, 1998, p. 395).

Trust is also a primary attribute of leadership. To maintain and promote trust, managers must be consistently open and honest in their relationships and transactions with employees and customers. Managers are role models who must demonstrate confidence in the integrity and ability of the people in the organization. Conflict is inevitable but when trust is present there is a foundation for resolution.

Communication. Family business functioning can be enhanced or weakened by the type and frequency of communication between the business' stakeholders. Stakeholders who are actively involved in a business are likely to have more up-to-date and detailed knowledge about the venture simply because of their role in it. A primary function of a communication strategy is to communication with family members not involved in daily business affairs.

A successful communication promotes open sharing of knowledge, beliefs, values and goals related to the organization through written documents and family meetings. The family's "rules of the road" can be communicated through documents such as a family constitution and family code of conduct. A wide range of family members should be involved in developing these documents so they reflect the family's shared commitment to specific norms and values. Firm performance and stakeholder satisfaction are enhanced when family documents such as the constitution are in alignment with the company's objectives.

Regularly scheduled meetings provide important opportunities for family members to discuss important issues. These meetings can range from annual retreats, which balance business discussion with fun activities designed to build relationships and to introduce younger family members to the firm, to quarterly family council meetings which provide opportunities for family shareholders to establish their goals and define their role with the business. These gatherings provide a safe place to resolve conflict and are also a forum for educating the next generation of family shareholders. Taken together, these communication tools support successful financial performance and the development of trust (Berent-Braun, & Uhlaner, 2010).

Succession Planning. Succession plays a critical role in family businesses. The company's success in the marketplace, family harmony, and financial results are all dependent on successful transition from one leader to the next. The average tenure of a family business CEO is more than 20 years so the transition from one leader to the next will have a significant impact on all stakeholders. In contrast, CEOs of publicly-traded non-family companies serve in that role for an average of six years.

Management succession is an important issue for all types of businesses but family business face additional challenges which may include a restricted pool of applicants, if the family is limiting potential successors to family members, as well as potentially sensitive relationships among incumbent leaders, potential successors, and family stakeholders.

Given these challenges, a best practice in succession is to view it as a dynamic process which extends over time and requires thoughtful planning rather than as a single event. Successful succession results from family employment policies which offer employment only to qualified and experienced personnel and family standing brings no special treatment. A second best practice for succession involves a committee of outside advisors in addition to family members playing a role in identifying the successor. For example, a steel manufacturer hired a search firm to evaluate all its executives and selected the most promising for membership on the executive committee. As part of the evaluations, some family and non-family employees were told that they did not have a future at the firm. Several years later, the new CEO was selected from among the members of the executive committee.

Questions for Students

1. How do family-owned or –controlled firms differ from management-controlled firms?
2. What is the resource based view and how does it differ between family and non-family business?
3. Would you want to work for a family business? Why or why not?

Exercise

American Chemsol Corporation (ACC), a successful chemicals and solvents manufacturer now in its third generation of family ownership, is preparing for its annual stockholder's meeting which will be held in four months. The CEO, President, and Chair of the Family Council are holding a planning session. As the meeting begins, it becomes apparent that the three individuals are not aligned in their thinking about the company's strategy for the future. At issue is whether the company should retain cash to buy out its soon-to-be-retiring CEO or invest in computer technology to improve business operations and customer relationships or do something else? Should the company consider debt financing so that it can do both? They must reach some agreement so they can prepare a proposal for the meeting.

Roles. The exercise has three character roles and one observer role. Each character role has their own view of what is in the company's best interest. The character's perspectives may not align with one another at first. However, the characters share the family values and traditions that are the foundation of the business and each of them is committed to its continuing success. During the role play, the shared values and commitment that each character has to the success of the company prompts them to move toward a position that is aligned with the positions of others.

Chair of Family Council. The chairperson represents thirty family owners who do not work for ACC. The Council facilitates communication between management and non-employee owners. The Chairperson is tasked with representing the Family Council's perspective to management. Council members hold 48% of ACC stock. Approximately half of the council members rely on their dividend checks to fund their lifestyle and are opposed to taking on debt or non-family partners.

Chief Executive Officer. The CEO has held this position for twelve years and is planning to retire within two years. With retirement just around the corner, the CEO wants to be sure that the company has sufficient reserves to buy his shares, and thus fund his retirement. The CEO has fought every effort to upgrade the company's computer systems. Under his leadership the company has retired all its debt and he has taken a neutral position on future corporate borrowing.

President. The President has worked in the company for ten years, five years in her current role. She has been very successful and both the Board and non-employee owners have agreed that she will serve as President and CEO when the current CEO retires. The President is concerned that American Chemsol is becoming less efficient and risks losing market share to the competition. The President wants to upgrade the company's enterprise software to help streamline and improve operations. She sees a lot of potential for the company and is willing to take on debt, especially now that interest rates are near historical lows.

Observer. The Observer is tasked with providing objective and impartial feedback. The Observer will track the role play, making note of each character's position and shifts throughout the role play, as described in the following procedure section. The Observe should also note areas of agreement and disagreement in the discussion. Consider how the systems theory model can help you understand the dynamics of the conversation.

Tips on Role Playing

- Be yourself as much as you can.
- Imagine yourself in your character's life. Consider your character's history with the company and their future plans.

Procedure. Each student will select a role and become familiar with it. Once the role play begins, the observer will track the time informing the group at five minute intervals. The role play lasts for ten to fifteen minutes. The three characters will first share their perspective on the company's strategy with regard to buying out the CEO and investing in software. The characters will then acknowledge their shared commitment to, and interest in, the success of ACC. Acting on this shared interest, the characters will propose steps which resolve their concerns relating to buying out the CEO, investing in technology and taking on debt. If time permits, they should draft the proposal to be presented at the Board meeting. The role play should be interactive and students are encouraged to ask questions of one another to learn more the various perspectives.

Feedback. The order of feedback begins with the participants and ends with the observer. The characters should address the following questions:

1. From your character's perspective, what is your reaction to the conversation with your colleagues? How was it different in the beginning, middle, and end of the role play?
2. Based on the conversation, what do you think the family's shared values are?

Case: Fasteners for Retail (FFr)

In December, 1999, Gerry Conway faced the toughest decision of his 37 years as an entrepreneur. Something had to be done about the long-term future of Fasteners for Retail (FFr), the business he had founded in 1962. The company had been extremely successful, with sales doubling every 5 years since the 1980s, and the market for the company's point-of-purchase display products was still growing.

With no dominant players in FFr's niche, Conway saw nothing but opportunity ahead. Still, he was concerned. The company had been debt-free from the start, but feeding its continuing growth would require an infusion of cash. At 69, Conway felt that this was more risky than he wanted to assume. An even more pressing concern for Conway is the recent announcement by his son, Paul, that he does not want to become FFr's next president and instead planned to leave the company. None of his other children were interested in becoming part of the leadership team. He mused:

> *I am a good entrepreneur but I don't like the managerial part of the business. I have a good manager here in Don Kimmel (the non-family company president). Until a year ago I was ambivalent about the future, but now I realize that I am ready to make a transition.*

Business History

Gerry Conway was the classic American entrepreneur—visionary, charismatic, driven, inpatient, and independent. He started a career in sales as a printing broker and, after a few years, hit upon the idea of adding display and merchandising accessories as part of the business. The advantage to selling accessories was that he could sell the same product to many companies, simultaneously, which was not possible in display printing.

Continued Growth at FFr

Within a decade, Conway began to focus exclusively on display accessories and fasteners within the point-of-purchase (POP) industry. POP products include the signs, displays, and devices, and structures that are used to merchandise products in retail stores. Conway listened to his customers and found that he was able to design new products to meet their needs. In a niche known for commodity products, FFr had almost 75 patents and patents pending. FFr's unique products and superior service also differentiated it from the competition.

FFr continued to grow rapidly. In the 1990s, Conway began to further professionalize the staff and named Don Kimmel as president. Kimmel was the perfect foil to Conway's creativity and vision. He introduced internal systems which matched the creative design and sales energy which had propelled the company for years.

Family Involvement

The Conway family was involved with the firm from the start. Early in FFr's history, the Conway children earned extra money by putting adhesive on the backs of fasteners. But of the seven children, only three worked in the business as adults. Kevin, the eldest, worked at FFr for many years as a salesman until health problems prompted him to resign. The fourth son, Neil, worked in the warehouse. He was diagnosed with schizophrenia during his first year in college and the structure of part-time employment worked well for him and for the company. Paul, the youngest son, had planned to join FFr from an early age. He joined the firm after having a successful career with another company. Paul came up through the marketing department. When Don Kimmel joined the firm as president, Paul was asked to become his assistant. The timing of the offer was designed to allow Paul to learn the business from a different vantage point and to take part in long-range planning. Bur now, Paul plans to leave the company.

Initially, Gerry Conway and his wife, Marty, were the owners of FFr. As part of their estate plan, they created a trust for each of their children and transferred a substantial amount of the value of FFr to them so as to avoid estate taxes, but without relinquishing control of the company. According to the trust agreement, a number of years, children over age 30 took their shares outright while those who were not yet 30 remained in successor trusts.

Succession Stories

Paul's Story. Paul admired his Dad and was happy to be working with him. Paul wanted to be perceived as contributing to the success of FFR and not working there just because he was SOB (son of boss). Initially, he saw his work with Don Kimmel as a potential launching pad for his new role at the company. Over time he became less interested in working at FFr. Paul came to believe that his Dad was able to manage the growing business because he grew with it, but he felt that he was less equipped than his Dad to manage what was now a large business.

Reflections from the Board of Advisors. Members of the advisory board felt that Paul could learn the job if he wanted to, and that having an experienced management team in place would give him time to learn. One member in particular recounted that Paul stated that he did not want to be in the position of making tough decisions. The member added that Paul may not have realized that he could do the job differently—in a more decentralized and collaborative way than his father.

Founder Gerry Conway's Dilemma

When Paul came to Gerry and said that he did not want to run the business, Gerry was disappointed but knew that Paul had not made this decision lightly. He wanted to support Paul and accept his decision. As Gerry Conway contemplated the future of FFr, his management team put the finishing touches on the company's new strategic plan. The plan made a strong and well-supported case for making a significant capital investment to develop fulfillment and to increase the product line through acquisition.

Conway intuitively knew that the time for the business to aggressively explore these growth opportunities had arrived. Funding the plan would take all the cash out of the business and would also require outside financing. Conway and his wife had given most of the non-voting shares of FFr to their children, but had retained all the voting stock. While the decision was his to make, it was decision that would impact the entire family. A family meeting was scheduled for the following week. It was time for Conway to decide what action to take.

Suggestions for Future Reading

Chrisman, J. C., Chua, J. H., & Steir, L. P. (2002). An introduction to theories of family business. *Journal of Business Venturing, 18*, 441–448.

Pieper, T. M. (2010). Non solus: Toward a psychology of family business. *Journal of Family Business Strategy, 1* (1), 26–39.

Ward, J. L. (2011). *Keeping the family business healthy: How to plan for continuing growth, profitability, and family leadership.* San Francisco: Macmillan.

References

Bertalanffy, L. V. (1972). The history and status of general systems theory. *Academy of Management Journal, 15*, 407–426.

Berent-Braun, M., & Uhlaner, L. (2010). Family governance practices and teambuilding: paradox of the enterprising family. *Small Business Economics, 38* (1), 103-119

Collis, D. H., & Montgomery, C. A. (2008). Competing on Resources. *Harvard Business Review, 86* (7/8), 140-150.

Habbershon, T. G. (2006). Commentary: A framework for managing the familiness and agency advantages in family firms. *Entrepreneurship Theory and Practice, 30*, 879.

Frank, H., Lueger, M., Nosé, L., & Suchy, D. (2010). The concept of "familiness": Literature review and systems theory-based reflections. *Journal of Family Business Strategy, 1* (3), 119–130.

Matthews, C. H., Hechavarria, D., & Schenkel, M. T. (2012). Family business: A Global perspective from the panel study of entrepreneurial dynamics and the global entrepreneurship monitor. In A. Carsrud & M. Brännback (Eds.), *Understanding Family Business* (Vol. 15, pp. 9-26): New York: Springer.

Mazzi, C. (2011). Family business and financial performance: Current state of knowledge and future research challenges. *Journal of Family Business Strategy, 2*, 161-181.

Poza, E. J. (2010). *Family business* (3rd ed.). Mason: OH: South-Western Cengage.

Rousseau, D. M., Sitkin, S. B., Burt, R. S., & Camerer, C. (1998). Not so different after all: A cross discipline view of trust. *Academy of Management Review, 23*, 393–404.

Stewart, A., & Hitt, M.A. (2012). Why Can't a Family Business Be More Like a Nonfamily Business?: Modes of Professionalization in Family Firms. *Family Business Review, 25*(1), 58-86.

Stockmans, A., Lybaert, N., & Voordeckers, W. (2010). Socioemotional wealth and earnings management in private family firms. *Family Business Review, 23*, 280–294.

Taguiri, R., & Davis, J.A. (1996). Bivalent attributes of the family firm. *Family Business Review. 9*, 199–208.

Weise, K. (2011). Behind five guys' beloved burgers. *Bloomberg Business Week*. Retrieved fromhttp://www.businessweek.com/magazine/behind-five-guys-beloved-burgers-08112011.html.

Wernerfelt, B. (1984). The resource-based view of the firm. *Strategic Management Journal, 5*, 171–180.

Zellweger, T. M., Nason, R. S., Nordqvist, M., & Brush, C. G. (2011). Why do family firms strive for nonfinancial goals? An organizational identity perspective. *Entrepreneruship Theory and Practice, 5*, 1–20.

PART VIII

Social Responsibility, Ethics, and Spirituality

18. Social Responsibility

Gilbert Tan
Singapore Management University

Ethan Chong Wei Nurn[1]
Civil Service College, Singapore

Monica Thiel
Independent Consultant

The Occupy Wall Street demonstrations started in the US on 17th September 2011, and spread worldwide to other countries across cities in Europe and Asia. The demonstrators wanted to restore social and economic justice in the society by protesting against lobbyists, corporate greed, and abuse of corporate power, especially in the financial industry. This series of demonstrations is an indication of the growing public disillusionment with business, and illustrates the need for corporate social responsibility (CSR) on the corporate agenda. Society is indeed becoming more wary and critical of business. As business becomes larger and more influential, society's expectations of business increase accordingly. However, the gap between societal expectations and social performance by business is increasing, as evidenced by the unethical business practices which led to the subprime mortgage crisis that started in 2008, as well as the collapse of Lehman Brothers. CSR can be viewed as attempts by companies to reduce the gap between societal expectations and their social performance. Business leaders are now paying more attention to CSR-related issues, such as fair labor conditions, product safety, corporate governance, environmental protection, and community welfare.

---

[1] The views expressed by the second author are done in his personal capacity and do not represent the official views of the Civil Service College.

Nature of CSR

Definition

Although there is no originating date of CSR, the notion that business has societal obligations can be traced to the aftermath of the Industrial Revolution in the 19th century. Essentially, CSR is about companies fostering social and environmental outcomes into their business operations, and enhancing the relationship between business and society. The definition of CSR is still evolving into multitudes of definitions and theories. Consequently, CSR is often used interchangeably with sustainability and sustainable development. Some early CSR scholars define CSR as the *commitment by business to seriously consider the impact of its actions on society and the natural environment.* Others define CSR as the *obligation of decision makers to take actions that protect and improve the welfare of society and the environment as a whole along with their own interests* (Davis & Blomstrom, 1975; Sarre, 1995).

Two popular CSR frameworks are Carroll's (1991) pyramid of CSR and Elkinton's (1997) triple bottom line (TBL). Carroll's pyramid of CSR gained much acceptance among academic scholars, as it was one of the earliest CSR frameworks that was theoretically coherent, and could guide both research and practice. Since then, researchers have conducted empirical studies based on the pyramid of CSR framework. In contrast, the TBL framework is a more practitioner-oriented framework that gained popularity in the late 1990s. In essence, these two frameworks embrace a multi-stakeholder view of corporate social performance and sustainability. Both frameworks explicitly specify that socially responsible companies must go beyond their obligation to make profits for their shareholders and emphasize the responsibilities that companies have to other stakeholders, such as employees, suppliers, government and community.

Pyramid of CSR

Carroll's (1979) four-part definition of CSR is one of the widely accepted definitions among management scholars. This definition focused on the types of social responsibilities business has—the economic, legal, ethical, and discretionary responsibilities—which mirror the types of expectations that society has of companies at a given point in time. This four-part definition gave rise to the *pyramid of CSR*, with economic responsibilities forming the base of the pyramid, and philanthropic responsibilities at the top.

Economic Responsibilities

These refer to business' responsibility to earn profits for its shareholders. To fulfill their economic responsibilities, companies should produce goods and services that society desires, and sell them at fair prices that society think represent the true value of the goods and services delivered, and provide businesses with sufficient profits to sustain its existence and growth to reward its investors. As the business environment becomes more and more competitive, the pressure on companies by their stockholders and investors to meet their economic responsibilities becomes more real. However, being profitable is not good enough, there are three other responsibilities that companies need to fulfill in order to gain acceptance and legitimacy from their stakeholders.

Legal Responsibilities

These refer to business' responsibility to comply with the laws of the societies they operate in as these laws reflect the societies' views of what are considered fair practices. However, legal responsibilities do not capture the full range of behaviors that society expects of business. This is because (a) the law cannot possibly address all the issues that business faces as new issues constantly emerge as the world constantly innovates and changes (e.g., social media, genetically modified food, e-commerce), (b) the law oftentimes lag behind changes in society's values or ethics as it takes time for changing social values to be reflected in the law, and (c) the laws may more accurately reflect the personal interests and political agendas of the legislators than what society deems to be appropriate.

Ethical Responsibilities

These include the standards, norms, values, and expectations that reflect what society regards as fair, just and consistent with the moral rights of all of business' stakeholders (e.g., employees, consumers, shareholders, community). In contrast to legal responsibilities, which often specify the minimum standard, ethical responsibilities go beyond what is required by law. For example, some companies take extra effort to implement environmental protection measures that are above legal mandates as a commitment to their ethical responsibilities to society. Ethical responsibilities are constantly evolving as societies' values change over time and differ globally.

Philanthropic Responsibilities

These refer to the obligations by business to undertake voluntary or discretionary activities for the betterment of the society and its stakeholders. These activities are not expected of business in an ethical sense and are not mandated by law. Examples of activities that companies undertake to fulfill their philanthropic responsibilities include corporate donations, product or service donations, and employee volunteerism. Philanthropic responsibilities are entirely discretionary activities undertaken by companies that are desired by society. They represent the companies' effort to do good works for their stakeholders, local communities and society at large.

The four components of the *pyramid of CSR* should be viewed as a unified whole, rather than as separate components of CSR. The challenge for companies is to make decisions and take actions that will simultaneously fulfill the economic, legal, ethical, and philanthropic expectations which society imposes on them. In other words, a company needs to be simultaneously profitable, law-abiding, ethical, and voluntarily contribute to society in order to be considered socially responsible.

The Triple Bottom Line

The triple bottom-line gained popular acceptance in the 1990s, and asserts that companies should take into account three types of performance—social, environmental and economic. Similar to the pyramid of CSR, the concept of the triple bottom line (TBL) is based on the observation that a company has responsibilities to multiple stakeholders instead of only to its shareholders. The TBL also captures the notion that economic measures are not the only measure for corporate success and sustainability. Shell popularizes the TBL concept, and calls it "people, planet, and profit." "People" refers to the social bottom-line directed at improving the quality of people's lives, labor conditions, and community welfare. It measures how the company impacts the community. "Planet" refers to the environmental bottom-line directed towards protecting and conserving the natural environment. It measures the company's impact on the natural environment. "Profit" refers to the economic bottom line in terms of the level of wealth and value creation. It measures the company's economic impact on the business environment.

Corporate Responses to CSR

The pyramid of CSR and TBL frameworks identify the accountabilities and obligations that business has to society, and define what constitute social responsibilities for businesses. In order to fulfill these responsibilities, companies have to take specific actions. These actions have been termed corporate social initiatives, which refer to activities and programs undertaken by companies in response to their various responsibilities to society, and in their efforts to be good corporate citizens of the local communities where they operate.

Kotler and Lee (2005) identifed six key types of corporate social initiatives:

Cause Promotion

A business engages in cause promotion when it provides financial and non-financial resources, such as corporate facilities and human resources to sponsor programs to enhance the awareness and concern for a social cause. The key focus is to direct attention to and create interests in a specific cause. Often, cause promotion involves activities such as fundraising and volunteer recruitment. For example, The Body Shop runs campaigns to encourage their customers to sign petitions for environmental and animal rights causes, and bans animal testing in its cosmetic products manufacturing process. The Body Shop is a good example of how a business initiates its own programs to support a cause that it endorses.

Cause-Related Marketing

A business engages in cause-related marketing when it makes a charitable contribution in support of a specific social cause for its own marketing purposes. Cause-related marketing has proven itself to be a powerful tool for stimulating sales, and therefore constitutes a win–win situation for both the social cause and the business. For example, Coca-Cola ran a program to make a donation of 15 cents per carton of Coke sold at Wal-Mart stores to Mothers Against Drunk Driving. It was reported that this program increased the sales of Coca-Cola by almost five times.

Corporate Social Marketing

This type of initiative involves a business developing and implementing comprehensive campaigns to change social behaviors directed at improving community well-being, and requires the most effort and commitment from the firm. In the past, it was predominantly the public sector agencies that were involved in corporate social marketing campaigns. However, things are now changing. Many socially responsible private companies are now actively participating in corporate social marketing campaigns on a broad range of issues—health, road safety, water conservation, crime prevention, organ donation, etc. Often, the company will partner with other public or non-profit agencies. For example, Subway partnered with the American Heart Association to run a corporate social marketing campaign to educate the public on how to engage in healthy heart habits.

Corporate Philanthropy

This involves business making direct contributions to a charity or cause, and is traditionally the most practiced form of corporate social initiatives. Examples of corporate philanthropy activities include giving cash donations, awarding scholarships to needy students, offering grants to a charity or non-profit organization, and giving donations in kinds, such as, donating products, services, technical expertise, etc.

Community Volunteering

Broadly, this involves the firm taking practical actions to encourage its employees, retail partners, and franchise members to donate their time and talents to support a charity or social cause. For example, store employees at The Body Shop were renumerated at the rate of a half-day's wage every week for volunteering in community services. There are many ways companies can help to promote community volunteering. This includes giving time-off to employees to participate in community services, identifying charities or social causes to support, partnering with charity organizations and activist groups to recruit employees as volunteers, and rewarding employees for their community services activities.

Socially Responsible Business Practices

These are good practices undertaken by companies that are not required by law, but benefit the community and promote the well-being of the companies' stakeholders. Companies can engage in a wide range of socially responsible business practices, each targeting a special social cause or stakeholder. For example, many companies implement elaborate recycling and waste management programs in response to the growing concerns on environmental issues. Some companies have specific human resource programs directed at improving employees well-being such as fair employment practices, work-life integration, work-place safety, and employee assistance programs. Further to this, some companies implement specific programs such as product safety, full disclosure of product information, etc., to protect the rights of consumers.

Outcomes of CSR

There are costs and benefits associated with CSR. Some people believe that CSR initiatives incur costs to companies. These costs include using up resources (e.g. increased wage cost to hire more people to drive CSR initiatives, time required to gain new competencies to implement CSR initiatives), decreased profits to stockholders, and the costs of CSR initiatives that may be passed on to consumers.

However, there is a body of research to support the business case for CSR. Companies can derive benefits from being socially responsible, and these benefits can be categorized into two categories: tangible and intangible benefits (Tan & Chong, 2009).

Intangible Benefits

These benefits are difficult to quantify, as they are non-physical in nature. The intangible benefits that CSR has been empirically shown to lead to include: increased corporate reputation (e.g., Logsdon & Wood, 2002), improved employee attitude (e.g., Fulmer, Gerhart, & Scott, 2003), attracting quality employees (Backhaus, Stone, & Heiner, 2002), and reduced business risk (Orlitzky & Benjamin, 2001). Other intangible benefits that CSR has been argued to enhance include: reduced government regulation, enhanced investors' confidence, reduced criticism from public, increased customer goodwill and loyalty, enhanced brand image, and increased employee motivation, morale, commitment, trust, and loyalty.

Tangible Benefits

These benefits are easily quantifiable in financial and physical terms. One of the most studied tangible organizational benefits of CSR is that of financial performance—much research has been done on the nature of the relationship between social performance and financial performance (Orlitzky, Schmidt, & Rynes, 2003), with inconclusive results. There are also studies which suggest that socially responsible companies perform no worse and usually perform better in the stock market than non-socially responsible companies (Domini, 2001). Other tangible benefits of CSR include enhanced market shares, increased sales revenue, and improved cost efficiency.

In addition, intangible benefits have been argued to lead to tangible benefits. For example, enhanced social reputation has been argued to result in repeat purchases by consumers and a company's ability to attract and retain better employees, thereby increasing profits in the long run. Also, increased employee learning was argued to lead to enhanced organizational capability, which leads to more efficient processes, utilization of resources, development of new resources, and increased productivity, ultimately reducing operating costs or increasing sales revenue (Kotler & Lee, 2005).

Implications for Management

As organizations and special interest groups are becoming more aggressive and powerful, managers have come to realize that the risk of not responding proactively to CSR-related issues (such as environmental protection, corporate governance, labor conditions, and human rights) is high and can be costly to the firm's reputation and financial performance. In response to this growing pressure for business to be socially responsible, some managers have adopted ad hoc measures to implement CSR programs in their companies to show that they are doing something about the issue.

Managers should not fall into this trap. Badly conceived and implemented CSR programs are often costly to businesses and fail to make any significant social impact. In order to do the most social, environmental, and economic good, managers must learn how to align their CSR programs with their business goals and activities. In other words, CSR programs must not be ad hoc but integrative. This calls for proper development and implementation of a comprehensive CSR approach. Specifically, this involves:

Identifying the Social and Environmental Causes to Support

Given the limited resources managers have, they need to be selective in their choice of which social and environmental causes to support. Companies will spread their resources too thin if they try to be involved in supporting too many causes. The most obvious criterion of which social and environmental causes to select is to select those that directly relate to the companies' business strategies (as reflected in their mission, values and operations). This will result in synergy. Also, some companies select social and environmental causes that are of relevance or concern to the companies' major stakeholders—employees, customers, powerful special interest groups, investors, and local communities, etc.—to obtain their support and cooperation.

Designing CSR Programs

In designing their CSR programs, it is helpful for companies to garner inputs from multiple stakeholders, including representatives from local communities or activist organizations. Involvement and participation at the early stage of

CSR efforts will help to reduce resistance at the implementation stage. The first step to designing CSR programs is to define clear goals in terms of measurable outcomes. The next step is to select the appropriate corporate social and environmental initiatives to meet the CSR goals. The corporate social and environmental initiatives chosen should 1) meet the needs of the social and environmental initiatives, and 2) relate to the business' objectives and goals, in order to harness the potential synergistic effect of the CSR efforts. For example, cause-related marketing is the most effective type of initiative for creating awareness and raising funds for social and environmental benefits. This is an excellent choice for businesses that are interested in improving sales and strengthening their brand image (Kujala, 2015).

Implementing the CSR Programs

Senior management support and effective communications are crucial to the successful implementation of CSR programs. Senior management support releases resources and lend credibility to CSR efforts. Effective communications facilitate the coordination and execution of successful CSR programs. Breakdown in communication often lead to confusion regarding roles and responsibilities, and may also lead to misunderstandings and conflicts among parties involved in CSR programs. It is important to hold regular meetings to gather feedback from all parties involved to identify problems and resolve issues.

Evaluating the outcomes

Evaluation can make people defensive. However, it is still necessary and companies should allocate sufficient resources for evaluation and reporting. The purpose of evaluation is to obtain information on whether the CSR programs have achieved their desired objectives and goals. This information then becomes input for more successful CSR efforts in the future, and is sometimes required for reporting to external stakeholders involved in the CSR programs.

Reporting the results

Reporting the results of a firm's CSR programs helps to improve communication with the stakeholders and consequently strengthen the level of stakeholder engagement. It is a good practice to report the evaluation results even if they are not positive. Transparency will help to improve the trust stakeholders have towards the firm in the long run. Managers should consider different levels of reporting (in terms of the level of detail) to different stakeholders. For example, in internal reporting, there should be detailed information for informed managerial decision-making and problem solving by relevant stakeholders. However, in external reporting, less details (but still sufficient for meaningful reporting) should be reported to ensure readability.

Sustaining CSR Efforts

Companies need both extrinsic and intrinsic drivers to sustain CSR efforts. An extrinsic driver of CSR efforts is the belief in the business case for CSR. The business case for CSR dictates that it is in the companies enlightened self-interest to engage in CSR due to the many tangible and intangible benefits associated with CSR practices. However, the relationship among social, environmental and financial performance is not straightforward. Past experience shows that companies do not obtain the immediate benefits of CSR in the short-run.

One intrinsic driver of CSR efforts is the belief in the normative case for CSR. This refers to the belief that companies should engage in CSR simply because it is the right thing to do. The normative case for CSR asserts that it is the moral duty of companies to be good citizens and do good works for the society. The foundation of the normative case is based on the notion of the social contract, which defines the relationship between business and society. The social contract refers to the shared understandings and mutual expectations between business and society. It defines what companies need from the society, and in turn specifies what they can give back to the society. From the social contract perspective, companies can only exist with the consent of society. They need the support and cooperation of employees, customers, suppliers, communities, special interest groups, government and other stakeholders to function in society.

Questions for Students

1. What is your definition of CSR?
2. Discuss Carroll's pyramid of CSR and Triple Bottom Line.
3. What activities can businesses and governments undertake to be socially and environmentally responsible?
4. How do businesses and governments benefit from fulfilling their social and environmental responsibilities?
5. What challenges do businesses encounter in fulfilling their CSR commitments?
6. Do you think that CSR should be an end in itself for businesses, and should not be used as a branding strategy to advance the business firm's competitive advantages? Please explain.

Exercise: An Organizational Assessment

Use the scale below to rate each of the 16 statements according to how accurately it describes the organization that you are assessing:

Strongly Disagree	Disagree	Neutral	Agree	Strongly Agree
1	2	3	4	5

____ 1. The primary goal of this organization is to make as much profit as possible.

____ 2. This organization strives to comply with all the state laws and regulations.

____ 3. The management of this organization does not compromise ethical norms of the society in order to achieve corporate goals.

____ 4. This organization contributes resources to the community.

____ 5. This organization strives to lower their operational costs.

____ 6. People in this organization operate strictly within the legal framework of the society.

____ 7. People in this organization always do what is right, fair and just.

____ 8. This organization strives to provide for community betterment.

____ 9. This organization strives for the highest returns to their shareholders.

_____ 10. People in this organization do not violate some laws and regulations even though it may be expedient to do so.

_____ 11. This organization avoids doing harm at all cost.

_____ 12. The management of organization actively promotes employee volunteerism.

_____ 13. This organization is not distracted from its economic function by solving social and environmental problems.

_____ 14. This organization adheres to all state rules and regulations even though it may be costly for them.

_____ 15. The management of this organization does not find it expedient to engage in questionable practices for economic gains.

_____ 16. This organization commits resources to support culture and arts.

(Source: Adapted from Tan, G., & Komaran, R. (2007). Perceptions of CSR in Singapore. _Journal of Asian Business, 23,_ 1–14.)

Exercise Instruction

This questionnaire measures the four components of corporate social responsibility (CSR), namely, economic, legal, social and philanthropic responsibilities. Sum up the scores of the items of each component. The higher the score, the stronger the organization is in that particular component of corporate social responsibility.

Economic Responsibility	Legal Responsibility	Ethical Responsibility	Philanthropic Responsibility
1.	2.	3.	4.
5.	6.	7.	8.
9.	10.	11.	12.
13.	14.	15.	16.
Total:	Total:	Total:	Total:

Questions for Students

1. Share your findings with your classmates.
2. Briefly describe the organization that you have assessed. What are its mission, vision, core businesses, and key CSR activities/programs?
3. Overall, what is your assessment of the organization's level of CSR? Is it a socially and environmentally responsible organization? Why or why not?

Case: Sony Electronics (Singapore) Pte Ltd, Energy Technology Singapore

Sony Electronics (Singapore) Pte Ltd, Energy Technology Singapore (SETS) was first incorporated under the name of Sony Display Device (SDS) in 1990, to manufacture Sony's Trinitron Cathode Ray Tube television. The SETS factory was subsequently converted to manufacture lithium ion batteries in 2008. Sony Electronics (Singapore) Pte Ltd is a member of the Sony group of companies in Singapore, which belongs to Sony Corporation, the Japanese multinational conglomerate headquartered in Tokyo, Japan.

SETS seeks to be an environmentally and socially responsible company, and places high importance on safety and community service activities. As a manufacturing firm, SETS is mindful of its environmental impact, and has invested heavily on environmental-friendly technologies to reduce its carbon footprint. SETS has an elaborate Environmental Management System (EMS) to implement its environmental policies. Structurally, the EMS is organized into 4 core groups, with the Managing Director at the head of the structure. The 4 core groups and their functions are: the Site Environment function is responsible for scheduling internal audits (for environmental, safety, quality, and occupational health); the Product Environment function is responsible for ensuring parts and materials from suppliers are free from banned chemicals; the Green Procurement function is responsible for ensuring that suppliers are environmentally-friendly; and the EMS workgroup function is responsible for carrying out SETS' environmental objectives (e.g. reduced energy and raw material usage).

SETS takes considerable efforts to comply with Singapore's laws and regulations. These regulations include those on environment pollution control, waste disposal handling and work place management. Activities to ensure the compliance with Singapore's laws include regular maintenance and checks on equipment, checking of samples from storm water discharge for contamination, and screening of noise levels by external parties. SETS' level of air emission, water samples, storm water discharge, and boundary noise has always been found to be within the limits of the national standards.

SETS is actively involved in community volunteering to foster positive relationships with its community stakeholders. It encourages its employees to take part in community projects such as fulfilling children's wishes on Christmas, delivering food packages to the poor, fund-raising walks, and making donations to causes such as disaster relief funds and charitable organizations. The Sony Group in Singapore was awarded the Arts Supporter 2008 Award from the National Arts Council for its generous sponsorship of the Singapore Visual Festival.

(The information provided in this case study is based on publicly available information obtained from the company's website: *www.sony.com.sg,* and its *CSR Report* 2009.)

Questions for Students

1. What are the key activities undertaken by SETS to fulfill its commitment to CSR?
2. What benefits can SETS hope to derive from its social and environmental activities?
3. What other CSR activities can SETS participate in to further its commitment to CSR?

Suggested Websites for Further Reading of CSR and Sustainability

1. 3BL Media: http://3blmedia.com/
2. CSR Asia: www.**csr-asia**.com/
3. World Business Council for Sustainable Development: www.**wbcsd**.org

References

Backhaus, K. B., Stone, B. A., & Heiner, K. (2002). Exploring the relationship between corporate social performance and employer attractiveness. *Business & Society, 41,* 292–318.

Carroll, A. B. (1991). The pyramid of corporate social responsibility: toward the moral management of organizational stakeholders. *Business Horizons, 34* (4), 39–48.

Davis, K., & Blomstrom, R. L. (1975), *Business and society: Environment and responsibility.* New York: McGraw-Hill.

Domini, A. (2001). *Socially responsible investing: Making a difference and making money.* Chicago: Dearborn Trade.

Elkington, J. (1997). *Cannibals with forks: The triple bottom line of 21st century business.* Oxford: Capstone.

Fulmer, I., Gerhart, B., & Scott, K. (2003). Are the 100 best better? An empirical investigation of the relationship between being a "great place to work" and firm performance. *Personnel Psychology, 56,* pp. 965–993.

Kotler, P., & Lee, N. (2005). *Corporate social responsibility: Doing the most good for you company and your cause.* Hoboken, NJ: Wiley.

Kujala, J. (2015). Branding as a Tool for CSR. In Wolf, R., Issa, T. & Thiel, M. (Eds.), *Empowering organizations through corporate social responsibility* (pp. 266–287). Pennsylvania: IGI Global.

Logsdon, J. M., & Wood, D. J. (2002). Reputation as an emerging construct in the business and society field: An introduction. *Business & Society, 41,* 365–370.

Orlitzky, M., & Benjamin, J. D. (2001). Corporate social performance and firm risk: A meta-analytic review. *Business & Society, 40,* 369–396.

Orlitzky, M., Schmidt, F. L., & Rynes, S. L. (2003). Corporate social and financial performance: A meta-analysis. *Organization Studies, 24,* 403–441.

Sarre, P. (1995). Towards global environmental values: Lessons from western and eastern experience. *Environmental Values, 4* (2), 115–127.

Tan, G., & Chong, W. N. (2009). Industry leadership in business: City Development Limited (CDL). In E. Wong (Ed.), *CSR for sustainability and success* (pp. 63–81). Singapore: Marshall Cavendish.

19. Ethics

Astrid Kersten
La Roche College

Even though ethical problems have been with us since antiquity, ethics violations are now as commonplace as the names of the companies implicated: financial fraud by Enron and Arthur Andersen, overseas bribery by Siemens, fraudulent government contract charges by Haliburton, Ponzi schemes by Madoff Investment Securities, consumer scams by Amway and Quixtar, mismanagement of government funds by Solyndra and AIG, human resource and environmental violations by Wal-Mart. The list goes on and on, feeding continuous news of new scandals to CorporateCrimeReporter, Corpwatch, CorporateNarc, and other watchdog organizations, that specialize in tracking corporate misbehavior. More recent violation of ethics and law include corporations such as GlaxoSmithKline, a giant global pharmaceutical company. GSK is under investigation by the UK's Serious Fraud Office regarding allegations of bribery in China and Poland (Snyder, 2014), as well as individual members of corporate upper management such as Wal-Mart's VP of Communications who recently resigned for making false statements on his resume (hrgrapevine.com, 2014). Even though many people argue that business ethics is an oxymoron, business ethics is studied and taught to prevent such scandals. Learning about business ethics helps us to understand how and why people make ethical choices, and how to promote ethical behavior in organizations.

Nature of Ethics

Definition

Business ethics is the study of moral behavior and decision-making in organizations—it helps people to determine what is right and wrong. People often experience ethical dilemmas in day to day life—conflicts between what we know we should do (*ethics*), what we want to do (*morality*), what we must do (*law*) and what we actually do (*ethos*). Ethics as field helps us to work through these dilemmas.

Ethics. This is the formal study of what people *ought* to value—using some general theoretical framework based in philosophy and the study of human behavior, ethics maps out what constitutes correct moral behavior. As we will see, different ethical frameworks result in different ideas about what is right and wrong, and why.

Law. This regulates individual and business behavior by stating what behaviors are and are not allowed in society. Law often provides a minimal standard while ethics goes beyond the law, recommending behavior based on moral principle or on collective interest. An ethical perspective may tell you it is wrong to cheat your customers. A legal perspective tells you what ways of cheating are and are not allowed by law.

Morality. A particular ethical framework becomes *morality* if it is adopted by a person or a company as their own guideline for right and wrong conduct. Companies often formalize morality into a code of conduct—rules and policies that specify to employees, suppliers and others what behavior is expected. Such codes often include legal guidelines but also additional standards for honest or compassionate behavior. For instance, a company code of conduct can include a vision statement about the company's commitment to honest business, legal guidelines against bribery, and company discipline policies prohibiting employees from accepting gifts from customers.

Ethos. Unfortunately, people do not always do what they should do, what they must do, or even what they want to do. Individuals sometimes ignore their conscience and in companies, formal codes of conduct sometimes are not followed because there are other, conflicting, and more central values operating. A desire for profit for instance may lead a person or a company to accept bribes in spite of legal guidelines, codes or morals. We talk about a personal or company *ethos* to refer to that set of values that *actually* guides and determines behavior (DesJardins, 2013).

Ideally of course, ethics, law, morality, and ethos are consistent and aligned. The field of ethics helps companies and individuals create such consistency by helping them think through the ethical dilemmas. For instance, business ethics can offer a perspective that shows the limitations of a pure profit motive, by pointing out the long term consequences of business choices, the social need for sustainable and ethical business practices, and the importance of a positive image of the company for customers and other stakeholders.

Kohlberg's Stages of Moral Development

At the individual level, one way to approach ethical decision-making is by looking at Kohlberg's (1981) model of moral reasoning. Kohlberg argued that as people grow and mature, they move through 6 sequential stages of development, organized into 3 levels of 2 stages each. At each level and stage, our reasoning about morality changes.

The Pre-Conventional Level. This is the first level which is essentially egocentric and focuses on external consequences, not on rules or principles. In stage 1, individual behavior is obedience and punishment driven: I will not lie, because my parents tell me it is wrong and because I am punished if I lie. In stage 2, the focus is on self-interest, determining "what is in it for me?" If I benefit from the behavior, it's a good thing, individually or in relation to others—"I'll protect you, if you protect me." Often times, pre-conventional reasoning is associated with children, but as we all know, sometimes adults can be stuck in this stage.

Conventional Level. This is the second level in which moral behavior is determined by looking to societal norms and expectations, often regardless of punitive consequences. Behavior is considered to be moral if fits the social norms. Stage 3 is driven by a relational desire to conform to social norms. This happens when we choose to act a certain way because we want to be considered a good person by others. Stage 4 by contrast is governed by a concern for law and order. We abide by the rules because rule-abiding behavior is necessary for an ordered and just society, not because we want to be accepted or liked by others.

Post-Conventional Level. This is the third level where people move from rules to principles. Recognizing that social rules may vary and that at times they may even be wrong, individuals come to select their own principles about what is right and wrong. Stage 5 is driven by social contract, meaning that decisions about what is right and wrong are governed by a desire to determine the greatest good for the greatest number of people. Stage 6, finally, is driven by universal ethical principles—the idea that we can determine right and wrong behavior through identifying just, moral principles to be upheld by all people, regardless of circumstances (see Gibbs, 2013 for further discussion, and Kohlberg's Theory of Moral Development. MP4 on YouTube).

Theories of Ethics

While Kohlberg focuses on individual moral reasoning as it relates to personality and personal development, ethical theory takes a different path. It argues that there are many different valid approaches to ethics, and until we make our own moral choices, there may not always be an easy answer to what is right and wrong. The world is full of ethical dilemmas. For instance, we all know that is wrong to lie and we have laws and codes of conduct that prohibit lying, but unfortunately, life is complicated. Is concealing facts the same as lying? And does the intention make a difference, for instance if I lie to save another person's life? Is it a matter of principle or do the consequences matter? Let's take a look at four different approaches to this issue (Ghillyer, 2010, 2013).

Virtue Ethics. This school of ethics argues that the ethical decisions in our life should reflect our personal commitment to certain ideals. If my *personal* ideal is to be an honest person, then this should be evident at all times in my character and behavior and hence, for me, it would always be wrong to lie. Similarly, a company is committed to honesty would expect all its officers and employees to be honest at all times and would reward honesty over profit, diplomacy, or company politics. If it finds a defect or a danger in one of its products, virtue ethics would demand honest disclosure based on commitment to the ideal.

Universalism. Another school of ethics holds that personal commitment is not the issue but rather, it is *universal duty* and obligation to certain moral ideals. Universalism argues that if something is right or wrong for some people, it is right or wrong for everyone. Universalism holds that it is possible to determine those universally right and wrong principles and that they apply regardless of individual particulars or circumstances. The idea that all business conduct must be based on honesty and good faith is one such principle, and in the case of finding a product defect, again, it would demand full and honest disclosure.

Utilitarianism. This school of ethics focuses on the *consequences* of actions rather than on the intentions, be they individual or universal. It argues that an action is ethical if it produces the greatest good for the greatest number of people. Again, if a company finds a product defect, it should provide honest disclosure, not necessarily on principle but rather because more people would benefit from telling the truth than from concealing it. Sometimes, utilitarianism is associated with muddled ethics, because it allows for the possibility that on a few occasions lying may be ethical. We should remember though that the key principle here is the common good, not individual interests or company profits.

Relativism. Finally, relativism would hold that ethical decision-making is shaped by one's *context*: time, culture, family and circumstances. What is right in some cultures may be wrong in others, and what is right in one situation, may be wrong in another. This does not mean that anything goes and that all ethical guidelines are thrown out the window. Instead, relativism says that we must allow for the possibility that different people and different situations may come to terms with ethics differently. In a given social context, such as in the example of a product defect, relativism would require that the company thoughtfully work through all elements of the situation, carefully weighing all interests, legal obligations, ethical principles, and cultural and legal responsibilities to arrive at a decision whether to disclose or not– a difficult and challenging task at best.

Regardless of the framework selected, it is important that companies—and individuals in the company—are conscious of their ethical choices, and reflect thoughtfully to make sure that ethics, laws, morality and ethos are consistent and aligned. This is not just a matter of principle; there are in fact many positive outcomes of such alignment as we will see later in this chapter.

Ethics and the Law

In the United States, an organization can be held liable for any criminal offenses that are committed by its agents. The United States Sentencing Commission (USSC) is the US Judiciary agency in charge of regulating and updating sentencing policies. The most common areas of legal misconduct include corruption and bribery in violation of the Foreign Corrupt Practices Act, violations of anti-trust legislation, violations related to privacy, intellectual property & security, and violations related to financial practice and corporate governance, regulated most recently in the Sarbanes-Oxley Act (SAO).

U.S. law not only punishes unethical behavior; it offers important incentives to companies that have strong and proactive ethics programs. If a convicted corporation can demonstrate that it had an "effective compliance program" prior to the violation, sentences may be reduced by as much as 95%.

The 2004 USSC Guidelines that were required as part of the SAO, list eight components of an effective compliance program: (1) clearly articulated "standards of conduct and internal controls," such as a company code of conduct or ethics; (2) high-level compliance oversight (e.g., a compliance or ethics officer, but more recently, also oversight by a Board of Directors or similar body); (3) carefully monitored delegation processes; (4) program implementation supported by "adequate resources, appropriate authority, and direct access to the governing authority"; (5) regular and updated compliance and ethics training at all levels of the organization; (6) auditing, monitoring and evaluation systems, and effective mechanisms to allow for and encourage reporting such as an ethics hotline and anti-retaliation mechanisms; (7) program enforcement through incentives and disciplinary mechanisms; and (7) appropriate reporting and corrective responses after detection (Commission, 1987; Johnson, 2004).

Having a proactive compliance program is important, legally and pragmatically, but organizations need to do more to prevent misconduct. One thing they can do it learn about how and why individuals made bad decisions in organizational settings.

Ethics, the Individual and the Organization

When ethical scandals hit the news, the first tendency is to look for so-called "bad apples"—to find self-interested individuals with faulty ethics that can be blamed for the incident, but things are rarely that simple. If it were, organizations could just screen job applicants using the popular pre-employment integrity tests and stop worrying about the problem. Aside from issues of cost, validity and reliability, however, these tests are limited by their focus on honesty, rule compliance, and impulse control, a limited and insufficient spectrum of ethical behavior (Hollwitz & Pawlowski, 1997).

Business Ethics Quarterly devoted a special January 2010 issue to looking at behavioral approaches to individual ethics, seeking to enhance our insight into why individuals in organizations engage in unethical behavior. They note that often times, individuals are not aware of acting unethically, do not see themselves as bad people, and are not really different from most other people

(Cremer, Mayer, & Schminke, 2010). Similarly, now famous Enron whistle-blower Sherron Watkins observes in a recent interview that most people see themselves as moral and ethical, yet all are capable of unethical behavior, given the right circumstances (Beenen, 2009). So what makes good people do bad things? In addition to the usual things like greed and bad leadership, Watkins identifies 3 factors identified by the Association of Certified Fraud Examiners: extreme performance pressure, opportunity for fraud, and rationalization. While most work situations include pressure and opportunity, organizations can limit the impact of these factors, for instance by having clear ethical guidelines and consistent rewards and punishments. Watkins also points to this when she discusses the excessive bonuses and other financial enticements at Enron: "employees become aligned with misdirected corporate values because of what it does for you personally" (Beenen, 2009, p. 277).

As more young people enter the workforce the modern workplace, a culture gap between older employees and so-called millennial may be developing. Recent studies by Bentley University indicate that millennials have a different conception of the "work ethic" than older employees. Millennials were also found to value "meaning and purpose" in work life more than mere climbing the corporate ladder. Working for a reputable and socially responsible/ethical company is a major priority. At the same time, millennials seem to have doubts regarding ethics in the business world (Ashgar, 2014).

Individual rationalization is also affected by the environment. Studies of rationalization and self-reinforcement tell us that we make decisions based on our interpretations of the consequences of our actions (Sepehri, 2011). Particularly important are perceptions of self-interest and internal consistency. People seek to align their self-image with how others see them, and with the way they justify behavior to themselves. That process in turn is strongly influenced by the organizational environment through such factors as performance evaluations, and opportunities for promotion and advancement. Attention must be paid to the role of positive and negative emotion and also to processes of sense-making and selective perception (Beenen, 2009). Clearly, the influence of organizational culture in the shaping of values and behavior is considerable, as is the role of company codes of conduct, and training and education.

Company Codes of Ethics. Company codes of ethics, also referred to as codes of conduct, identify clear legal, procedural and behavioral guidelines designed to help employees to be ethical. Company codes usually focus on the behavior of employees, not the leadership or the company as a whole. This is reflected in the typical topics covered, such as avoiding conflict of interest, protecting company property, preventing employee theft, protecting confidential information, restricting competition, and avoiding bribes.

Sadly, company codes—and the legal frameworks that shape them- have done little to limit *managerial* "mischief"—illegal or questionable practices on the part of managers. For instance, Enron, one of the most famous recent dramas of ethical wrongdoing, prided itself on an exceptional code of ethics, based on "human rights principles" and values of respect, integrity, communication, and excellence. The irony was not only in its failure to control employee behavior. It was also, and more importantly, in the way in which its definition of company success circumvented and subverted ethics. In Enron's corporate culture, making profit was not only justified, it was required, exalted and not subjected to ethical scrutiny.

Sometimes companies formulate a vision and mission based position on ethics— Google for instance, summarizes its position as "Don't be Evil" and this is helpful as an informational and a cultural narrative tool. Ekmak, an Italian manufacturer of machinery and equipment for maintaining green spaces, uses the mantra "We Care!" to express their concern for environmental sustainability. However, vision statements or ethics codes are not effective in and of themselves—they must be a part of a comprehensive ethics and compliance program. Priest and Kaplan (2003) report that they conducted company assessments only to find that employees did not receive the Code, did not understand the Code, or merely made fun of the Code, citing both violations and management's failure to respond to violations. Unless company leadership is committed to ethics and expresses this commitment in all company practices, even the best code will be ineffective.

Ethics, Rights and Responsibilities

Even though individual rights are rarely discussed in company codes of ethics, they are a key component of organizational morality. Companies that want to be ethical need to reflect upon and clearly articulate rights and responsibilities in the relationship with their employees.

Rights. There are 5 areas of individual rights that should be considered (Ghillyer, 2013; DesJardins, 2013; Fisher & Lovell, 2012). The first is the *right to equal treatment*, free from discrimination. In the U.S., this right is established in the Civil Rights Act and related pieces of legislation. What is often not understood though is that this right, as legislated, is in fact very limited. While morally, it may be argued that all people have the right to be treated equally;

this right is limited to those areas specified in the law, such as race, religion, and disability. An organization would do well to consider equal treatment as a general ethical principle structuring its dealings with all employees.

Second is the *right to work*, including such issues as people's right of access to employment, but also, once employed the right to job security, the right to meaningful work, and the right to a clear employment contract DesJardins (2013). In most cases, the right to work is very limited and many states have "employment-at-will" laws that allow organizations to fire employees for any reason or no reason at all, provided it is not discriminatory.

A related right is *the right of due process* which requires that employees are treated in a consistent, procedural manner, not subject to arbitrary authority and decision-making. Most often, issues of due process arise in the context of discipline and termination. Organizations that clearly outline behavioral expectations and rules, and that have established policies and procedures to deal with discipline and termination do not find due process to be a challenge, provided of course managers consistently adhere to the process.

Fourth is *the right to a safe and healthy workplace*. This area is regulated by the Occupational Safety and Health Act (OSHA) and other pieces of legislation, but we still find regular reports of company violations that endanger the lives and well-being of employees. Companies that are committed to ethics often go beyond the narrow provisions of the law and work on ways to ensure employee well-being, including a high quality of work life, positive work life balance, and good health benefits.

Fifth and last is *privacy in the workplace*. This right has been very controversial because most legal interpretations do not guarantee privacy within the organizations. Companies are usually given the right to inspect everything on their premises which includes employee lockers, bags, desks, and the content of their computers and electronic mail, again as long as such inspections are not discriminatory. It is good ethical practice to clearly inform employees of the limits to their privacy, and to let them know if, when and how inspections might occur.

Responsibilities. Individuals and companies not only have rights, they also have responsibilities. Both have a responsibility to follow the requirements of their employment agreement. For individuals, this means to carry out the tasks for which they were hired, but also, a duty of trust, obedience and confidentiality with regard to their employer (DesJardins, 2013). Individuals may have additional responsibilities defined by their professional roles, such as a lawyer's rules regarding client privilege. Loyalty to the company may conflict with loyalty to one's profession.

People also have responsibilities as citizens. If they witness violations of the law, they have a responsibility not to comply and a responsibility to report, i.e. blow the whistle. To the extent that whistleblowing responsibilities might endanger their job security, this in turn could conflict with responsibilities they may have in their personal life, to support themselves and their families. And finally, people have loyalties to themselves, to their own principles and codes of ethics which may be at odds with any of the responsibilities outlines above. Conflict between different important ethical requirements, principles and loyalties is of course what often lies at the heart of "ethical dilemmas." Learning about how to deal with ethical dilemmas is an essential responsibility of managers and students of management.

Learning about Ethics Many people have argued that at least some of the responsibility for the ongoing business ethics scandals must go to education. Ciulla (2011) for instance says that financial disasters and business scandals are rarely the result of poor accounting skills but often the result of executives not being trained in history and ethics. Others like Ghoshal (2005) argue that business schools teach theories of human behavior that implicitly accept and thereby condone unethical behavior. Himsel (2014) says that despite trying, business schools often fail ethics education as well as the creation of an "ethical business climate." This situation needs to change not only because it is the right thing to do, but also because unethical behavior can land corporations into major financial, public relations, and legal problems.

A first step is to make sure that ethics is a key part of all business courses and texts, such as this one. Beenen and Pinto (2009) argue that in learning about ethics, managers—and students of management- need to move beyond a mere theoretical understanding of what is right and wrong. They need to become resistant to corrupt practices, through what they call a "4P" approach: perceive, probe, protest, and persist. The first step, perceiving, requires that managers understand what constitutes corruption and what form it takes, that they become mindful and attentive to their surroundings, and learn to gather information and ask questions. If they think misconduct might actually be happening, the second step is probing: systematically asking questions and collecting reliable, accurate data on the situation. This process of "due diligence" needs to happen, regardless of personal interest. Especially when we ourselves stand to profit from misconduct, probing is an essential step in ensuring ethics and integrity.

If probing makes it clear that an ethics violation has taken place, the next step becomes protest. It helps if students learn ahead of time that whistleblowing is difficult. There is a potential of damage to the company and to one's own interests and relationships. And even though there are legal protections for whistleblowers, they often times to do not work sufficiently to keep individuals free from harm. It also helps if people know how to protest—if they know the various steps that should be followed in terms of internal and then external reporting mechanisms. Finally, individuals must persist. Here, it helps to be clear about one's own ethical values and commitments but also, to have courage. Even more helpful is coalition building. People that blow the whistle together are not only more successful but also better able to persist.

In her interview with Beenen and Pinto (2009), Sherron Watkins indicates that she does not think that management education can make an unethical person ethical. In this sense, your ethical character and choices may be your own. However, educational institutions have a requirement to enforce ethical policies and a zero tolerance policy on cheating and other forms of unethical behavior may go a long way towards weeding out unethical business executives (Beenen & Pinto, 2009).

In the final analysis, business ethics is a collaborative effort, requiring the active involvement of government, lawmakers, business executives, managers, individual employees, customers and educational institutions. In this effort, all stand to benefit from ethical behavior but only through active learning and involvement.

Outcomes of Ethical Behavior

Positive Impact on Individuals

For individuals, ethical behavior is important for peace of mind, human development, and consistency. The *"New York Times"* test is often suggested in this regard, asking people to think about how they would feel if their behavior would appear on the front page of the *NYT*. If you would not want your mother to read that page, don't do it! Ethical reflection also adds to the development of empathy because, as Kohlberg (1981) would argue, we can determine what is right and just by looking at a situation through the eyes of another person.

Finally, it is important that we grow morally, because people tend to be consistent in their decision-making with their choices reflecting their developmental stage about two thirds of the time (Colby et al., 1983).

Positive Impact on Organizations

Much research has surfaced over the last decade that suggests that strong company ethics can be very beneficial for business. The most important argument is an intrinsic one that comes from the study of organizational cultures, suggesting that successful organizations often have a strong commitment to clear values (Collins, 1994). These core values shape the identity of the organization and the behavior of its members.

There are also more instrumental reasons for good ethics. First, ethics affect one's consumer base. There is a growing "ethical consumer" movement that reflects the impact of a positive company image on consumer choices. While many consumers still make buying decisions based on a limited self-interest, shaped by price and product availability, there is an increasing awareness of the ways in which consumer choices can shape company ethics—whether through organized boycott of specific products or companies, or more generally, through the impact of company reputation on customer loyalty, and buying behavior.

Second, company ethics affect employees. Companies with an ethical image are more successful at attracting job applicants, many applicants will consider working for ethical companies even if the pay is lower, and once employed, they will respond positively to an ethical culture, showing enhanced loyalty, productivity and engagement (Center, 2009).

Third, company ethics affect the bottom line. One organization studying corporate ethics and bottom line impact is Ethisphere, an international research institute that focuses on identifying best practices in the areas of organizational ethics, social responsibility, sustainability, and anti-corruption. As part of its research effort, Ethisphere annually identifies the 100 top ranking ethical organizations across the globe. Since 2007, it has compared the performance of all publicly traded companies on its top ranking list against the S&P500, and has observed differences in the rate of return of + 5% in 2007 to +45% in 2011 (BusinessWire, 2011).

Implications for Managers

Managers today must learn all they can about ethics. Not only must they know the legal context of business ethics, they must also know what mechanisms, structures, and processes promote the development of ethical cultures, how to create a code of conduct, and how they themselves can be effective advocates for ethics, modeling ethical integrity through an active process of resistance to corruption and misconduct.

Creating Ethical Cultures

Rewards and punishments are important in shaping individual behavior, but they are not the only important factors. In fact, an over-reliance on these may encourage employees to operate at Kohlberg's earliest stages of moral reasoning, i.e. doing things only because they are rewarded or punished, not because they are right. Organizations need to develop truly ethical cultures.

The Components of an Ethical Culture. The first thing that comes to mind when we think about ethical companies is organizations with strong core values that are articulated and promoted by top leadership (Collins, 1994). However, if Enron has taught us anything, it is that "*strong* cultures" can also be very *wrong* cultures, if there is no critical reflection and no oversight. Many other factors also come into play.

Ethisphere annually publishes a list of what it calls "the world's most ethical companies." More than 3000 companies from more than 100 countries and 36 industries are rated on its Cultural Ethics Quotient (CEQ). In 2014, the top CEQ list contained 144 companies including both US and foreign companies.

Ethisphere's CEQ evaluation framework shows the 5 main categories that managers need to work on in order to make a company culture ethical:

1. *Ethics and Compliance programs* (25%), based on best practices and the standards set by the SEC Federal Sentencing Guidelines, discussed earlier;
2. *Reputation, Leadership and Innovation* (20%), which includes the company's reputation and its track record of legal compliance, litigation and ethics, and innovative initiatives that promote ethics, good governance, transparency and social responsibility
3. *Governance* (10%), in particular governance related to oversight and risk management

4. *Corporate Citizenship and Responsibility* (25%), incorporating sustainability, citizenship and social responsibility practices, such as environmental stewardship, community involvement, corporate philanthropy, workplace well-being and supply chain engagement and oversight.
5. *Culture of Ethics* (20%), looking at value-based culture, ethics codes, and practices both inside and outside the organization. (Ethisphere, 2014)

In addition to these CEQ areas, managers that want to create ethical companies need to pay attention to three additional factors (Laczniak & Murphy, 2004). The first factor is measurement and assessment. Case studies of ethical failure, more often than not, show companies obsessed with limited measures of what constitutes company success, often focused on financial indicators. Organizational success must include a more balanced measure, such as the balanced scorecard approach, which measures success by balancing financial measures with measures of internal process, customer satisfaction, and learning and growth. The second factor is leadership. In many cases of ethical failure, the company leader had a cult-like personality following and was surrounded by people who could or would not question. Stringent company oversight will begin to curtail such practices but beyond that, managers must grow a culture that rewards critical thinking, independent judgment and the rights of individuals. The third factor is creating an effective company code of conduct.

Company Codes of Conduct. In formulating codes of conduct, managers must identify clear legal, procedural and behavioral guidelines to help their employees to be ethical. There are many resources available to managers that demonstrate how to write effective company codes of conduct, what should be in them, and how to train employees in following these codes, including institutes of ethics, sample codes, ethics consultants and ethics bookstores. In writing codes of conduct, managers must carefully consider the law, the company mission statement, and company and individual rights and responsibilities.

In order for codes of conduct to be useful, they must be linked to the company mission and vision. They must also include key elements such as how to safely report misconduct, how employees are protected against retaliation, and company rewards for ethical behavior. Codes of conduct must be followed up with regular training and reinforcement in order to be meaningful and effective. Finally, the leadership at the top must be committed to ethics and must express this commitment in all company practices.

Questions for Students

1. What kinds of unethical behavior have you witnessed, on the job or in your classes? Did this behavior always involve "bad" people? What could the organization have done to prevent the misconduct or to remedy it?
2. How does theoretical perspective affect how we perceive misconduct? How does one's personal perspective affect perception? Are there certain things that you would always consider to be right? Wrong?
3. Some organizations use social media like Facebook to screen potential or current applicants on their ethics. Do you think this is good practice? If you were screened, and the company had access to *all your information*, what would be the result?
4. Have you ever been in a position to "blow the whistle"? How would learning about the 4 Ps have helped you in that position?
5. Groups like *The Yes Men* and *Adbusters* take an activist, culture jamming approach to exposing and criticizing what they see as a lack of corporate ethics. Do you think this is a positive, useful contribution to the ethics debate or not?

Class Exercise

In her interview, Enron whistleblower Sherron Watkins gives an interesting example of the problems in ethical decision-making. After she gave a university lecture, the professor asked the students if they would have done what Ms. Watkins did, and all 400 students said they would have. The professor then asked how many of them would report a fellow student for cheating, and only 2 said they would. He then said that only those 2 followed Ms. Watkins' example. In small groups, discuss the parallels and differences between the 2 situations.

Chapter Research Assignment

One useful way to learn about company ethics is by looking at actual Best Practices. Research an existing company, focusing in particular on their mission statement, code of conduct and ethical practices. You can often find these by exploring different elements of the company website, including employee guidelines and information for investors. You can also google the company name and "lawsuits." It helps to visit the website for Ethisphere and review its 2014 ranking of companies: http://ethisphere.com/worlds-most-ethical/

Case: New Dawn

You are an accountant for a firm that works on corporate restructuring efforts. Your firm specializes in organizations that provide health services, day care, housing and rehabilitation for the elderly. As part of the normal due diligence process, you have been reviewing financial records, assets and HR records for New Dawn, an organization that is currently in financial trouble, in part because they often provide care for homeless and indigent elderly people that usually fall between the cracks. One of the ways New Dawn has been able to do this is by creatively diverting government and insurance funds received on behalf of some clients to the care of clients who are not government by any public or private provisions. Another is by unofficially employing individuals who may not have been fully qualified or had proper working papers.

New Dawn has asked your firm to assist in restructuring the firm. The ultimate goal of this restructuring is to make New Dawn eligible for other government and private sector financial support that would allow it to make its support of the indigent part of its official mission, while continuing quality care for all its clients.

In going over the records, you have noticed many irregularities, all of which supposedly took place for a good purpose. However, if the extent of the irregularities is revealed and documented, New Dawn may be in danger of losing licenses, certifications and may not be able to stay in business.

Case Questions:

What is lost if New Dawn closes its doors?
What is your obligation, 1) to yourself—what moral codes or responsibilities do you hold to in your life as an individual? 2) your profession as an

accountant—what codes apply here? 3) to your organization—see sample company code of ethics below; and 4) to society—what laws, ethics or rules apply?

Suggestions for Further Reading

Beenen, G. and Pinto, J. (2009). Resisting an epidemic of organizational-level corruption: An interview With Sherron Watkins. *Academy of Management Learning & Education,* 8 (2), 275–289

Ciulla, J. B. (2011, April 1). Is business ethics getting better? A historical perspective. *Business Ethics Quarterly*, 21 (2), 335–345.

Jennings, Marianne. (2006) *the Seven Signs of Ethical Collapse: How to Spot Moral Meltdowns in Companies... Before It's Too Late*. New York: St. Martin's Press.

References

A List of Corporate Scandals (2013). Retrieved from http://theeconomicrealms.blogspot.com/2013/01/a-list-of-corporate-scandals.html

Ashgar, R. (2014). Study: Millennials' Work Ethic Is In The Eye Of The Beholder. Forbes.com. Retrieved from http://www.forbes.com/sites/robasghar/2014/01/29/study-millennials-work-ethic-is-in-the-eye-of-the-beholder/

Baucus, M., & Beck-Dudley, C. (2005). Designing ethical organizations: avoiding the long-term negative effects of rewards and punishments. *Journal of Business Ethics, 56*, 355-370.

Beenen, G., & Pinto, J.. (2009). Resisting an epidemic of organizational-level corruption: An interview With Sherron Watkins. *Academy of Management Learning & Education, 8*, 275–289.

BusinessWire (2011). Ethisphere Announces 2011 World's Most Ethical Companies, Retrieved from http://www.businesswire.com/news/home/20110315006776/en/Ethisphere-Announces-2011-World%E2%80%99s-Ethical-Companies#.VE_1nT90xD8

Center, E. R. (2009). *Ethics and employee engagement.* http://www.ethics.org/files/u5/NBESResearchBrief2.pdf.

Ciulla, J. B. (2011, April 1). Is Business Ethics Getting Better? A Historical Perspective. *Business Ethics Quarterly*, 21 (2), 335-345.

Colby, A., Kohlberg, L., Gibbs, J. & Lieberman, M. (1983). A longitudinal study of moral judgment. *Monographs of the Society for Research in Child Development, 200*, 48, 11–96.

Collins, J. (1994). *Built to last: Successful habits of visionary companies.* New York: Harper Collins.

Commission, F. S. (1987). *Federal sentencing guidelines. Chapter 8.* Retrieved from http://www.ussc.gov/2004guid/tabconchapt8.htm.

Cremer, D., Mayer, D., & Schminke, M. (2010). Guest editors' introduction: On understanding ethical behavior and decision-making: A behavioral approach. *Business Ethics Quarterly, 20,* 1–6.

DesJardins, J. (2013). *An introduction to business ethics.* Boston: Mc Graw-Hill.

Ethispere. (2014). *World's most ethical companies 2014.* Retrieved from http://ethisphere.com/worlds-most-ethical/scoring-methodology/

Farkas, A. D. (2004). A few bad apples? An exploratory look at what typical Americans think about business ethics today. New York City: A report for the Kettering Foundation from Public Agenda.

Fisher, C., & Lovell, A. (2012). *Business ethics and values: Individual, corporate and international perspectives* (4th ed.). New York: Prentice Hall.

Frenkel, D.J. (2013). The greatest business ethics scandals of the 21st century. Retrieved from http://prezi.com/z2kgdfif4gxn/the-greatest-business-ethics-scandals-of-the-21st-century/

Ghillyer, A. (2013). *Business ethics now.* Boston: McGraw-Hill

Ghillyer, A. (2010). *Business ethics: A real world approach.* Boston: McGraw-Hill.

Ghoshal, S. (2005). Bad management theories are destroying good management practices. *Academy of management learning and education, 4,* 75–91.

Gibbs, J. C. (2013). *Moral development and reality: Beyond the theories of Kohlberg, Hoffman, and Haidt.* New York: Oxford University Press.

Himsel, D. (2014). Business schools aren't producing ethical graduates. Retrieved from http://www.businessweek.com/articles/2014-08-06/business-schools-dont-teach-ethics-effectively

Hollwitz, J., & Pawlowski, D. (1997). The development of a structured ethical integrity test for pre-employment screening. *Journal of Business Communication, 34,* 203–219.

hrgrapevine.com (2014). Wal-Mart VP resigns over CV lie. Retrieved from

HR Grapevinehttp://www.hrgrapevine.com/markets/hr/ article/2014-09-16-walmart-vp-resigns-over-cv-lie

Johnson, K. (2004). *"Federal sentencing guidelines: Seven minimum requirements. "* Retrieved from http://www.ethics.org/resource/fsgo-series-part-3

Josephson Institute, Center for Business Ethics (2014). Corporate Scandals and their consequences. Retrieved from http://josephsoninstitute.org/business/resources/corporate-scandals.html

Kohlberg, Lawrence (1981). *Essays on moral development* (Vol. I: *The philosophy of moral development.* San Francisco: Harper & Row.

Kohlberg's Theory of Moral Development.MP4. (video) http://www.youtube.com/watch?v=PuhgBujkD10

Laczniak, G., & Murphy, P. (2004). Ethical leadership for improved corporate governance and better business education. In R. A. Peterson, & O. Ferrell (Eds.), *Business ethics: New challenges for business schools and corporate leader* (pp. 175–195). Armonk, NY: M. E. Sharpe.

Priest, S., & Kaplan, J. (2003). *On codes of conduct in light of Sarbanes-Oxley, NYSE listing requirements and the SEC.* http://www.ethicalleadershipgroup.com/articles/Codes of Conductarticlewithrevisions.

Rollert, J. P. (2014). An ethicist on Wolf of Wall Street: The most anti-greed movie ever? *The Atlantic.* Retrieved from http://www.theatlantic.com/entertainment/archive/2014/02/an-ethicist-on-em-wolf-of-wall-street-em-the-most-anti-greed-movie-ever/283806/

Sepehri, M. S. (2011). A micro level view of the self-reinforcement process. *SAM Advanced Management Journal*, 76 (2), 29–37.

Snyder, B. (2014). British officials begin investigation into GlaxoSmithKline, Fortune.com. Retrieved from http://fortune.com/2014/05/27/ british-officials-begin-investigation-into-glaxosmithkline/

20. Workplace Spirituality

Gilbert Tan
Singapore Management University

Eugene Geh
University of Virginia

Annette E. Craven
University of the Incarnate Word

Management scholars tend to ignore the significance of spirituality in organizational lives. For example, the scientific school of management adopts the machine model of human productivity. The administrative school of thought views humans as rational beings. Both of these schools downplay the emotional aspects and ignore the fact that humans have social and emotional needs. In contrast, the human relations school recognizes the importance of workers' feelings and social needs. Spirituality in the workplace acknowledges the importance of attending to the soul of employees in organizations. It understands that employees yearn for meaning in work-life and connection with themselves, others, nature and some supernatural forces beyond oneself. It is important to pay attention to workplace spirituality because people bring their full selves, including their souls, to work. As people spend more time at work, they do not want to waste their lives chasing after empty and meaningless goals in the corporate world. Managers and employees alike long for fulfillment and purposeful lives at work. Even in times of financial crisis and economic upheaval, their concerns are largely on non-material issues. They care about their inner life and relational values such as, love, relationships and positive motivations. People cherish peace, connectedness, hope, and personal development.

Nature of Workplace Spirituality

Definition

Even though the quest for spirituality is as old as humankind, there is no consensus on the definition of workplace spirituality. Management scholars and practitioners struggle to describe exactly the full meaning and scope of this concept. The myriad of definitions of workplace spirituality tend to be centered on the following themes:

Inner Life—the feeling of inner peace and the sense of purpose in life.

Interconnectedness—the inherent human need to feel connected with one's authentic self, others, the entire universe, or some higher power.

Values and Spiritual Principles—the emphases on ethics, virtues, wisdom, intuition, and human emotions as one's moral compass.

Lived Experience—the actualization of the values and spiritual principles, i.e., living out the deeply held values and spiritual principles in one's life.

For the purpose of this chapter, we adopt Ashmos and Duchon's (2000) definition of workplace spirituality as "the recognition that employees have an inner life that nourishes and is nourished by meaningful work that takes place in the context of community" (p. 137). Organizations that promote workplace spirituality attend to the spiritual needs of their employees and take effort to nourish their inner life. These organizations emphasize a sense of community among their employees and provide them the opportunity to experience meaning and purpose at work.

Religion vs. Spirituality

Although there is some overlap between religion and spirituality, research studies confirm that people do differentiate between the two (Mitroff & Denton, 1999). These studies suggest that people tend to have a negative view of religion. Many feel that it is inappropriate to introduce religion into the workplace. Religion involves rituals. The practices of the rituals are conducted publicly and in an organized manner. Hence, religion is seen to be dogmatic and divisive. In contrast, spirituality is more positively regarded. People feel that it is more appropriate to introduce spirituality in the workplace since it is non-denominational, tolerant, and inclusive. Spirituality practices tend to be personal and informal. It is a response to people's yearning for meaning and purpose in life.

Spirituality can be thought of as either faith-specific or non-faith specific. Faith-specific spirituality is the overlap between religion and spirituality. Even though faith-specific spirituality involves public practices of religious faith and rituals, the emphasis is on the inward transformation and inner peace that are based on a personal relationship with God. However, spirituality can also be experienced naturalistically rather than in a theistic way. Non-faith specific spirituality is not based on the teaching and dogma of any specific religion. Its foundation is derived from moral values and ethical principles. Non-faith spirituality is probably the kind of spirituality that is perceived to be most appropriate for the workplace since it is non-religious and non-denominational.

Spiritual Leadership

There is a need for spiritual leadership. Leadership plays an important role in fostering workplace spirituality in an organization. Figure 1 shows the latest version of Fry's Spiritual Leadership Theory. The theory is based on the observation that humans have intrinsic needs for spiritual well-being (SWB). The development of spiritual leadership involves the fostering of altruistic love and hope/faith among employees in pursuit of a shared vision. Spiritual leadership attends to the followers' desires for spiritual well-being (SWB) by cultivating a sense of calling and membership. Individuals with a high sense of calling derive meaning and purpose in life and believe that they can make a difference at work. Individuals with a strong sense of membership feel understood and appreciated in the organization. The theory hypothesizes that spiritual well-being (SWB), i.e., calling and membership at work, would lead to higher organizational commitment and performance. Fry's Spiritual Leadership Theory has been empirically tested and supported (Fry, Hannah, Noel, & Walumbwa, 2011).

Figure 1
Fry's Spiritual Leadership Theory

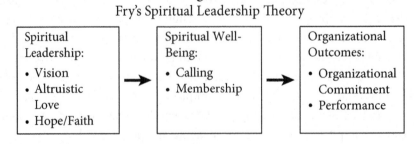

Note: Adapted from Fry et al., 2011, p. 261

Fry's Spiritual Leadership Theory specifies two important tasks that leaders need to do in order to apply spiritual leadership in their organizations. Specifically, spiritual leaders have to:

1. Provide a strong vision to inspire a sense of calling and purpose in the followers. The vision must make the followers feel that what they are doing is meaningful and that their work can make a difference.
2. Cultivate a strong culture in the organization so that employees can develop a sense of belonging and membership. This is achieved by fostering alturistic love among members in the organization whereby leaders and followers genuinely care for and appreciate one another.

To perform these two tasks, the leader needs to have certain values, attitudes, and behaviors that help to promote a sense of calling and membership among members in the organization. Leaders that practice spiritual leadership must exercise genuine care and concern to their followers in order to nurture a culture of altrustic love in the organization. In addition, they have to embrace the values of honesty, integrity, compassion, forgiveness, and kindness to build trust and loyalty. To foster hope and faith in the organization's vision, spiritual leaders have to be endurant, perserverant, and set high standards of excellence.

Organizational Culture and Spirituality

Organizational cultures consist of cognitive systems explaining how people think, reason, and make decisions. At the deepest level culture consists of a complex set of values, assumptions, and beliefs that define the ways in which a firm conducts its affairs. A spirituality-friendly organizational culture has more impact on worker productivity, ethics, values, exercise of authority, innovation, etc., than the economic–political environment. Jurkiewicz and Giacalone (2004) provide a values framework of workplace spirituality culture. Currently, this framework is at its infancy of theory development, and the extent to which it can lead to desirable organizational outcomes such as quality of products and services and customer satisfaction still needs to be empirically tested. The following values are indicative of a spiritual workplace:

Benevolence. Benevolent activities promote positive emotions and result in improved employee attitudes. These include being kind toward others and doing things to promote the happiness and prosperity of employees and other stakeholders:

Generativity. Individuals who are high in generativity are concerned with the long-term consequences of their actions. They are interested in leaving something behind for future generations.

Humanism. This seeks to bring about the greater good in humanity. It is expressed in practices and policies that promote dignity and worth of every individual in the organization. Personal growth and development of members is just as important as achievement of an organization's performance goals.

Integrity. An organization that values integrity will adhere closely to high standards of ethical conduct. Deceptive, insincere, and manipulative behaviors will not be tolerated in the organization that values integrity.

Mutuality. There is emphasis on interconnection and interdependence among employees. The organization balances the needs and contributions of employees and stakeholders. There is a feeling of shared goals, and people work for the common good.

Justice. A just organization values fairness and impartiality. Employees will be treated in an even-handed manner. Rewards and punishments will be equitably distributed.

Receptivity. The presence of receptivity is characterized by openness, supportive relationships, flexibility, and calculated risk-taking. Employees dare to challenge norms and practices. They behave spontaneously and adapt readily to changing environments.

Respect. There will be mutual respect and consideration for others. Everyone in the organization will behave civilly and regard each other with esteem.

Responsibility. Employees take personal responsibility to overcome obstacles in the attainment of organizational goals. They are interested in doing what is right, rather than focusing only on doing the right thing.

Trust. High trust organizations are characterized by employees feeling secure to depend on others, acting more cooperatively, and engaging in less political behaviors.

Alternatively, Rhodes proposed six components which constitute a model for workplace spirituality (2006).

An emphasis on sustainability. In this sense, Rhodes ties limited to resources to the greater good. This involves strategic, long-term thinking which takes into consideration the impact of organizational actions on society, individuals, and the environment.

Values contribution. This component manifests the concept of *live local, think global*. A spiritual organization engages in community and volunteer service. The servant leadership style would be prevalent in a spiritual organization.

Prizes creativity. When spirituality is considered as a phenomenon separate and apart from religion, and leaders recognize that promoting spirituality invites the employee to contribute holistically of their talents, creative potential can be unleashed. This can lead to innovative thinking which can improve an organization's ability to navigate changing environments.

Cultivates inclusion. In a world where diversity can become synonymous with individuality, if the culture does not include spirituality, shared life experiences and lessons learned can fall by the wayside. Exclusivity based on differences can prevent inclusivity which is a key characteristic of a sense of community. A spiritual organization is an intentional organization in building a culture of care that emphasizes that the very differences which make employees diverse as individuals also make them creative as a community.

Develops principles. The concept of cognitive dissonance can be used to explain when an employee's core values are not aligned with an organizations espoused values. Creating a culture of spirituality can help an organization channel the focus from what the stated values are to the focus of using values in the workplace. It can also diminish, even eliminate, the sense of disconnect an employee may feel when their individual values are similar to, but not exactly like, the organization's values.

Promotes Vocation. C12 Group is an organization whose mission is *Building GREAT Businesses for a GREATER Purpose* (http://www.c12group. com/about-c12/). The organization serves business leaders who consider the act of doing business to be the act of ministry. Though admittedly faith-based, with activities grounded in biblical teachings, the leaders and CEOs who belong to this organization do much more than study the Bible. They not only lead organizations which embrace workplace spirituality, but they also consider it their vocation to promote spirituality as leaders. In doing this, these leaders manifest what Rhodes sees as the promotion of a vocation.

An Approach to Workplace Spirituality

Vallabh and Singhal have taken the concept of workplace spirituality, and working from the works of others, have proposed a way to facilitate workplace spirituality using a person-organization fit approach (2014). They contend that both individuals and organizations travel a path to spirituality; the larger

Figure 2
Workplace Spirituality

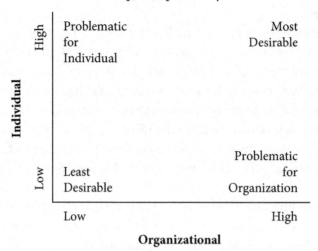

Note: Adapted from Vallabh & Singhal, 2014, p. 197

the organization, the greater the number of individuals in varying stages of spirituality. How then, does an organization create a culture that is appropriately responsive both at the community and individual levels to the varying levels of maturity in spiritual development? The researchers propose that there are two continuums—individual and organization—along which either or both could range from low to high in workplace spirituality.

Vallabh and Singhal use the four scenarios depicted in Figure 2 to propose how a person-organization fit approach can be successful in facilitating workplace spirituality, acknowledging that these are but a few of the many places along the continuum of maturity either may presently be at in a stage of development. They also suggest a variety of ways to conduct the facilitation, through communication in company core values and mission statements or codes of conduct, as an HR practice using policy to reinforce spiritual values, or in the use of interventions at the intrapersonal, interpersonal or group levels. The key is in organizational commitment to workplace spirituality.

Outcomes of Workplace Spirituality

The burgeoning interest in workplace spirituality which has escalated since the Enron disaster and the emergence of Sarbanes-Oxley might be attributed to the popular belief that a spiritual work environment creates a win–win situation for both employees and the organization. Many practitioners adopt the optimistic view and believe that workplace spirituality can lead to desirable individual and organizational outcomes. Proponents of workplace spirituality believe that employees are likely to be more productive, more creative, and more fulfilled if they are working for an organization that meets their spiritual needs. They reason that personal fulfillment and high morals are closely linked to outstanding performance and hence, have a direct impact on an organization's financial success. The linkage between workplace spirituality and desirable outcomes is not just based on practitioners' experiences and observations. There is a growing body of research to support this belief (Karakas, 2009).

Individual Outcomes

There have been ample studies on the impact of workplace spirituality on employee attitudes and behaviors. Workplace spirituality has been theoretically and empirically linked to the following individual outcomes:

Personal Satisfaction and Wellness. Today's corporate world puts much emphasis on material wealth and financial profitably. Workplace spirituality enables employees to gain a sense of personal satisfaction at work and provides them with a deeper sense of purpose in life (Dehler & Welsh, 1994). When work takes on new meaning, it will have a positive impact on employees' sense of well-being.

Sense of Interconnectedness and Community. Employees have social and emotional needs. Life in the materialistic corporate world can be cold and lonely. Workplace spirituality enables employees to feel emotionally supported and that they belong to a community. It gives them a sense of connectedness to themselves and others (Milliman, Czaplewski, & Ferguson, 2003).

Loyalty and Commitment. Workplace spirituality provides meaning and purpose to the worklife of employees. In turn, this feeling of meaning and purpose will enhance loyalty and commitment by fostering positive affective bonds between the employees and their organization (Milliman et al., 2003).

Performance and Productivity. There are two ways to evaluate employee performance— in-role behavior and extra-role or organizational citizenship behavior (OCB). In-role behavior refers to the performance of tasks/roles that are formally expected of the employees. Productivity is a good example of in-role behavior. Organization citizenship behavior (OCB) refers to the performance of discretionary behaviors beyond the job scope of employees but are beneficial to their organizations. Workplace spirituality will enhance individual performance and productivity because when employees feel fulfilled, connected, and committed, they are more likely to give their best to their work and demonstrate organization citizenship behavior (Karakas, 2009).

Organizational Outcomes

The workplace spirituality movement is gaining momentum in the business world. Well-known corporations like Intel, Coca-Cola, Boeing, and Sears have incorporated workplace spirituality programs and practices in their organization. Obviously, these corporations believe that workplace spirituality has a desirable impact on organizational performance using the triple bottom line approach. This triple bottom line approach defines performance on the basis of the economic, social, and environmental impact of the organization. There is a body of research to support the notion that workplace spirituality positively contributes to organization performance.

Economic Performance. Workplace spirituality helps to improve the finanical performance of an organization through its positive influence on the employees in terms of morale, commitment, and the willingness to go the extra-mile for the organization. When morale and commitment are high, it helps to reduce absenteeism and employee turnover in the organization. All of these will lead to a positive impact on the financial performance of the organization.

Social and Environmental Performance. Workplace spirituality promotes values that look beyond the material realm and focus on interconnectedness with self, others, and the entire universe. These values will direct the organizations to consider the community and environment in their decisions. Organizations that promote spirituality at work have good corporate values and honor ethical principles. Workplace spirituality promote values such as fairness, community, and responsibility in the organization. These values help businesses to be more socially and environmentally responsible. Tom's of Maine is a good example of how workplace spirituality helps to improve social performance. Its corporate values and actions supports the philosophy of "doing well by doing good" (Chappell, 1993).

Implications for Management

Fostering Workplace Spirituality

There is no quick fix method to nurture workplace spirituality. Managers cannot expect instant results. Workplace spirituality takes time, effort, and resources to develop in organizations. Top management must be willing to invest their time and commit financial and human resources to plan and implement change strategies to foster workplace spirituality in the organization. It calls for a holistic approach that views the organization as an open system and emphasizes the interconnectedness among the various subsystems of the organization, namely, leadership, culture, structure, and people (Tan, 2007). A holistic approach understands the complexity involved in large-scale organizational change. It calls for multiple interventions targeting different parts of the organization to achieve sustainable changes. Since organizations function as a system, any changes in one part of the organization have to be reinforced by coordinating changes in other parts. For example, the single intervention approach of training, in and of itself, may not be effective in fostering workplace spirituality because training is only targeting at the people subsystem of the organization. The impact of training may not last if the existing culture of the organization is hostile to workplace spirituality. Specifically, a holistic approach to fostering workplace spirituality involves the following:

1. assessing the organization's readiness for workplace spirituality;
2. sesigning programs to foster workplace spirituality;
3. implementing the programs; and,
4. evaluating the effectiveness of the programs.

Managers need to assess the organization's readiness before deciding on what programs to implement to promote workplace spirituality. In assessing the organization's readiness, managers need to examine the obstacles to spirituality of their organization's subsystems. A thorough examination of these factors will improve the chances of successful implementation of programs to foster spirituality in the organization. For example, the top management team in the organization may be supportive of workplace spirituality, but the organization has a very competitive and political culture. In this case, even though the leadership is ready for workplace spirituality, any attempt to introduce programs to foster workplace spirituality may be hampered by the organization's competitive and political culture.

After identifying the obstacles to spirituality, the next step is to design appropriate programs to remove these obstacles and to prepare the organization to embrace workplace spirituality. Frequently, this would mean rewriting the organization's mission statement to embrace spiritual values and principles. Examples of workplace spirituality programs include team-building to foster a sense of community, leadership development workshops to promote spiritual leadership, and changes in the reward and appraisal systems to recognize employees and managers who are supportive of workplace spirituality.

There are practical issues that managers need to consider when implementing workplace spirituality programs. For example, managers need to prioritize which program to implement first. It can be overwhelming for the organization if all the spirituality programs are implemented simultaneously. Early involvement by employees and relevant stakeholders during the design phase of workplace spirituality programs will help in their implementation. There should be frequent communications between management and employees during the implementation phase to identify problems and resolve issues. Managers must be seen to be receptive to the feedback from employees and relevant stakeholders.

Finally, evaluating the effectiveness of spirituality programs requires managers to determine whether the programs have achieved their intended objectives. For example, if the purpose of a particular spirituality program is to promote a sense of community in the organization, managers can design a survey to track changes in perceptions of sense of community before, during, and after the program. The results from the survey can help managers know what works and what do not.

Pitfalls of Workplace Spirituality

Managers should be mindful of the potential pitfalls of workplace spirituality. Workplace spirituality values employee wellness over material wealth. It goes against the core value of workplace spirituality if managers are only interested in employee productivity and performance. Workplace spirituality should be pursued as an end in itself and not as a means to financial gain. It may backfire if managers view workplace spirituality as an administrative tool to enhance employee productivity and performance. Employees will react adversely if they feel that managers are using workplace spirituality programs to manipulate them to work harder and more productively. Workplace spirituality programs have to be implemented in an authentic manner, and the beneficial influence on employees and the organization will naturally follow.

Ill-conceived and badly implemented workplace spirituality programs can also lead to divisiveness, discrimination, and abuse. Managers must prepare their organizations to embrace workplace spirituality. Since spirituality is value-based, it can be controversial and divisive. Management must develop consensus among members on the scope and nature of spirituality to be embraced in the organization to avoid misunderstanding and ill feelings. Some organizational members may inevitably feel discriminated against if they do not agree with the scope and nature of spirituality that is practiced in the organization. Over enthusiasm in implementing workplace spirituality programs can lead to abuse when organizational members feel coerced to participate in the programs. Misguided workplace spirituality programs may cause organizational members to feel spiritually or religiously harassed.

Managers need to consider potential legal repercussions when they introduce spirituality programs in organizations (Giacalone & Jurkiewicz, 2010). The United States Constitution dictates the separation of church and state. This poses a problem when organizational members view spirituality and religion as synonymous. Managers must be careful that the workplace spirituality programs are broadly conceived to incorporate the diverse spiritual needs of organizational members. Managers cannot be seen as favoring one spiritual perspective over others as this could be construed as discriminatory. Special care must also be exercised such that these programs do not follow any religious faiths or practices.

Questions for Students

1. How to you define workplace spirituality? How is it different from religion?
2. Briefly explain Fry's spiritual leadership theory.
3. What can you do to develop spiritual leadership?
4. Would you want to introduce workplace spirituality in the organization? Justify your answer.
5. How would you promote workplace spirituality in an organization?
6. Do you agree that workplace spirituality should be an end in itself and should not be used as a managerial tool for organizational performance?

Case: The Presbyterian Community Services

The Presbyterian Community Services (PCS)[1] was founded in 1974 by the Presbyterian Churches in Singapore. They are one of the largest community service providers in Singapore comprising 28 services in the areas of infant care, integrated children care, and elderly care. The organization is very much influenced by Christian teachings and values as reflected in its vision: "To honour and magnify the Name of our Lord through the services of PCS."[2]

PCS derives its financial resources from donations and revenue from their child-care education services. The Executive Director (ED), Mr. Laurence Wee, fosters an open and supportive work environment. Employees feel safe to voice their opinions and suggestions freely in the organization. He praises and affirms them for their hard work and good performance. He values all his staff as worthy individuals. He is attentive to their needs and concerns. He spends time bonding with his staff and colleagues through informal interactions and lunch treats. As a result, organizational trust increases and people feel a sense of belonging in the organization.

To enhance their professional development, the ED creates opportunities for his staff to work with experts and specialists. The ED takes it upon himself to personally conduct training sessions to develop their professional skills. The ED cares about spiritual development too. He conducts regular bible studies to share how Christian teachings can be applicable at work. He also encourages his staff to attend Christian seminars and workshops conducted by external consultants on management and leadership topics.

The ED leads by example through living out the 'fruits of the spirit' which include values such as love, joy, peace, forbearance, kindness, goodness, faithfulness, gentleness and self-control. The ED believes in giving his staff autonomy and freedom to complete their tasks. He takes effort to explain the rationales of his decisions. He wants this staff to understand how each of them fits into the larger picture. This will ensure them to feel that their jobs are meaningful and serve a larger purpose. The ED does not believe in micro-managing as he understands the detrimental effects of excessive monitoring of his staff. The ED sees himself as a 'father' of the organization and personally ensures that his staff are well taken care of. When asked about his leadership style, he states: *"I give them empowerment. I believe in giving my staff my trust. I know*

---

[1] This case is adapted from a Student Independent Study Project by Au Yeong Yuen Mun under the supervision of the first author, Gilbert Tan.

[2] http://www.pcs.org.sg

the importance of going above nagging. I just tell them to go and get the goals. I don't just nag"

Questions for Students

1. Do you think the ED practices spiritual leadership at PSC? Elaborate.
2. How would you react to the ED's leadership style?
3. What would be the potential problems with the ED's leadership style?

Exercise: An Organizational Assessment[3]

Using the scale below, rate each of the 15 statements according to how accurately it describes the organization that you are assessing:

Strongly Disagree	Disagree	Neutral	Agree	Strongly Agree
1	2	3	4	5

_____ 1. Employees in this organization experience joy in work.

_____ 2. This organization values working cooperatively with others.

_____ 3. Employees feel hopeful about life in this organization.

_____ 4. Give work that is connected to what employees think is important in life.

_____ 5. People in this organization feel part of a community.

_____ 6. Employees rely on their spiritual values to influence the choices they make.

_____ 7. People in this organization look forward to going to work.

---

[3] Adapted from Asmos, D. P., & Duchon, D. (2000) Spirituality at work: A conceptualization and measure. *Journal of Management Inquiry*, 9, 134–145; and, Czaplewski, M. J. , & Ferguson, A. J. (2003). Workplace spirituality and employee work attitudes: An exploratory empirical assessment. *Journal of Organizational Change Management*, 16, 426–447.

_____ 8. Employees support each other in this organization.

_____ 9. This organization allows employees to show their spiritual side.

_____ 10. Employees see a connection between work and the social good.

_____ 11. This organization links employees with a common purpose.

_____ 12. Prayer is an important part of employees' life in this organization.

_____ 13. Employees can see what gives their work personal meaning.

_____ 14. People in this organization genuinely care about each other.

_____ 15. People care about the spiritual health of their colleagues in this organization.

Exercise Instruction

This above questionnaire measures three components of workplace spirituality, namely meaningful work, sense of community, and inner-life. Sum up the scores of the items of each component after placing the score you assigned to each item in the questionnaire in the appropriate box below. The higher the score, the stronger the organization is in that particular component of workplace spirituality.

Meaningful Work	Sense of Community	Inner-life
1.	2.	3.
4.	5.	6.
7.	8.	9.
10.	11.	12.
13.	14.	15.
Total:	Total:	Total:

Share your findings with your classmates. Do you consider the organization that you have assessed a spiritual or non spiritual organization? Why?

Suggestions for Further Reading

Mitroff, I. I., & Denton, E. A. (1999). *A spiritual audit of corporate America: A hard look at spirituality, religion, and values in the workplace.* San Francisco: Jossey-Bass.

Fry, L. W. (2003). Toward a theory of spiritual leadership. *Leadership Quarterly, 14,* 693–727.

Tan, G. (2007). Towards a holistic framework in fostering spirituality at work. *Current Topics in Management , 12,* 213–227.

References

Ashmos, D. P., & Duchon, D. (2000). Spirituality at work: A conceptualization and measure. *Journal of Management Inquiry 9,* 134–145.

Chappell, T. (1993). *The soul of a business: Managing for profit and the common good.* New York: Bantam Books.

Dehler, G. E., & Welsh, M. A. (1994). Spirituality and organizational transformation: Implications for the new management paradigm. *Journal of Managerial Psychology, 9,* 17–26.

Fry, L. W., Hannan S. T., Noel, M., & Walumbwa, F. O. (2011). Impact of spiritual leadership on unit performance. *Leadership Quarterly, 22,* 259–270.

Giacalone, R. A., & Jurkiewicz, C. L. (2010). The science of workplace spirituality. In R. A. Giacalone & C. L. Jurkiewicz, *Handbook of workplace spirituality and organizational performance.* New York: M. E. Sharpe.

Jurkiewicz, C. L., & Giacalone, R. A. (2004). A values framework for measuring the impact of workplace spirituality on organizational performance. *Journal of Business Ethics, 49,* 129–142.

Karakas, F. (2009). Spirituality and performance in organizations: A Literature Review. *Journal of Business Ethics, 94,* 89–106.

Milliman, J., Czaplewski, A. J., & Ferguson, J. (2003). Workplace spirituality and employee work attitudes: An exploratory empirical assessment. *Journal of Organizational Change Management , 16,* 426–447.

Mitroff, I. I., & Denton, E. A. (1999). *A spiritual audit of corporate America: A hard look at spirituality, religion, and values in the workplace.* San Francisco: Jossey-Bass.

Rhodes, K. (2006). Six components of a model for workplace spirituality. *Graziadio Business Review,9(2).* Retrieved March 20, 2015 from http://gbr.pepperdine.edu/.

Tan, G. (2007). Towards a holistic framework in fostering spirituality at work. *Current Topics in Management , 12,* 213–227.

Vallabh, P. & Singhal, M. (2014). Workplace spirituality facilitation: A person-organization fit approach. *Journal of Human Values, 20(2),* 193–207.

PART IX

Stakeholders, Sustainability, and Performance

21. Stakeholder Management

Dawn Keig
Brenau University

Rosalyn Rufer
SUNY Empire State College

Managers are constantly bombarded with conflicting expectations from different individuals and companies with which they interact. One way to view these influences are from a stakeholder perspective. Effective decision makers understand the importance of balancing and protecting the interests of various stakeholders, including investors, employees, the community, local and state governments, suppliers, funding sources, various interest groups and, of course, the client or customer. As such stakeholder management provides a lens through which a manager can examine and effectively balance and respond to the wide variety of the internal and external pressures that every business faces.

Nature of Stakeholder Management

Definition

Individuals and groups who are impacted by an organization's actions can be considered *stakeholders*. As the name implies, stakeholders have a 'stake' in or a claim to some aspect of an organization's efforts. In the broadest sense, a corporation's stakeholders are comprised of "any individual or group who can affect or is affected by the achievement of the firm's objectives" (Freeman, 1984, p. 46). This chapter first considers the concept of stakeholder at the firm level, examining and contrasting the stakeholder orientation with other more traditional views of the firm. The intent is to reinforce a principle-driven but very practical and relevant set of stakeholder management principles and techniques that the reader can apply at multiple levels and contexts of management.

Dimensions of a Stakeholder Orientation

To appreciate the benefits associated with a stakeholder orientation requires an understanding of some of the more traditional input–output views of the firm. In the most basic *production view* of the firm, the firm is seen primarily as a vehicle by which raw materials from suppliers are converted into products that can be sold to customers. Resources come in; products go out. From this production view, external stakeholders such as suppliers to the firm and the customers can easily be identified.

Of course, this early manufacturing-centric view is overly simplistic in that it does not take into account other critical aspects of the firm, such as its internal stakeholders: managers, employees, and owners (shareholders). Therefore, the more comprehensive *managerial view* of the firm emerged to recognize these additional important dimensions. And although the managerial view recognizes the influence and impact of the firm's efforts on managers, employees, and shareholders, the *shareholders'* interests are considered to be the most important and are considered to be of *primary* importance.

Under the managerial view, maximizing *shareholder* value becomes the primary goal of the firm. However, as noted by Berman, Wicks, Kotha & Jones (1999), the best way to improve the performance of the firm and thus the shareholder value is to pay attention to all stakeholders' concerns, not just select internal or external stakeholders. The stakeholder theory of the firm proposes that maximizing *stakeholder* value should be the primary goal of the corporation (Donaldson & Preston, 1995). Shareholders are certainly considered important stakeholders; but to place sole consideration on these stakeholders does not maximize the value of the firm (Harrison & Wicks, 2013). To better understand how to maximize the value of the firm, we must first identify who are our stakeholders.

Who Are the Stakeholders?

Revisiting the broad definition of stakeholder, the firm should consider *all* individuals and groups that may affect or may be affected by the firm's actions as potential stakeholders. This means that in addition to suppliers, customers, managers, employees, and shareholders (private and institutional investors), the firm may also consider their stakeholders to include appropriate governmental and regulatory agencies; community and social elements; special interest groups, consumer advocates, environmentalists, and other non-governmental organizations (NGOs); and any allied partner (Gnan, Hinna, Monteduro, & Scarozza, 2013).

Furthermore, stakeholder management is not only a concern for large corporate enterprises. Small businesses that are organized as partnerships, for example, are also influenced by a variety of different stakeholder groups. Consider the case of a professional accounting partnership. In addition to client and employee stakeholders, the accountants' behavior is subject to governmental stakeholders, such as the influence of changing tax codes and other regulations.

Even a single-person business operation can benefit from a stakeholder orientation. For example, Julio's Shoe Repair, a sole proprietorship in a small town, may not have employees or shareholders, but Julio has other stakeholders to consider, such as his customers, the community chamber of commerce, his banker, government regulations, and maybe even the local community college. Small business owner/operators can maximize the value of knowing and serving their current and future stakeholders through stakeholder management.

Balancing Different Stakeholder Interests

Under stakeholder theory, shareholder interests should be balanced appropriately with other stakeholder interests and the value that the relationship brings to both the firm and to its stakeholders. Rather than automatically subordinating one stakeholder group to another, the firm should seek to understand, integrate, and optimize multiple stakeholder perspectives. This is not always an easy task, as there are often competing pressures from different stakeholder groups. An organization that wishes to act socially responsible may do so to sustain a positive image with its customers and community. However shareholders may view the extra costs as less than beneficial. Take for example the case study of GE in their Hudson Falls, New York operations. For years they chose to pollute the Hudson River instead of putting place extra environmental protections that would ultimately diminish the profitability of the operation. After pressure from the community and the government, GE was forced to clean up the PCBs that they had previously dumped into the river.

How to balance pressures from different stakeholder groups and maximize the value of the organization is a concern of decision makers. Donaldson and Preston's (1995) elaboration of the stakeholder view of the firm provides a framework within which managers can answer important questions that impact firm strategy, including:

1. *Descriptive* questions (Should this particular stakeholder's interests be considered?);
2. *Instrumental* questions (What impact does this stakeholder have on the work at hand?); and
3. *Normative* questions (Why should a particular stakeholder's interest be taken into account if the firm cannot yet identify a specific benefit in doing so?).

Once the critical stakeholders are identified, Harrisons and Wicks' model (2013) focuses on creating stakeholder value for those stakeholders. They identify four areas from which value can be derived: 1) stakeholder utility associated with actual goods and services, 2) stakeholder utility associated with organizational justice, 3) stakeholder utility from affiliation, and 4) stakeholder utility associated with perceived opportunity costs. As firms look to manage their stakeholder relationships, they need to develop a reciprocal relationship: one in which the stakeholder creates value for the firm and one in which the firm creates value for the stakeholder. This increases the utility associated with the firm and its products. Ethical behavior is also recognized by Harrison and Wicks (2013) as key to maximizing the value of the firm. Besides improving the image of the organization to its external stakeholder, ethical behavior also increases the utility associated with organizational justice. Ultimately the utility from a positive affiliation with the organization further increases stakeholder engagement.

Components of Stakeholder Management

To be able to effectively manage stakeholders, the manager must first identify the universe of relevant potential stakeholders, and then he or she must thoughtfully consider how those stakeholders might affect and/or be affected by the organization's goals and objectives for which the manager is responsible. Thus the first step in stakeholder management is to identify the critical list of stakeholders. The second step is to assess their impact on the strategy of the organization and impact of the organization's strategy on the relationship with the stakeholder. The third step in the process is to identify effective ways to build the relationship, such as improvements in communication, improvements in increasing the value provided to the stakeholder (Harrison & Wicks, 2013), or increasing stakeholder engagement (Dawkins, 2014).

Stakeholder Identification

The groups commonly identified as key stakeholders often include the internal stakeholders such as the employees, the managers, and the stockholders; the external stakeholders often include the customers, the community in which the organization operates, the government (s) that oversee that community, the suppliers to the firm, and other partnerships, such as allied firms, universities, and even unions. To identify the stakeholders critical to a function or project, the manager should first consider all individuals and groups that are *Involved* in, *Impacted* by, and/or can *Influence* the strategy of the firm. This "I–I–I" framework for stakeholder identification ensures that as comprehensive an understanding as possible is developed in terms of who might potentially be a stakeholder with expectations or influence that could impact the success of the organization.

It should be noted that impact and influence does not always mean in a positive way! The impact may be positive or negative. For example, the manager of a project to implement a new system should identify the end users of the system as stakeholders; however, some of those users may be excited about an impending system change, and others may be less enthusiastic. Or consider the example of outsourcing. A manager has decided to outsource a certain function in the department to a third party organization. It is obvious in this example that the employees that are being displaced are highly impacted by the outsourcing decision. The manager may be able to influence whether this impact is a positive or negative experience for those stakeholders based on how their stakeholder interests are considered in the outsourcing process.

Assessment of Impact of Stakeholder Relationships

Freeman (1984) described a simple two-dimensional framework to help managers assess the relative risks and opportunities associated with different stakeholder groups. One dimension assessed the degree of *cooperative* orientation associated with the stakeholder (high or low), and the other identified the degree of *threatening* orientation (high or low). The resulting 2x2 matrix provides four descriptive quadrant groupings of stakeholder influence, each having a distinct corresponding stakeholder management strategy.

On the other hand, we most frequently see a similar 2 × 2 matrix showing power (or influence) and interest (Mohan.& Paila, 2013). This 2 × 2 matrix was adapted from the early work of Mitchell, Agle, and Wood (1997). Mitchell et al. (1997) looked at the relationships with stakeholders in terms of power, legitimacy, and urgency. The commonly used power and interest tool, as seen in Figure 1, helps decision makers assess the strength of each relationship and how to best manage it. Common strategies for managing stakeholders, which have high power and high interest in the firm (actively engaged), are to manage those relationships closely because of their importance. Those relationships with low power and low interest require minimal effort and are often just monitored. Stakeholders with low interest but with high power are best managed by keeping the stakeholders satisfied with the relationship. This often includes

Figure 1
Stakeholder Power Tool

	Low	High
High	Stakeholders with the most control over the firm	Stakeholder which the firms must manage closely
Low	The least significant stakeholders	Stakeholders where the firm has the most control

Power

Interest

Source: Adopted from Mohan & Paila (2013)

increasing the engagement of the stakeholder in order to increase the interest. Lastly those stakeholders with high interest and low power can best be managed by increasing communications in order to keep these stakeholders informed.

In addition to managing stakeholders though 2 × 2 matrixes, we can often find decision makers that prefer the use of a table. Tables are commonly used in managing constructions projects because of the complexity and inter-connectivity between stakeholders. When using tables the first column is the list of critical stakeholders; the second is often the interest. Using a table to describe interest can provide more information beyond the strength of the interest. Similarly the third column is usually the strength of the power and once more a short narrative can provide additional information about the power beyond the high and low strengths. Other columns might include positive impact on the firm, with another assessing the negative impact. A subsequent column could then address the net impact. In most construction projects, there is most often a column identifying the interconnectivity of the relationships with other stakeholders. The last column in the table would provide for a strategy for managing the stakeholder (or sometimes labeled: moving forward). Here the decision maker can identify which stakeholders should be further engaged, which require additional communications, and which should be monitored (see Table 1)

Outcomes of Stakeholder Management

Organizations that make stakeholder concerns a strategic priority may achieve advantages over competitors. As noted earlier, an important consideration in stakeholder management is the perception of ethical behavior of the organization (Harrison & Wicks, 2013). If the organization is view by its stakeholders as behaving ethically, greater value is perceived in the relationship. As a result of interconnectivity between stakeholders, this helps to strengthen the relationships with all stakeholders.

In addition to behaving ethically from a stakeholder perspective, the decision maker must take care to balance the needs of the various stakeholder constituents (Bourne & Walker, 2005). As noted by Harrison & Wicks (2013), the utility obtained from organizational justice, helps to sustain stakeholder relationship. This is closely aligned with the perception of ethical behavior.

A savvy manager understands the power and influence dynamics of his or her organizational environment and hence alertly and proactively seeks out opportunities to align interests and balance potential conflicts. The most positive

Table 1

Table Assessment of Stakeholder Relationships

Stakeholder	Influence	Power	Positive Benefit	Negative Benefit	Net Benefit	Relationship with others	Management Strategy

outcomes of stakeholder management come when the firm not only balances specific competing stakeholder claims and expectations, but actually creates a stakeholder culture that permeates the organization and its ways of working (Jones, Felps, & Bigley, 2007).

Implications for Management

A stakeholder orientation can provide a useful philosophy for general management at all levels, from the firm level to the departmental, team, or even project level. A skilled manager seeks all feasible opportunities to maximize value for all stakeholders. This requires the manager to holistically identify all potential internal and external stakeholders of the organization, as well as to accurately assess how they may impact and/or be impacted by other stakeholders. All stakeholder groups are ultimately comprised of sets of individuals, and the better a manager is at understanding people and their motivations, fears, expectations, and priorities, the more effective that manager can be.

Whether a manager is responsible for a small staff, a medium-sized project, or an entire department or division, understanding and applying stakeholder principles to the management process can lead to greater organizational success. In order to manage stakeholder expectations, managers must first *identify* their stakeholders and stakeholder groups. A comprehensive stakeholder *analysis* process helps managers better understand and manage expectations from the start. We have identified several ways to assess stakeholder relationships and subsequent strategies to manage those relationships. Some of these strategies include increasing communications; increasing engagement; or increasing the value of the relationship for both the stakeholder and the organization. Managers should also be aware that stakeholders develop and refine perceptions over time regarding their own expectations and thus the strategies may require modifications.

It is also recognized that stakeholder priority is a relative concept, and during certain times in the lifecycle of a firm certain stakeholders may be more important than others (Jawahar & McLaughlin, 2001). For example, during the *start-up stage* of the business, availability of adequate funding and a customer market for the company's product may determine whether the firm even survives, thus elevating the relative importance of investor (and creditor) and customer stakeholders. During the *emerging growth stage* of the business, as survival concerns have stabilized and expansion becomes the primary strategic focus, more relative stakeholder attention may be paid to employees, management structures, and supplier relationships. As the business lifecycle enters the *maturity stage*, the firm may operate with its most balanced treatment of stakeholder interests, but as the firm moves into *decline*, the issue of survival may again raise the relative priority of certain stakeholders.

The stakeholder analysis process is key to ensuring managers focus on the most impactful stakeholder risks and opportunities. The challenges associated with balancing diverse stakeholder interests reinforce the importance of developing and maintaining integrity as a manager related to stakeholder management. Managerial credibility is key in establishing a positive enduring reputation with stakeholders (Mahon & Wartick, 2003).

Questions for Students

1. Think about the cell phone industry. What are some of the potential internal and external stakeholder groups that Apple might need to consider in its stakeholder management plan? Would the potential stakeholders for Verizon or AT&T be different? Why or why not?
2. How can a manager determine which stakeholder or stakeholder group is *most* important to their area of responsibility? What influences may alter this importance?
3. How does a thorough understanding of organizational power and influence dynamics relate to effective stakeholder management?
4. What are the types of utilities for creating value in stakeholder relationships? How can a decision maker increase the value for a given stakeholder relationship?

Exercise: Stakeholder Analysis

Hyundai Motor Company was established in 1967 (About Hyundai); by 2007 they were the world's fifth largest auto producer. Hyundai has three plants in Korea, but in order to serve their global customers better, they established plants in the U.S., India, China, Turkey, the Czech Republic, Russia and most recently Brazil.

The first plant in the United States was built in 2005 in Alabama. The Hyundai Sonata rolled off the production line in 2006. Hyundai is proud of their facility in Alabama, as seen in a YouTube video at https://www.youtube.com/watch?v=KH-QJLewLnk . When the recession heavily impacted the U.S. automakers, this new plant brought economic growth to the Alabama community (Bunkley, 2011). However not everyone was happy when this plant was first built, including the unions. Unlike the automobile manufactures in Detroit Michigan and several other manufacturing plants, throughout the United States, workers were not interested in Unionizing. In spite of the strong opposition from the United Automobile Workers union, Hyundai's strategy for global growth has succeeded, including an additional manufacturing facility in Georgia, and design and testing sites in California and Michigan.

If you worked for Hyundai in 2005, what decisions would have to be made to support this global growth? What would your stakeholder analysis look like?

Exercise Questions

1. Who were the primary internal stakeholders for growth within the United States? Who were the external important external stakeholders?
2. Which stakeholders had the most potential influence (power) over the success of Hyundai's project? Which stakeholders had the most potential interest over the success of Hyundai's project? Using the 2 × 2 power matrix tool discussed earlier, position each stakeholder on the matrix and identify the strategy you would use to manage these stakeholders.
3. Would there have been a benefit from using a table instead of the matrix? Why or why not?
4. If you were going to later build the plant in Georgia, would you have used the same stakeholder analysis as you did in 2005? Why or why not?

Case: Malaysia Flight MH370

March 8, 2014 Malaysia Flight MH370 disappeared over the Indian Ocean. One year later we still know very little about what happened to the 227 passengers and 12 crew members. What we do know is that air traffic controllers lost contact with the plane two hours after takeoff in Vietnamese air space. After much miscommunication, satellite data indicates that it veered off course shortly after losing contact. At first local officials searched for the plane but when it was believed to veer off course, the Australian government stepped in to help in the search with their advanced technology. The Unites States was also involved because it was a Boeing 777 aircraft. However as of March 2015, the plane has yet to be found. It is now believed that the battery on the plane's data recorder expired one year prior to the disappearance of the plane.

There has been much criticism on the communication strategy of CEO Ahmad Jauhari Yahya (Hildebrand, 2014). Early communication failed to address the concerns of the families. In fact, there were several statements issued that just led to the confusion, including when contact was lost and the last known location of the plane. All the families knew was that they were to come to Beijing for information about the flight. However when arriving, there was no additional information; Malaysia Airlines was accused of shielding families from correct information. In fact, CEO Yahya used Facebook to notify families that the plane was missing. It seemed as if the only stakeholder with whom CEO Yahya communicated effectively was the Malaysian Government, the major stockholder of the airline.

Since this incident, Malaysia Airlines stock has been devalued; it has been forced to lay off 6000 employees. Was it wrong of CEO Yahya to focus on the stockholder? Did CEO Yahya act responsibly in his treatment of the families of the passengers? What was the impact of strategies used in the treatment of Malaysia Airline's stakeholder in the global community? It has been suggested that CEO Yahya should have hired a crisis communication team to address stakeholder needs. If you were part of this team, what steps would you have taken to improve stakeholder relationships within this troubled Airline?

Suggestions for Further Reading

Carroll A., & Buchholtz, A. (2012). Business and society: Ethics, sustainability, and stakeholder management (8th ed.). Australia: South-Western, Cengage.

Gnan, L., Hinna, A., Monteduro, F., & Scarozza, D. (2013) . Corporate governance and management practices: Stakeholder involvement, quality and sustainability tools adoption. *Journal of Management & Governance, 17* (4), 907-937.

Howitt, M. & McManus, J. (2012). Stakeholder management: An instrument for decision making. *Management Services.* 56 (3), 29-34.

References

About Hyundai Motor Company. (n.d.). Retrieved March 16, 2015, from http://www.hmmausa.com/our-company/about-hmma/hmc-fact-sheet/

Berman S. L., Wicks A. C., Kotha S. & Jones T. M. (1999). Does stakeholder orientation matter? The relationship between stakeholder management models and firm financial performance. *Academy of Management Journal, 42*, 488-506.

Bourne, L., & Walker, D. H. T. (2005). Visualising and mapping stakeholder influence. *Management Decision, 43*, 649–660.

Bunkley, N. (2011, February 18). Hyundai's swift growth lifts Alabama's economy. *New York Times*. Retrieved March 16, 2015, from http://www.nytimes.com/2011/02/19/business/19hyundai.html?pagewanted=all&_r=0

Dawkins, C. (2014) The principle of good faith: Toward substantive stakeholder engagement *Journal of Business Ethics. 121,* 283-295.

Donaldson, T., & Preston, L. (1995). The stakeholder theory of the corporation: Concepts, evidence, and implications. *Academy of Management Review, 20*, 65–91.

Freeman, R. E. (1984). *Strategic management: A stakeholder approach* (Vol. 1). Boston: Pitman.

Harrison J.S. & Wicks A.C. (2013) Stakeholder theory, value and firm performance. *Business Ethics Quarterly.* 23 (1) 97-124.

Hildebrant, A. (2014, March 13). Malaysia Airlines MH370: How to make a crisis worse. Retrieved July 15, 2014, from http://www.cbc.ca/news/world/malaysia-airlines-mh370-how-to-make-a-crisis-worse-1.2570213

Howitt, M. & McManus, J. (2012). Stakeholder management: An instrument for decision making. *Management Services.* 56 (3) 29-34.

Jawahar, I., & McLaughlin, G. (2001). Toward a descriptive stakeholder theory: An organizational life cycle approach. *Academy of Management Review, 26*, 397–414.

Jones, T., Felps, W., & Bigley, G. (2007). Ethical theory and stakeholder-related decisions: The role of stakeholder culture. *Academy of Management Review, 32*, 137–155.

Mahon, J. F., & Wartick, S. L. (2003). Dealing with stakeholders: How reputation, credibility and framing influence the game. *Corporate Reputation Review, 6*, 19–35.

Mitchell, R.K., Agle, B.R. and Wood, D.J. 1997. Toward a theory of stakeholder identification and salience: Defining the principle of whom and what really counts. Academy of Management Review, *22*, 853-886.

Mohan, V. R. M.& Paila, A. R. (2013). Stakeholder management in infrastructure/construction projects: The role of stakeholder mapping and social network analysis (SNA). *Aweshkar Research Journal, 15* (1) 48-61.

22. Sustainability

Sanda Kaufman
Cleveland State University

Samuel Gómez Haro
Universidad de Granada
Campus Universitario de la Cartuja s/n

John Grant
Visiting Fellow
Colorado State University

Sustainability—the ability to last for a long time—is a business goal for most organizations. In the past, lasting in time referred to the economic health of a business. Successful organizations carry out their activities for many years, and the longer they do so the more we believe they are indeed successful. In other words, the very ability to stick around for long time periods becomes a measure for the quality of products or services and management of a business. We have always valued sustainability even when we did not have a name for it. What contributes to business sustainability? This chapter discusses the meanings of sustainability, its dimensions, and organizational strategies that promote it.

Nature of Sustainability

Definition

Sustainability is a broad term: applied to ever more contexts, it sounds so familiar that definition seems hardly necessary. Looking closer, however, we find that it has different meanings for different people. In general, *sustainability is the capacity of a system—whether ecological, social or economic—to function and serve its purposes in the long run.* Such long-term functional survival hinges on systems' ability to use wisely the resources upon which they depend. This means not only not exhausting such critical resources in the short run, but also managing their flow and quality so they continue to serve in the future. Therefore an organization's sustainable behavior has to be purposeful, targeted, and active, rather than a passive consequence of other processes.

Since all human activities are embedded in our shared natural environment, sustainability has come to refer especially to maintaining and improving the local to global natural ecosystems that supply us with vital resources. Ecosystems consist of interlinked living organisms and their habitats working together as systems with numerous and necessary components without which they get disrupted, sometimes irreversibly. We alter and even deplete these ecosystems through production and consumption of goods and services. In the past, the scale of ecosystems exceeded by far the scale of human activities. Therefore the possibility of exhausting them was difficult to imagine. Nevertheless, since the dawn of history people destroyed their host environments through unsustainable agricultural practices (Diamond, 2005). Population growth, the industrial revolution and advances in transportation and materials processing technologies led to sharp increases in the demand for, and capacity to use, natural resources. In the last one hundred and fifty years, global use of natural resources has accelerated. Renewable resources—such as plants that can grow back—have been exploited at rates exceeding the speed of regeneration. Economic globalization and new transportation, information and communication technologies appeared for a while to increase our ability to secure natural resources; but the accompanying global interdependence of production and consumption systems is now becoming a limiting factor. It is no longer possible to keep any portion of the planet safe from consequences of unsustainable practices elsewhere. As we deplete our natural environment, we reduce the ability to sustain in the long run businesses that depend on it.

Two sustainability characteristics are shared by all contexts in which this term is used. The first is that we consider sustainability *desirable*. We would be hard-pressed to find anyone in the private or public sector claiming to pursue lack of sustainability. The second is that sustainability is by definition linked with *time*. Since it means providing conditions for a system to last, it requires predicting what the future holds, and preparing for it; and, it is not a short-range outcome: sustainability is achieved over the long haul, sometimes beyond the life of those who promote it. Together, the positive connotation of sustainability and its link to time give rise to a paradox: the decision to achieve the much-desired sustainability is difficult to sustain!

In 1987, the United Nations' World Commission on Environment and Development issued the Brundtland Report that captured the meaning many attach to sustainability. It deemed development sustainable if it "meets the needs of the present without compromising the ability of future generations to meet their own need" (p. 1). This rather utilitarian definition reflects a broadly shared view of nature as having value only insofar as it serves human purposes. It also reminds us that sustainability is about the long run.

Sustainability does not mean "staying the same." Rather, for socio-economic systems including business organizations, it requires ability to adapt or change practices, institutions, and rules, to enhance our collective capacity to meet challenges in order to continue desired activities in time. It also means putting up the fewest possible barriers to future choices.

Before proceeding, we should ask "sustainability of what?" As students of management, we may be inclined to focus on the sustainability of organizations. However, sustainability is sought for ecosystems, as well as for businesses, communities, cities, regions, or the entire globe; it may refer to economic, social, or environmental assets and/or to relationships. For ecosystems, sustainability means retaining functionality and the ability to restore themselves despite continued extraction of some components, or destabilizing shocks. A city or region is sustainable if it manages in the long run to provide the quality of life its residents seek, despite changes in the larger context in which it is embedded, and without undermining the future generations' ability to do the same.

Businesses function within social–economic systems whose sustainability they enhance or undermine through their use of resources and waste production. A business is sustainable if over extended time periods it produces needed goods or services efficiently, providing value to those invested in it, and if it contributes to the sustainability of its broader contexts—from local to global. To sustain a business, managers have to understand not only the goals, needs, and inner workings of their own organization, but also how it relates to its economic, social, and environmental contexts. Can businesses conduct their activities without attention to the contexts in which they operate? We propose here that while it is not impossible (for a while), such businesses are not sustainable because ignoring their interdependence with the natural environment and with their host communities would bring about their demise. Owing to the complexity of this subject and to the functional interrelatedness of natural and socio-economic systems, we cannot hope to offer here complete coverage of all the facets of sustainability. We focus on how managerial decisions can foster or undermine environmental sustainability. Many of the ideas that follow transfer to other types of sustainability.

Dimensions

At its publication, the UN's Brundtland Report (1987) represented a milestone: it was the first time the international community expressed collective awareness and readiness to address the impacts of economic development on global shared and limited natural resources. There is now widespread recognition that sustainability of our societies and economies is fundamentally dependent on practices that sustain the capacity of the earth's ecosystems to support human communities. Therefore, promoting sustainability amounts to conducting business activities without reducing or compromising their resource base. The report identified three key sustainability dimensions:

The Environmental Dimension refers to resource conservation and pollution prevention, in order to satisfy demand for products and services without exceeding the carrying capacity of the natural environment—its ability to support human activities without being degraded or depleted.

The Social Dimension refers to justice aspects of production and consumption of goods and services. Besides consumption, other sources of satisfaction include social cohesion and equity with respect to fundamental rights, equal opportunities, and poverty eradication. Thus socially sustainable businesses promote democracy, human rights, equity, peace, respect for cultural diversity and regional identity, as well as broad access to information.

The Economic Dimension refers to factoring the costs of maintaining the quality of shared natural resources (air, water, soil) into the price of goods and services, instead of considering these resources free public goods. It entails avoiding negative environmental effects of unconstrained economic growth.

To take into account the three dimensions of sustainability, businesses need awareness of the social and natural systems they affect, as well as the resources necessary to nurture them. These resources are more available in affluent countries than in developing countries, which tend to be less able to afford sustainable practices, though they too need to preserve their natural environment. This explain partly why industries apply different standards of operation in different countries, and locate production facilities where dire poverty forces people to accept damage to ecosystems and to human health that would not be tolerated in developed countries.

Components

Some of the key components of the environment in which businesses operate include water, soil, air, and plant and wildlife. Businesses need to sustain these components through their practices.

Water is limited and unevenly distributed across the globe. Growing populations and fast-paced economic development are straining its availability; current economic activities are overdrawing or polluting rivers and lakes, at times to irreversible levels. The Aral Sea in Uzbekistan offers a striking example: its feeding rivers having been diverted for irrigation, it has now approximately 10% of its original size, when it ranked among the four largest lakes in the world. The Great Lakes and many American rivers are heavily polluted. Worldwide, water use patterns are unsustainable: if trends continue unabated, water for drinking and agricultural use will become increasingly expensive or even unavailable in arid areas. The environmental and economic consequences of running out of clean water are catastrophic. We could buck the trend through policies and actions that protect and sustain water resources. Some of the barriers to action will be discussed here.

Soil. Local unsustainable practices have global consequences. For example, the desertification occurring in North Africa and portions of Asia is due to unwise agricultural practices. The ensuing severe famine in places no longer able to grow enough food causes political unrest that can destabilize an entire continent and lead to war. Soil salinization, also found in North Africa as well as China, has similar disastrous consequences for food production.

Air. The hole in the atmosphere's protective ozone layer (resulting in high rates of skin cancer around the world), high rates of morbidity and mortality, and global climate change are a few global consequences of production and consumption practices that pollute the shared atmosphere we all need for our existence, or change its composition with deleterious effects.

Plants and Wildlife. The ability of healthy natural ecosystems to sustain plants and wildlife and offer economic value can be severely reduced or even irreversibly destroyed. For example, responding to high demand for wood for construction, some developing countries cut down their forests in quest of much-needed cash for food and development. The zealous tree-cutting outpaced the speed of regrowth, exhausting a resource that could have served well in multiple ways in the long run, had it been sustainably exploited. A similar story of depletion through overharvesting can be told about the few remaining tuna fisheries once abundant around the world.

Other quickly diminishing resources include non-renewable (fossil) energy sources, some construction materials, and minerals critical to various production processes including phosphorus for agriculture and metals used in the manufacturing of electronics.

Sustainability of any resource or human activity is the cumulative result of *joint decisions*, actions and practices by individuals, businesses small and large, communities and government agencies. No one can bring it about by acting alone. Instead, numerous individual and collective choices contribute to sustainability or undermine it in time. For example, some managers decide that paying a penalty for infringing on regulations (e.g., by illegally dumping industrial effluent in a river) is less costly to their company in the short run than abiding by rules. Others seek competitive advantages by providing products that are "green," or meet their social responsibilities by joining forces with their host communities to protect scarce or endangered natural resources.

The larger the *scale* we consider, the more difficult it is to draw a simple list of what it takes to promote sustainability or to assess it. For example, how to tell if a country's economy is sustainable before clear signs of failure become evident? Is the population of this planet managing available resources in ways that will allow it to continue to live within its bounded means? Answers to these questions entail not only *descriptive* challenges of understanding of how ecological and socio-economic systems interact, but also normative (value-driven) issues about how they should interact, and *prescriptive* questions of how they need to interact to achieve sustainability of social-ecological systems. We also need measures or indicators to inform us reliably if we are making progress or slipping off the paths to sustainability.

In general, as our understanding of ecological systems and of our dependence and impact on them increases, we would expect our ability to foster sustainable ecosystems and social–economic structures within them to be greatly enhanced. We now know, for example, what causes irreversible damage to wetlands, or what leads to failure of businesses and public institutions, and even of entire national economic systems. Nevertheless, we continue to engage individually and jointly, in private and public domains, at all scales from local to global, in actions that predictably undermine our systems' ability to endure. In what follows we discuss some threats to environmental sustainability that might account for our seeming inability to promote it at all scales. Understanding these obstacles may lead to strategies to overcome them.

Threats to Sustainability

In the past, unsustainable activities were due to lack of knowledge about cause-and-effect links to environmental impacts. For a long time people did not understand that their agricultural practices led to desertification or that animals could be hunted into extisnction. More recently, as resource limits have become visible, people have grown increasingly aware of their own global interdependence as well as the links between people and their natural environment. The perception has gradually set in that human decisions and activities can have unwanted, at times irreversible consequences; the continuity of human societies depends on the health and quality of their natural environment. In countries with relatively high standards of living (achieved by depleting natural resources around the world) people value their quality of life and understand how the natural environment contributes to it. They are searching for ways to lessen their impact on the environment. In contrast, in developing countries where many have yet to eat enough to relieve their hunger, there is relatively less awareness of the negative health consequences of the activities that provide sustenance, and less willingness to devote scarce resources to any other purposes than aggressive economic development.

Besides awareness, obstacles to acting sustainably at the individual or societal levels stem largely from the complexity of the systems within which we function and their intricate relationships and delayed feedbacks. For example, the sustainability of a business organization depends not only on direct managerial decisions but also on indirect decisions by competitors or government regulators. The sustainability of natural ecosystems such as watersheds depends directly on the decisions of those who use/exploit/manage them, and indirectly on political decisions to allocate public funds to watershed protection or cleanup. Consequences of any decisions and actions accrue slowly in time, leaving us uncertain about the effectiveness of our sustainability decisions.

The earlier example about managers dumping industrial effluent in a river even if they have to pay ensuing penalties illustrates the obstacles to sustainability and the dilemmas it poses. These managers are responding to poorly structured regulatory incentives that make it more worthwhile to pay penalties than to heed rules. They are rewarded for short-run successes and lack long-run incentives. They are perhaps not haunted by ethical dilemmas, or by the lasting consequences to ecosystems and human health of dumping toxic effluent. They are responding as many do when faced with the temptation of the immediate competitive edge obtained by getting away with more than those who comply with regulations; or they do not want to be law-abiding when others are exploiting opportunities for quick gain. To succeed, sustainable management strategies have to address such obstacles and the incentives that privilege the short run.

Some of the obstacles to sustainable management are psychological, inherent in our ways of thinking. Other difficulties are institutional, inherent in the structure of political and economic incentives, and rules within which managers operate. Finally, some difficulties stem from the very nature of the ecosystems we wish to sustain, and from the interdependence between economic, social, and natural systems. As well, knowing how well we are doing when acting sustainably is challenging on two counts. First, environmental processes are very slow-changing, so there is almost no immediate feedback from our action. Too often, only later generations bear/reap the costs/benefits of our current choices. Second, although several indicators have been devised for assessing various aspects of sustainability, they are yet to be widely accepted. We discuss next a few common obstacles to sustainable management behavior.

Psychology: "I'll gladly pay you Tuesday for a hamburger today." J. Wellington Wimpy, a "Popeye" cartoon character, gave voice to our tendency to sharply discount benefits or costs the further in the future we reap them. Environmental consequences of how we use natural resources or of how we pollute soil, air and water become visible years from when we implement our decisions. We are hard-pressed to expend resources now to prevent damage in the (often distant) future. Difficult economic times only accentuate our Wimpy-like preference for benefits now and costs later. Even knowing that continued discharge of polluted effluent may exhaust a lake's ability to repair itself, the practice goes on because in the moment it appears more cost-effective than acting to protect the lake. The current heavy pollution in the Great Lakes is the result of many preceding decades during which they served as a low-cost means of waste disposal for abutting industries.

Psychology: "If we run with scissors. ..." Bazerman and Watkins (2004) suggest that we should not be as surprised as we are by many of the crises we face—environmental, economic and social—because they are predictable if we heed their signs. We understand well many of the factors contributing to environmental degradation, and how our activities cause irreversible damage or exhaust the resources we need for our activities. However, psychological and organizational dynamics stack the odds against timely preventive or mitigating action (Kaufman, 2011).

Besides overly discounting future benefits of current costly actions, both individuals organizations tend to be overconfident in the plans we devise to reach our goals. We rarely have a Plan B, and we fail to learn from the past (Bazerman & Watkins, 2004). Production of goods and services still relies heavily on the continued availability of cheap fossil fuels, even after we experienced the distressing effects of shortages during the 1967 and 1973 oil crises. We should have learned and prepared but we still failed to predict the next crisis in 2008, when oil prices skyrocketed and dealt a global economic blow. For the first time in the US oil demand dropped significantly. Consensus developed around the need to seek alternative energy sources. But only several weeks later oil prices dropped drastically, if temporarily. Resolve to act and change petered out. The next fuel supply crisis is waiting in the wings, and we will be surprised—as usual.

There is a good example of a timely collective response to a predicted crisis, but its uniqueness reflects how difficult it is to act before crises hit—although it is often less costly than fixing the damage later. The so-called Y2K crisis threatened critical, interlinked data sets that support the functioning of vital private and public organizations and the essential services they provide. The trigger would have been the transition from 1999 to 2000 (Y2K), expected to cause irreversible damage to data because of the internal representation of dates in computers. Predictions of immediate, far-ranging economic and functional losses caused direct stakeholders to rally and act to prevent the crisis. However, judging by public reactions at the time and since then, we did learn a lesson but it was the wrong one. Instead of realizing how effective and efficient it is to forestall crises before they happen, we learned that since the dire predictions did not materialize, the costly prevention measures had been wasteful and unnecessary.

Similar attitudes underlie widespread perceptions that (costly) measures to forestall or to mitigate climate change consequences are not necessary and that we can handle problems if and when we see them. While not all proposed solutions to climate change are necessarily cost-effective or sure to work as planned and to achieve their goals, neither is inaction a wise strategy. Since currently few are inclined to act, many more unpleasant but predictable surprises are in store for our environmental and socio-economic systems at all levels.

Incentives Structure: "I'll sneak another cow on the commons and hope nobody notices." This logic underlies the Tragedy of the Commons, a story G. Hardin (1968) told to illustrate the effect of incentives on people's decisions. In the story, there is a pasture (commons) in town that can support only one grazing cow per neighbor. The temptation is great for one neighbor to add a second cow to this free pasture, since the added damage is minimal while the benefit is substantial. However, everyone is similarly tempted—and gives in. In Hardin's words, "Therein is the tragedy. Each man is locked into a system that compels him to increase his herd without limit—in a world that is limited. Ruin is the destination toward which all men rush, each pursuing his own interest in a society that believes in the freedom of the commons" (p. 4).

The natural environment is our *commons*. Individuals and businesses face the temptation to over-consume scarce resources—lest someone else do and gain competitive advantage—or to pollute in all media, since everyone else does. Overfishing of tuna and sea bass in international waters is a replay of the *commons*: to secure one's share when faced with competition, everyone harvests too much fish, until the fish populations are exhausted, as is the livelihood of those who depended on them. Examples of such actions and outcomes abound.

The Commons incentives to overconsume or overuse are exacerbated by lack of mutual trust and lack of ability to enforce oversight through regulations or treaties. A global-scale example is the failure of nations to agree on reductions in the emission of greenhouse gases, to reduce predicted consequences of global climate change. If all countries agree on emission limits, the temptation is great for each country not to do its share. Since the other countries are suspected of releasing more than their share of greenhouse gases (equivalent to adding cows to the commons) each country concludes it should do the same, instead of being the only one that imposes economic hardships on its population to save the planet. Neither will any country retaliate on others for not carrying out the treaty: countries beset by many problems and with diverse and divergent interests have a poor record of forming durable coalitions to impose sanctions on those who default on commitments. Thus most see cheating as being cost-free while living up to commitments is very costly both politically and economically. The choice is clear! However, as in the Tragedy of the Commons, should predicted consequences of climate change materialize, globally shared outcomes will be dire.

Economics: "Air, soil, and water are ours to use." Air, soil and water are used in the production of goods as ingredients or as storage for waste. They have long seemed abundant and free, therefore not included in the price of goods and services. The price of disposable products does not include the cost of disposing of them. The price of electricity does not include the price of loss of salmon at river dams or loss of aquatic fauna and flora due to discharge of hot nuclear reactor cooling water into lakes. However, we are paying for pollution and overuse through the costs of healthcare, of transporting resources over longer distances, or lack of land for agriculture and development. In hindsight, given the choice we might have preferred to pay (possibly less) for sustainable practices to avoid the consequences of pollution, some of which are irreversible.

Pricing that includes the costs of maintaining and improving air, soil, and water quality has long been proposed as a means to enhance environmental sustainability. However, most consumers prefer to pay as little as possible for goods and services. Businesses competing to respond to demand seek to lower their production costs. The recent trend to produce food locally through sustainable farming is a step in the direction of including the real production costs into the price of goods. Locally produced food has other beneficial side-effects such as reducing the cost, energy use, and pollution associated with hauling goods over long distances, and making the food supply less vulnerable to crises (plant diseases, hurricanes, etc.) through production decentralization. However, this trend has yet to reach the scale at which it can make a meaningful difference to the environment, not least because only the relatively wealthy can afford farmer market prices.

Ecosystem Processes: "What we don't know won't hurt us." Owing to global availability and accessibility of information, ideas and knowledge spread faster than ever. As a result, one idea taking hold broadly is that human activities are contributing to greenhouse gas emissions that are causing global climate change. Although predictions vary, they point consistently in the direction of widespread negative, destabilizing consequences for many parts of the world. Yet at every decision level—from country to regional, local, organizational, and individual—there has been much talk and little preventive or remedial action. Compounding the Wimpy factor, the commons incentives and pricing issues is the slowness inherent in natural environmental processes, with ensuing *low feedback* about consequences of our choices.

Effects of our actions accrue gradually over many years, often beyond our lifetime. As a result, our ability to assess success and benefit from it is low. So is our ability to be concerned about the predicted long-term consequences of inaction and our willingness to prioritize them above our daily challenges. It is as difficult for managers as it is for elected officials to justify expenses whose benefits are uncertain (because far in the future) and for which they will receive no credit. Moreover, since ecosystem feedback is very low in the short and medium run, we quickly tend to conclude that our actions have no impact and therefore a change of strategy is in order. There is also a mismatch between our attention to issues and the time necessary for assessing whether measurable changes are in the desired direction. Our resolve is undermined by the seeming lack of environmental response to our (often costly) actions. In the absence of evidence of results, we give up too soon and thus fail to foster environmental sustainability.

Systems and Their Interconnectedness vs. Mental Models: "One cause and one solution." There is a gap between the complexity of ecosystems and their interrelatedness with social and economic systems, and our mental models of (how we think) they work. The complexity and interconnectedness give rise to so-called *wicked problems* difficult to resolve because our interventions often have unforeseen negative consequences that exceed the expected benefits. Adding to this problem, we have a tendency to assume that observed events have one cause and we focus on it alone as we devise solutions. To prevent climate change, the focus has been on reducing the *carbon footprint* (carbon dioxide emissions) although several other greenhouse gases and water vapor are also serious contributors. Solutions address reductions both in use of fossil fuels to generate energy, and in energy consumption. On the generation side, wind turbines were deemed ideal until side effects surfaced, including relatively large land needs, noise, and the killing of migratory birds—all predictable, had attention not been focused only on expected benefits. On the consumption side, incandescent light bulbs were replaced with fluorescent bulbs, but focus on benefits has ignored the fluorescents' mercury content posing health dangers. Besides the hazardous material cleanup necessary when breaking fluorescents, the switch from incandescents has moved pollution from air to soil, as fluorescents pose landfill problems.

Systems and their Interconnectedness vs. Mental Models: "There is no free lunch." The examples above illustrate one last obstacle to environmentally sustainable business practices. Changes in the ways that we consume, produce and price goods, or manage organizations have not only benefits we seek but also costs, at times unexpected. For changes to be implemented there has to be broad understanding of costs and consensus that the benefits are worth the price.

Crises can sometimes bring about rapid consensus for change. Environmental problems occasionally reach crisis level and mobilize attention, resolve, and the sense that the price of response is justified by the needs. More often, long-term environmental issues have difficulty attaining the salience and perceived urgency necessary for action (Layzer, 2012), and quickly fall in priority behind pressing short-range problems such as economic crises, unemployment, poverty, health care or education.

Having listed several dimensions of sustainability related to the natural environment and some obstacles to it, we address next some practical management aspects, including sustainability outcomes, indicators and strategies.

Outcomes of Sustainability Strategies

Let us imagine that we have overcome many of the hurdles just described. Individuals, private and public organizations and governments around the world are now poised to act in ways that promote environmental sustainability. In fact, several countries and some American cities and regions are engaged in sustainable development practices. How can we monitor progress toward various sustainability goals—whether reducing waste, containing the demand for energy and water, or reducing greenhouse gas emissions? We need baseline measures (i.e., where we were when we began to act) and practical indicators (reliable and using accessible data) at different scales, to link corporate social and financial performance. Of the numerous indicators proposed (Chao & Lam, 2011), some are helpful in overcoming obstacles to managerial decisions that sustain the environment. We give below two examples: the ecological footprint and the ecological backpack. We follow up with a few strategies that can help businesses self-monitor and engage in sustainable practices.

Indicators of Business Sustainability

The Ecological Footprint assesses the strain various human activities cause to natural ecosystems. It measures the biologically productive area required to produce agricultural crops, meat, fish, or wood, or to provide infrastructure services and to absorb carbon dioxide emissions from burning fossil fuels. The global ecological footprint (also called natural capital) has nearly doubled since

1961, meaning we have almost doubled the strain. Since the 1970s, had everyone in the world consumed on average the same amount of natural resources as the inhabitants of developed countries, we would have needed the resources equivalent to two additional planets Earth (WWF 2004 Annual Report).

The ecological footprint can be computed for a specific organization, family or individual. It communicates effectively the need to treat lightly on the natural ecosystems that host our activities. This indicator can also be used to assess an organization's progress toward reducing its consumption of resources and its output of greenhouse gases.

The Ecological Backpack measures the total amount of natural material disturbed in its natural setting by production activities. It consists of the total input—from cradle to readiness for use—necessary to generate a product, less the weight of the product itself. It can also be used to assess the resources needed to provide services, including those that are often not given a value, such as air or water.

These two examples illustrate how difficult it is to capture in a single measure all aspects of sustainability. Moreover, such quantitative indicators fail to include intangibles such as the aesthetic value of natural landscapes lost because of development or mining activities, or justice issues. Nevertheless, these indicators reflect at least some of the costs we fail to take into account through traditional approaches.

Strategies Fostering Sustainability

Several business concepts and approaches to sustainability have been effective. We offer here four examples. They are not universally applicable: the best sustainability approach is likely the one designed to serve a specific business, its stakeholders and its environmental context.

The 3Rs (Reduce, Reuse, and Recycle) Initiative, proposed by Japanese representatives to the 2004 G8 Summit, aims to foster responsible individual and organizational consumption habits by reducing waste. Businesses can reduce their costs of production, a short-run incentive beyond the satisfaction of contributing to long-run environmental sustainability. Such strategies are easier for businesses to adopt precisely because of the short-run economic benefits that appeal even to those uninterested in sustainability.

The Precautionary Principle entails avoiding certain risks to ecosystems and to human health before conclusive scientific evidence becomes available.

In matters of high risk (threats to large populations or unique natural resources, and/or severe or irreversible impacts) the precautionary principle has been widely accepted. When an outbreak of animal disease is suspected to be linked to imports from a specific country, trade restrictions are imposed before further information is obtained about the precise source of the outbreak and its extent—better safe than sorry. However, we also need caution to avoid engaging too hastily in costly remedies. In the US, the discovery of clusters of cancer cases among people living around high-voltage transformers led to calls to move everyone away. This costly remedy was eventually discredited with scientific evidence. Waiting for more information paid off in this case; haste was also unwarranted because illnesses such as cancer develop from long-term exposure to carcinogens. In other instances where effects accrue rapidly, preventive action should also be quick.

Biomimicry entails applying solutions from nature including biological principles, biostructures and biomaterials to various human problems. For example, economic activities could mimic how almost any residue from biological processes is used by some animals or plants in a natural recycling of sorts. Some restaurants have been using their spent cooking oil to supply part of the energy they need. Here again, short-run cost cutting incentives make this strategy easier to adopt than diffuse benefits that materialize only in the long run.

Triple Bottom Line (TBL) Accounting entails measuring a company's performance along the three dimensions of sustainable development, instead of focusing only on economic outcomes. The principle underlying TBL (also called "people, planet, profit") is that corporate sustainability depends on balancing economic, social, and environmental responsibilities (Elkington, 1998; Grant, 2008). TBL may promote businesses' consciousness about the need to sustain their host environments and communities and also leads to concrete actions. A company using a TBL reporting format will strive to generate economic benefits for its shareholders as well as behave responsibly towards everyone it affects through its activities.

Implications for Management

We have discussed so far the need to promote the long-term goal of (mostly environmental) sustainability and some obstacles to sustainable business decisions. We offered examples of indicators and tools for assessing progress and for reframing organizational goals to include environmental impacts. However, managers' awareness of environmental consequences of their decisions is not sufficient to steer decisions toward sustainability because managers do not make their decisions in a vacuum. They operate in a broad socio-economic context where other decision makers—stakeholders—also act to protect their economic and social interests and their values.

Stakeholders are the individuals and public and private organizations who affect or are affected by an organization's activities. Their interests, demands and expectations, and the power each wields in this network of relationships play key roles in shaping business strategies. From an organizational perspective, stakeholders can be seen (framed) as direct - providers, users - and indirect influencers—the public, media, and members of governance structures such as elected officials. Podnar and Jancik (2006) classified stakeholders by their relationship with the organization. This relationship can be inevitable with competitors, customers, regulators, employees, suppliers, and shareholders; necessary with labor unions, schools and universities, media, local communities and the natural environment; or desirable with employees' families, other companies, nonprofits, cultural organizations, political parties, opinion leaders, and various advocacy groups. The perspective adopted, with its specific categories, contain implicit prescriptions for the interests managers take into account in their decisions. When the natural environment does not make their stakeholder list, it signals lack of intent to strive for its sustainability.

How then to manage the different classes of stakeholders, and balance their various interests? Traditional approaches prescribed focusing only on shareholders. Sustainable approaches prescribe taking into account not only shareholders but also other stakeholders to whom an organization may have a moral responsibility. Initiatives such as the European Commission's Green Paper, the United Nations Global Compact, or the Global Reporting Initiative generated debate on responsible corporate governance that is accountable to the society to which it belongs, to its legitimate stakeholders, and to the natural environment.

Stakeholder management can be very complicated for socially responsible organizations. Designing creative paths to sustainability is becoming ever more necessary as the public's awareness of it increases, and as communication technologies afford cheap, real-time participation in decisions of large numbers of people around the globe. Many stakeholders prefer organizations they view as socially responsible. In addition, the more organizations adopt sustainable practices, the fewer regulations may be necessary to ensure the protection of natural environments. Examples of positive consequences of industry-wide sustainable practices are found in the hotel industry and more generally in the tourism sector, as well as in the apparel sector (see the *Patagonia* case below). The *Pikolinos* shoe company illustrates socially responsible management of stakeholding relationships for sustainability. It collaborated with the Association for the Cohesive Development of the Amazon (ADCAM) to create a new shoe model and having it manufactured by women in Maasai Mara (Kenia). This project provided Maasai tribe members with sustainable employment consistent with their traditional life-style.

The many positive examples of management and initiatives that sustain the natural environment are not sufficient to overcome either the Wimpy syndrome or the Commons incentives that drive businesses to focus more on the short run and to compete for resources by any means regardless of long-run consequences. Global sustainability—the use of limited resources to satisfy current needs without compromising the future or exceeding the resources of the one planet we have—cannot be achieved unless the sustainability ethos percolates, becoming the dominant approach to the conduct of business.

Questions for Students

1. What is your "working definition" of sustainability? (Please indicate the level of analysis you are addressing in terms of geography, scale, etc.)
2. How does time affect business decisions that contribute to, or detract from sustainability of the natural environment? (Differentiate the descriptive and the normative in your answer).
3. How does/should the need for environmental sustainability affect the conduct of business?
4. Find two business examples in which Commons-like incentives lead to negative collective environmental outcomes.
5. Find another sustainability indicator and give an example of where it might be used.
6. What are the advantages and disadvantages of the TBL accounting approach?
7. Investigate the cradle-to-grave and the cradle-to-cradle product design approaches and how they might contribute to business strategies for environmental sustainability.
8. In what ways is the Pikolinos Maasai project socially responsible? How is it contributing to the company's sustainability? Are there any environmental benefits of this project?

Exercise

Select a type of business of interest either because you have experience in it or because you plan to work in it.

- Analyze how it affects the natural environment. Consider for example (if applicable) its inputs and their sources, the production processes and their by-products, the energy necessary for transportation of raw materials and products and for the production process, the handling of waste, and issues related to the product's life-cycle and its disposal.
- Using readily-available data, propose some measures for making it sustainable in any or all aspects of production, use and disposal (you may want to consider using the Trendalyzer tool (http://www.footprintnetwork.org/en/index.php/GFN/page/trendalyzer).
- Explore obstacles to the implementation of your proposal, and ways to overcome them.

Case: Patagonia Company

Patagonia is a company based in California that designs, develops and markets clothing and gear for outdoor sports, travel and daily wear. It is known for innovative designs, quality products and environmental conscience.

Patagonia's mission states that building the best possible product must cause no unnecessary harm; and, that the business should inspire and implement solutions to environmental problems. Consistent with its mission, Patagonia uses environmentally sensible materials, such as organic cotton, recycled and recyclable polyester. It also sponsors and participates in environmental initiatives, and gives $40 million in grants and in-kind donations to grassroots environmental organizations. Patagonia considers its employees to be its "internal clients" who are very important to the organization. The nearly one thousand people working directly for Patagonia are paid fairly, with benefits, health care, flexible work schedules and paid time off for environmental internships. Patagonia seeks employees who share its values regarding quality and environmental causes.

Patagonia does not make the products it sells. Rather, it enters into agreements with more than 70 factories world-wide, including countries such as

Vietnam or China where there are cases of bad labor practices. But since Patagonia's commitments are not limited to its organization, it works with factories that share the values of integrity and environmentalism. Their case shows that it is possible to make good products and to lower employee turnover by treating everyone humanely, in contrast to common practices in the apparel industry where some businesses have mistreated their employees with excessive work hours, unsafe work conditions, low salaries, and even child labor.

Patagonia's path to responsibility began when it was still a small organization. It decided to test and formalize its vision and management processes while growing. In the 90s it reviewed factory conditions agreements, quality standards, and labor conditions. It developed a "contractor relationship assessment" using scorecards to review factories' performance in different areas related to its mission, including the responsible side of social compliance.

There was also a setback in Patagonia's history. The number of factories with which it worked grew rapidly. It lost track of the information about new factories and the ways in which they had worked for a number of years. As a result, Patagonia was even dropped from the Fair Labor Association (FLA). To regain the employees' and factories' confidence regarding social and labor issues, the company hired a social responsibility manager.

Nowadays, the company trains its staff and employees about Patagonia's Workplace Code of Conduct. It works closely with suppliers (three of whom are FLA members) and factories, auditing them and reducing their number in order to facilitate monitoring. Corporate responsibility is integrated in Patagonia's outsourcing strategy and in its strategic management practices. Its Social/ Environmental Responsibility (SER) team can veto a decision to work with a new factory that does not fit in with the company's policies. The SER team is revising conduct codes and publishing a Footprint Chronicles website, in which they trace the environmental and social impacts of products. The Footprint Chronicles is the equivalent of a corporate responsibility report. The website is also a model of corporate transparency and of commitment to exercise social responsibility through actions, processes, management style and consequences. This type of industry needs more such good models of how to begin about change and solve environmental, manufacturing, and labor responsibility problems.

Suggestions for Further Reading

Savitz, A. W., & Weber, K. (2006). *The triple bottom line: How today's best-run companies are achieving economic, social and environmental success—and how you can too.* San Francisco: Wiley.

Busch, T., & Hoffman, V. H. (2011). How hot is your bottom line? Linking carbon and financial performance. *Business & Society, 50,* 233–265.

Griskevicius, V., Tybur, J. M., & Van den Bergh, B. (2010). Going green to be seen: Status, reputation, and conspicuous conservation. *Journal of Personality & Social Psychology, 98,* 392–404.

Marshall, G. (2014). *Don't even think about it.* New York: Bloomsbury.

References

Bazerman, M., & Watkins, M. (2004). *Predictable surprises: The disasters you should have seen coming, and how to prevent them.* Cambridge, MA: Harvard Business School Press.

Chao, Y. L., & Lam, S. P. (2011). Measuring responsible environmental behavior: Self-reported and other-reported measures and their differences in testing a behavioral model. *Environment and Behavior, 43,* 53–71.

Diamond, J. (2005). *Collapse: How societies choose to fail or succeed.* New York: Viking.

Elkington, J. (1998). *Cannibals with Forks: the Triple Bottom Line of 21st century business.* San Francisco: Wiley.

Grant, J. (2008). *Organizational performance in an interdependent world. Current Topics in Management, 13,* 35–58.

Hardin, G. (1968). The commons dilemma. *Science, 162,* 1243–1248.

Kaufman, S. (2011) Complex systems, anticipation, and collaborative planning for resilience. In Goldstein B. (Ed.), *Resilient organizations: Social learning for hazard mitigation and adaptation* (pp. 61–98). Boston: MIT Press.

Layzer, J. A. (2012). *The environmental case: Translating values into policy.* Washington DC: CQ Press.

Podnar, K., & Jancik, Z. (2006). Towards a categorization of stakeholder groups: An empirical verification of a three-level model. *Journal of Marketing Communications, 12,* 297–308.

United Nations General Assembly (1987, March 20). Towards sustainable development. *Report of the World Commission on Environment and Development: Our common future* (Annex to document A/42/427–Development and International Co-operation: Environment; Our Common Future (Chap 2, Para 1). New York: United Nations General Assembly.

23. Performance Measures

Ismail Civelek
Western Kentucky University

Performance measures are quantitative tools for helping organizations to understand how well their products and services are doing; and investigate possible improvements in an organization. Increasing quality, engineering, environmental, and customer satisfaction requirements force organizations in progressing towards objectives in their production processes, manufacturing facility's safety, and yield. Performance measures let organizations make intelligent decisions to meet external and internal goals; and improve their business practices and customer satisfaction. In an organization, performance measures contribute to more informed organizational performance appraisals, accountability, responsibility, and better decision-making.

Nature of Performance Measures

Defining Performance Measures

A performance measure is defined for evaluations to meet an objective or improve a process in the organization. Performance measures need to be defined by a *number* (magnitude) and a *unit* of measure (term). For instance, highway mileage is a performance measure for cars to evaluate their fuel economy. 2015 Toyota Camry has 35 miles per gallon (mpg) mileage on the highway; 35 define the magnitude of the miles per gallon and mpg is a term used to evaluate the fuel economy of a car.

In organizations, performance measures are always associated with a *goal* or *objective* or *target*. Performance measures are usually represented by multi-dimensional units of measure. For example, 35 *miles per gallon* mileage for the Toyota Camry is a two-dimensional performance measure. However, single dimensional units are used in organizations with the variation for design or engineering standards. For instance, the goal for the percentage of deficient products out of the daily yield in a manufacturing plant can be 4% ± 0.8% of products manufactured in a shift or day.

Attributes of Performance Measures

There are numerous attributes of a performance measure based on organization, product, service, process or environment. However, there are six attributes expected from a performance measure in any type of evaluation in an organization: compatibility, understandability, basis for decision-making, broad application, precision, and cost-effectiveness.

Compatibility. Any performance needs to be measured with existing tools in the organization. In some situations, especially in manufacturing environments, investment might be needed in new machinery or training of labor to measure the performance metric.

Understandability. An ideal performance measure needs to be understood easily by people within the organization. Since performance measures are geared towards a target or objective, any confusion or doubt in an organization would undermine the success of a performance measure.

Basis for Decision-Making. Managers in an organization use performance measures to reach a target for a process, product or service; thus, they have to provide an agreed basis for decision-making in such organization.

Universal. A performance measure can be applied broadly in an organization. Even if every performance measure can't be applied in every product, service or process of an organization, an ideal performance measure needs to be interpreted broadly in different practices of an organization.

Precision. A performance measure is expected to be precise in interpreting results or decision-making. Managers in an organization do not rely on non-precise performance measures in their decision-making.

Economical. A performance measure needs to be cost effective in order to be used in evaluating any product, service or process.

In addition to six important attributes of performance measures, managers in an organization prefer valid, reliable, responsive, functional and credible performance measures. Also, the attributes of performance measures change with respect to market, product structure and strategy of an organization.

Categories of Performance Measures

Categorization of performance measures often changes depending on organization, product, service, and process. However, most performance measures can be grouped into six general categories: productivity, quality, timeliness, effectiveness, efficiency, and safety.

Productivity. Measures the rate of value added products or processes per unit of input, such as labor and capital.

Quality. There are numerous definitions provided for quality in the past century. Quality is the degree to which a product, service or process conforms to design or customer specifications. Quality is a matter of *production function*, in which it measures the fitness of a product, service or process for use, of an organization (see DeVor, Chang, & Sutherland, 1992).

Timeliness. Based on customer requirements, timeliness measures whether a process was completed on time and within target design specifications.

Effectiveness. This category is sometimes put under quality in different resources. Effectiveness measures the degree to which a product, service or process meets the design requirements.

Efficiency. Measures how cheap an organization creates value. Efficiency is often considered jointly with productivity in organizations.

Safety. Measures how dangerous or healthy the working environment is within an organization. Especially in manufacturing plants, a performance measure called *days without an accident* is widely used to increase safety awareness among workers.

Outcomes of Performance Measures

In a competitive world, organizations that measure performance better are more successful than companies that do not use any systematic performance measure. The most important outcome of using systematic performance measures for an organization is integration of a *quality* philosophy with the company's product and service. The other important outcome of performance metrics plays a key role in the supply chain of the organization.

Quality Control

Quality is often defined as the level of conformance to customer requirements. Every product or service is designed to serve a particular type of customers. Quality design is basically how well a product's or service's design can capture its customer requirements. For example, Progressive insurance company targets fast response time, so its design quality is focused on time as well. Southwest airline targets price and convenience sensitive customers; hence its design is geared towards low cost and convenience. In quality control, there are numerous concepts and techniques that use performance measures such as *total quality management* and *Six-sigma*.

Total Quality Management. Defined as "managing the entire organization so that it excels on all dimensions of products and services that are important to the customer" (Jacobs, Chase, & Aquilano, 2008). Total quality management has two essential objectives: careful design of the product or service, and guaranteeing that the company's overall system can use the design consistently.

Six-sigma. Six-sigma is a philosophy and set of methods to eliminate defects and waste in product or service processes. Six-sigma is originally developed by Motorola, USA in 1986 due to increasing complaints from the field sales force about warranty claims, but was used extensively with *continuous improvement* and *lean manufacturing* by Toyota, Japan. Six-sigma basically seeks to reduce variability in the processes that lead to defects.

Outcomes of Performance Measures in Supply Chain

There are various categorizations of supply chain management performance metrics in the literature based on organization's products, market, and customer segmentation. Gunasekaran, Patel, and Tirtiroglu (2001) provide five main categories of supply chain management performance metrics: *order, supply, make/assemble, delivery* and *customer*.

Order. Performance measures, which are related to order planning, are at the beginning of performance evaluation in the supply chain link of an organization. The most important performance measure at this stage of the supply chain is *order lead-time*, which is the time gap between when an order is placed and it is received. Reductions in total order lead-time or variability of the order lead-time are considered very significant competitive advantages for any organization trying to improve efficiency in its supply chain.

Supply. In the past, supplier evaluations are based only on price. In addition, price variation, on-time delivery, quality, and reliability are now also used in business practices. Also, suppliers are evaluated by an organization in three different levels: *strategic, tactical,* and *operational. Strategic* level performance measures include supplier pricing against competitors in the market, quality level (quality standards or certificates), cost saving, and environment protection initiatives. *Tactical* level performance measures rely on capacity flexibility, efficiency of order cycle lead-time, and quality assurance methodology of a supplier. In addition to strategic and tactical level performance measures, *operational* level performance measures cover efficiency of scheduling activities in a supplier's manufacturing facility and rate of deficient-free replenishments.

Make/Assemble. A product is either manufactured or assembled in a plant before it is delivered to customers. Performances of products and processes in manufacturing facilities have the most important impact on overall performance, particularly on production cost, quality and delivery reliability, of an organization. The most important performance measures at this stage of supply chain are *range of products* and *capacity utilization*.

Delivery. The effectiveness of delivery directly affects customers, thus delivery is the most important factor in analyzing customer satisfaction. Speed of delivery, variability in delivery and cost of delivery are major performance metrics in evaluating delivery performance.

Customer. Customer requirements make organizations change their products, services or processes. The most desirable performance measure is flexibility of an organization based on individual customer needs.

Implications for Management

Performance measures are used to evaluate products, services, processes, and workers' appraisal within an organization. Hence, managers use extensive data from supply chain, retailers, and customers to improve their organization's performance measures. Managers generally add new performance measures to improve their decision-making. The most significant implications of performance measures for managers arise during *supply chain strategy, outsourcing,* and *new product development* decisions.

Supply Chain Strategy

Supply chain strategy lets an organization make structural decisions about its supply chain over the next several years and these decisions are very expensive to alter on short notice. For example, location of manufacturing plants and warehouses is a typical strategic decision about an organization's supply chain (see Chopra & Meindl, 2010). There are several performance measures related to supply chain strategy depending on organization, market and product, but *inventory turnover, cycle inventory,* and *fill rate* are common in practice (see Jacobs, Chase, & Aquilano, 2008).

Inventory Turnover. Inventory turnover is a performance metric to measure how many times goods-inventory is sold in a time unit. Inventory turnover is directly related to the efficiency of supply chain management due to inventory investment, which can be monitored easily in supply chains.

Cycle Inventory. Cycle inventory is the average amount of inventory used to satisfy customer demand between consecutive shipments from the supplier. The amount of cycle inventory is directly affected by *batch size*. The basic performance issue organizations face in practice is the size of cycle inventory and *ordering cost*. When cycle inventory is high, organization keeps higher inventory but it saves from the ordering cost; when cycle inventory is low, it keeps lower inventory, but it incurs more ordering cost (see Chopra & Meindl, 2010).

Fill Rate. Fill rate measures the fraction of customer demands (replenishment orders) that were satisfied on time from organization's (supplier's) inventory. Fill rate is averaged over a specified number of units of demand (replenishment orders).

Outsourcing

Outsourcing is a business decision to move some internal activities of an organization to outside providers. There are numerous reasons why organizations outsource some of their operations depending on the source such as organizational, financial, revenue or cost. Outsourcing also helps organizations to improve quality, productivity, and cycle times. For example, organizations outsource their cleaning process instead of hiring employees of their own.

New Product Development

New product development is a major competitive tool and has a direct impact on an organization's long-term success. Organizations introduce new products to respond to changes in customer needs and strategic moves from their competitors. For example, new product development is a key factor in drug companies' success in a highly competitive market. Since the number of new technologies and products has dramatically increased over the last twenty years, aligned with development of e-commerce, organizations critically need to respond to fast-pace changes in the market. The most important performance measures for new product development projects are time to market, productivity, quality, and profitability of new product introduced (see Jacobs, Chase, & Aquilano, 2008)

Questions for Students

1. Why do organizations need performance measures? Give two examples of performance measures used by an organization.
2. Which attributes of the performance measures are more important for an organization?
3. What is the relationship between product's quality and flexibility to meet customers' needs?

Exercise

Compare 10 different companies with 6 different performance measures. Put an X into corresponding company's cell if you think that it has a better specific performance measure than its competitor (Put N/A if you think the performance measure is not applicable):

	Quality	Flexibility	Safety	Reliability	Price	Delivery
Facebook						
Myspace						

Netflix						
Blockbuster						

Chrysler						
Honda						

Target						
Walmart						

Best Buy						
Amazon						

Case: Performance Measures as Dimension of Being Lean

"DETROIT—A quarter century ago, people in this city not only bashed the surging Japanese car companies with words, they also vented their frustration by swinging sledgehammers at Japanese cars, a way for some to raise money for charity (three swings for $1 at one event)" ("Move over GM," 2007). Toyota moved to the top of the list of biggest car manufacturers of the U.S. in 2007 by passing GM. There are various reasons that Toyota is the biggest car seller in the country, but the main reason is still quality.

In mid 1980s, American car companies tried to decode Toyota's success in producing the most reliable cars. Over 5 years of study in MIT, Womack, Jones, and Roos (1990) reported that:

- Toyota Takaoka auto assembly plant in Japan was twice as productive as the General Motors Framingham auto assembly plant.
- The quality of the Takaoka plant was three times better than that of the Framingham plant

The Japanese assembly plants (in both Japan and North America) reported both high productivity and high quality. Manufacturers from other parts of the world tended to have high quality or high productivity, but not both. Womack and coworkers attributed the superior performance of Japanese plants to the *lean production systems*.

Suggestions for Further Reading

Chopra, S., & Meindl, P. (2010). *Supply chain management strategy, planning, and operation.* New Jersey: Prentice Hall.

Kleijnen J. P. C., & M. Smits, T. (2003). Performance metrics in supply chain management. *Journal of the Operational Research Society, 54,* 1–8.

Shutler M., & Storbeck, J. (2002). Part special issue editorial: performance management. *Journal of the Operational Research Society, 53,* 245–246.

References

DeVor, R. E., Chang, T., Sutherland, J. W. (1992). *Statistical quality design and control, contemporary concepts and methods*. New Jersey: Prentice Hall.

Gunasekaran, A., Patel, C., & Tirtiroglu, E. (2001). Performance measure and metrics in a supply chain environment. *International Journal of Operations & Production Management, 21* (1/2), 71–87.

Move over GM, Toyota is No. 1. (2007). *The New York Times Online* (http://www.nytimes.com/2007/04/25/business/worldbusiness/25iht-25auto.5431609).

Jacobs, F. R., R. B. Chase, & N. J. Aquilano. (2008). *Operations and supply management*. New York: McGraw-Hill Irwin.

Walleck, S., O'Halloran, D., & Leader, C. (1991). Benchmarking world-class performance. *McKinsey Quarterly*, 1, 2–5.

Womack, J. P., D. Jones, & D. Roos. (1990). *The machine that changed the world*. New York: Rawson.

CPSIA information can be obtained
at www.ICGtesting.com
Printed in the USA
LVOW03s0320200816

501102LV00010B/53/P

9 781631 895418